End of Time Prophecies

A Study of Daniel and Revelation

Lowell S. R. Litten, Jr.

End of Time Prophecies

A Study of Daniel and Revelation

All Scripture is taken from the New King James Version Bible, unless noted. Copyright © 1982 by Thomas Nelson, Inc. Used by permission. All rights reserved.

> The text of the New King James Version® (NKJV®) may be quoted or reprinted without prior written permission with the following qualifications: (1) Up to and including 1,000 verses may be quoted in printed form as long as the verses quoted amount to less than 50% of a complete book of the Bible and make up less than 50% of the total work in which they are quoted; (2) all NKJV quotations must conform accurately to the NKJV text.

King James Version taken from a PDF Version. Original Publish Date: March, 2001, Revised: January 2004

> The text of the King James Version (KJV) of the Holy Bible is in the public domain. You may copy and publish it freely.
>
> This Portable Document Format (PDF) version of the King James Holy Bible is also placed into the public domain. It was created directly from the public domain text and converted to PDF format using "DaVince Tools", a software product that converts text files and other file formats into PDF (http://www.davince.com).

I want to thank my Father, Ms. Pein (WCI instructor), my Mother, Michael, and the Little Flock Seventh-day Adventist Church inside of Western Correctional Institution, for assisting me in the endeavor to turn my study of Daniel and Revelation into this volume of text.

Copyright © 2016: Lowell S. R. Litten Jr.

Book Design: Russell Publishing ©2016
Library of Congress Control Number: 2016917308

For my wife,

"I thank my God upon every remembrance of you, always in every prayer of mine making request for you all with joy, for your fellowship in the gospel from the first day until now, being confident of this very thing, that He who has begun a good work in you will complete it until the day of Jesus Christ;" (Philippians 1:3-6).

For my children,

"My son[s and daughters], if you receive my words, And treasure my commands within you, So that you incline your ear to wisdom, And apply your heart to understanding; Yes, if you cry out for discernment, And lift up your voice for understanding, If you seek her as silver, And search for her as for hidden treasures; Then you will understand the fear of the LORD, And find the knowledge of God" (Proverbs 2:1-5).

Contents

Preface	1
The Hebrew Captives (Daniel Chapter 1)	9
The Metal Statue (Daniel Chapter 2)	13
The Fiery Furnace (Daniel Chapter 3)	23
Nebuchadnezzar is Humbled (Daniel Chapter 4)	27
Prophetic Timings (A Day for a Year Concept)	33
The Fall of Babylon (Daniel Chapter 5)	37
Daniel and the Lion's Den (Daniel Chapter 6)	41
Cartoon Beasts (Daniel Chapter 7)	45
Translations of the Bible (Why are there so many?)	55
Rams and Goats (Daniel Chapter 8)	59
The Little Horn of Prophecy (Daniel Chapters 7 & 8)	61
The Seventy Week Prophecy (Daniel Chapter 9)	71
The Cleansing of the Sanctuary (Daniel 8:14)	83
Time-lines of Prophecy (Important Dates in History)	91
Daniel Mourns Three Full Weeks (Daniel Chapter 10)	99
Daniel's Last Vision (Daniel Chapter 11)	103
Michael Stands Up (Daniel Chapter 12)	129
Michael Our Prince (Who is like God?)	131
Counterfeit Prophecy (Wheat versus Tares)	135
Israel in Prophecy (A Counterfeit Concept)	139
Introduction to Revelation (The Apocalypse of Christ)	153
The Seven Churches (Revelation 1-3)	165
The Seven Seals (Revelation 4,5 & 6)	179

The Antichrist (1 John 4:3)	193
The 144,000 (Revelation 7)	197
The Seven Trumpets (Revelation 8, 9 & 11)	203
The Rise of the Empires (A View of History)	215
The Little Book and the Seven Thunders (Revelation 10)	219
The Two Witnesses (Revelation 11:1-13)	223
The Dragon's War (Revelation 12, 13, & 14)	229
The Seal of God (The Sabbath)	241
The Last Angel Messengers (Revelation 14, 18)	247
The Last Plagues (Revelation 15, 16)	257
Armageddon (A Mount Carmel Experience)	269
Who is Babylon the Great? (Revelation 17, 18)	273
The End of Time (Revelation 19, 20)	287
The End of Time Outline	297
A Time-line for the End of Time (The Prophecy of the Future)	299
The Second Coming of Christ (The Gathering of His Saints)	313
Hell and Death (The Biblical Truth)	317
The New Jerusalem (Revelation 21)	327
A New Heaven and a New Earth (After the End of Time)	333
Index	337

Preface
End of Time Prophecies

The End of Time is near. Events in the world, including— wars and rumors of war, global warming, pandemic diseases, weird weather patterns and more— are beginning to unsettle both the religious and non-religious alike. You do not have to be a Christian to see that there are changes to the world we live in. The earth is in a state of turmoil that has not seen its equal since time began. Nature is becoming more unpredictable, seasons are not as distinct as they used to be, and human nature is rapidly declining at every turn. For the Christian this is scriptural. These events have been foretold in the amazing book called the Bible.

"But as the days of Noah were, so also will the coming of the Son of Man be. 38For as in the days before the flood, they were eating and drinking, marrying and giving in marriage, until the day that Noah entered the ark, 39and did not know until the flood came and took them all away, so also will the coming of the Son of Man be" (Matthew 24:37-39).

"Then the LORD saw that the wickedness of man was great in the earth, and that every intent of the thoughts of his heart was only evil continually" (Genesis 6:5).

The increased wickedness of mankind is one of the signs that the coming of the Son of Man— Jesus Christ is getting closer.

The End of Time

What does this mean?

When will it be?

What events will take place?

The Bible answers these questions. They are revealed through the study of prophecy. There are prophecies within the Bible that have been proven accurate down to the exact day. This book will look at two books of the Bible that carry most of these prophecies: Daniel and Revelation.

End of Time Prophecies

This is not your average book on prophecy. The interpretations of Biblical prophecy found within these pages will differ from many of the current, mainstream and popular interpretations that exist. The Bible warns us that we are to take nothing at face value, but in all things we are to search the Scriptures to see if they are true (Acts 17:11). Truth is absolute and it does not change. Truth can allow itself to be critiqued and tested, but it will always remain truth. Challenge what you hear and read. Question traditions, sermons and all books (including this one). Compare everything with the plain Word of God.

This book was written when I had a lot of free time to study and read; I was in prison. Daniel, Revelation and End of Time prophecy has always fascinated me, but I never took the time to do an in-depth study. With time on my hands I set about to understand prophecy. The Bible is designed to be read as a complete book, both the Old Testament and the New Testament are necessary for a proper understanding of biblical beliefs and practices. All of the answers needed are found within the Scriptures. Isaiah 28:10 outlines the method of study required to understand all scripture: *"For precept must be upon precept, precept upon precept, Line upon line, line upon line, Here a little, there a little."*

One of my frustrating pastimes is to watch the church channel on TV and listen to the various pastors, authors and prognosticators throw out their own views of the End of Time. These people annoy me. They take a single text, and then without scriptural support they throw out ideas or guesses on what they think it means. My cell-mate always asks me why I torture myself with watching these people. I suppose I hope to find someone who might have biblical or historical evidence that would counteract the interpretations that have been revealed from scripture. More often than not I find nothing to support their claims.

This book is a culmination of many exhaustive line by line studies of the Bible as well as research into history, languages, dates and times.

Preface

It is my hope that anyone, beginner included, can understand the messages of the prophets as they speak about the End of Time.

The Study of Prophecy

The study of prophecy is arguably the most debated topic in all of theology, and yet it does not need to be so confusing or troublesome. Prophecy is a part of the Scriptures.

"All Scripture is given by inspiration of God, and is profitable for doctrine, for reproof, for correction, for instruction in righteousness, 17that the man of God may be complete, thoroughly equipped for every good work" (2 Timothy 3:16,17).

How much of prophecy is profitable?

"All Scripture is profitable" (Verse 16).

What is the purpose of studying Scripture, prophecy included?

"That the man of God may be complete, thoroughly equipped for every good work" (Verse 17).

All Scripture is profitable, this includes the endless lists of who begat whom, the Levitical laws, Christ's parables, and the symbolic visions included in prophecy.

Scriptures *"are written that you may believe that Jesus is the Christ, the Son of God, and that believing you may have life in His name" (John 20:31).*

This is the purpose of every word written in the Bible. The Bible points us to Jesus Christ. This is the purpose of prophecy as well—to point us to Jesus Christ.

Prophecy, like parables, appear confusing at first glance. When Jesus Christ walked this earth His own disciples questioned Him about this and why He spoke in parables.

"And He said, 'To you it has been given to know the mysteries of the kingdom of God', but to the rest it is given in parables, that 'Seeing they may not see, And hearing they may not understand'" (Luke 8:10).

End of Time Prophecies

Christ's answer gains more clarity when we read the passage from Isaiah that Christ was copying.

"Make the heart of this people dull, And their ears heavy, And shut their eyes; Lest they see with their eyes, And hear with their ears, And understand with their heart, And return and be healed" (Isaiah 6:10).

This statement is one of opposites or reverse psychology given to the prophet Isaiah to share with his listeners. God's people were looking for the easy path in life and had neglected the desire to understand, search and study the Word of God. Instead of returning to God, and building a relationship with Him, they were satisfied with their dull understanding. They were enjoying their heavy ears that desired smooth words, and their blindness to His Word, hoping that this would hide their sins. They were enjoying the feelings and emotions involved in their lives and were not focused on truth.

Belief in Jesus is not based on feelings or emotions. While emotions will exist and may help in our belief, our salvation comes from a complete trust in Him—this is faith. We are to have faith that He is our Savior, even when all earthly indications point to something else.

When Christ was on earth some followed Him simply because of the amazing miracles and magical events that He performed. They saw with their eyes and enjoyed the show.

"But although He had done so many signs before them, they did not believe in Him, 42Nevertheless even among the rulers many believed in Him, but because of the Pharisees they did not confess Him, lest they should be put out of the synagogue;" (John 12:37,42).

Jesus Christ knows that appreciation of the Bible grows with its study. Speaking in parables requires that His believers search, seek and find the truths hidden in His Word. It does not take anything but our time in reading the Scriptures. It is our privilege to understand both parables and prophecy. Satan has blinded the minds of many so that they are glad for any excuse to not study. The devil knows that each fresh search for truth and understanding will reveal something more that will counteract his acts of deception. Christ knows that the subject of truth is inexhaustible and that it will carry us through eternity—if we believe, and in faith follow His Word.

Three Tools to Interpret Prophecy

Three tools are needed for us to study and understand prophecy:

1. We are to call upon God. Before you pick up the Bible or this book to read, pray for the Holy Spirit to be present and ask Him to guide you into all understanding. He will show you great and mighty things.

"Call to Me, and I will answer you, and show you great and mighty things, which you do not know" (Jeremiah 33:3).

2. We are to search the Scriptures for our answers. Specifically we are to study precept upon precept and line upon line.

"You search the Scriptures, for in them you think you have eternal life; and these are they which testify of Me" (John 5:39).

"These were more fair-minded than those in Thessalonica, in that they received the word with all readiness, and searched the Scriptures daily to find out whether these things were so" (Acts 17:11).

"Whom will he teach knowledge? And whom will he make to understand the message? Those just weaned from milk? Those just drawn from the breasts? 10For precept must be upon precept, precept upon precept, Line upon line, line upon line, Here a little, there a little" (Isaiah 28:9,10).

3. We are not to guess! The secret things belong to the Lord. The things which are revealed belong to us.

"For there is nothing covered that will not be revealed, nor hidden that will not be known" (Luke 12:2).

"The secret things belong to the LORD our God, but those things which are revealed belong to us and to our children forever, that we may do all the words of this law" (Deuteronomy 29:29).

If God has not revealed the interpretation to us then we must wait for the event to pass so we can know its meaning. Some prophecies have definite interpretations revealed from God for us to know. Other prophecies have no prior interpretations and are only to be understood once the foretold event has passed.

End of Time Prophecies

Prophecy as a dictionary word is simply: "a prediction of something to come" *(Merriam-Webster)*. Biblical prophecy adds to this definition by focusing on the past more than upon the future.

"And now I have told you before it comes, that when it does come to pass, you may believe" (John 14:29).

The Gospel of John tells us plainly that prophecy foretells history so that when you see the event turning out exactly as the Bible outlined, then you may have a boost to your faith, to your belief in the Word of God and in Jesus Christ as God.

When we read prophecies that were written over 2500 years ago and they come true exactly as foretold this adds strength that the Word of God is truth and not some novel guess or idea. Truth is 100% accurate, all of the time, or else it is not truth.

It is crucial that if we do not have a direct interpretation we are *not to guess* at its fulfillment. There is no guessing with God. This is where my angst with the TV evangelists develops. Many read a passage of prophecy and with no direct *"Thus saith the Lord"* from scripture they guess at what the prophecy is trying to foretell. This is not scripturally sound.

It is interesting to note that even Christ, when He was tempted by Satan did not use His own words. Christ used the already written Word of God to refute each temptation. By His example, we are to run our lives. We cannot guess at meaning. God's Word is complete and it will reveal every detail and secret that God desires for us to know.

As we study Daniel we will use these tools to unravel prophecy. We will see that some visions have their full meaning and purpose revealed to us by the Word of God. The visions of Daniel 4 and the writing on the wall of Daniel 5 were prophecies that were meant to be understood and interpreted within Daniel's life time. In the case of the writing on the wall, the interpretation was meant for that very evening. Other prophecies, like the one of a metal statue in Daniel 2, only has a portion of the meaning revealed to us by God. To properly interpret this vision, we must wait for it to come to pass

Preface

and then, looking back, we can see its perfect predition. Today we have the luxury of history and can now look back at the prophecies of Daniel and conclude with perfect precision the exact meaning of the prophecies. We will revisit this concept in more detail when we get to each vision.

God's Word is not given to obscure, hide or divide; and yet great divisions have occurred because men reason out what they believe to be the balance of unrevealed truth. Randomly guessing at scriptural interpretation is dangerous and inaccurate. In fact the Bible warns of making false interpretations.

"For I testify to everyone who hears the words of the prophecy of this book: If anyone adds to these things, God will add to him the plagues that are written in this book;" (Revelation 22:18).

Here are a few heinous plagues described in the Bible that God might add to those who purposely pervert the Word of God.

"And this shall be the plague with which the LORD will strike all the people who fought against Jerusalem: Their flesh shall dissolve while they stand on their feet, Their eyes shall dissolve in their sockets, And their tongues shall dissolve in their mouths" (Zechariah 14:12).

"So the anger of the LORD was aroused against them, and He departed. 10And when the cloud departed from above the tabernacle, suddenly Miriam became leprous, as white as snow. Then Aaron turned toward Miriam, and there she was, a leper" (Numbers 12:9,10).

The study of biblical prophecy adds a blessing to all who study it. In fact the book of Revelation was designed to be read aloud in the churches.

"Blessed is he who reads and those who hear the words of this prophecy, and keep those things which are written in it; for the time is near" (Revelation 1:3).

When was the last time you heard Revelation read in your Church?

All Scripture is profitable for our spiritual growth—prophecy included. When God is able to foretell future events with precision it shows us that God is omnipotent (all powerful), and omniscient (all knowing). When we read of God's promises coming true exactly as foretold, we gain faith and hope that God's future promises will also come to pass. When we read of God's warnings and His promises to watch and care for us as the troubles mount, we can gain strength to know that He will not give us more than we can endure and that we have a Father in heaven who watches over us.

It is my prayer that this book will lead you into a better understanding of God, of His love, His order, His perfection, and His grace—that is, the gift of salvation that is free to all, no matter how degenerate you are. All He asks is that you believe on His name and hold on by faith that His word is accurate and complete.

The Hebrew Captives
Daniel Chapter 1

We begin in the book of Daniel. This book of the Bible was designed by God to be our tutor, teaching us how to understand and properly interpret all other prophecy found in the scriptures. The focus of our study will be how to understand biblical prophecy in relation to our known history.

Our focus is on prophecy, but there is so much more within the books of Daniel and Revelation. Daniel's life is an excellent example of living the Christian life. He holds true to the words, doctrines and beliefs as given in God's Word. He and his friends cooperate in prayer with God and stand united though strangers in a foreign land. Glancing ahead to the book of Revelation we will read that simply reading prophetic text is enough to impart blessings. I emphasize that you return and study these books for other lessons in life including your spiritual growth.

Introduction to Daniel

Daniel's experiences are without parallel in providing modern Christians with insight into principles of practical Christian living. He endured multiple kingdoms, castration, captivity and torture that many will never have to experience. Through it all he gave thanks to the God of heaven and creation.

"In the third year of the reign of Jehoiakim king of Judah, Nebuchadnezzar king of Babylon came to Jerusalem and besieged it. 2And the Lord gave Jehoiakim king of Judah into his hand, with some of the articles of the house of God, which he carried into the land of Shinar to the house of his god; and he brought the articles into the treasure house of his god" (Daniel 1:1,2).

The book of Daniel begins as the fulfillment of a previous prophecy.

"Then Isaiah said to Hezekiah, 'Hear the word of the Lord: 17Behold, the days are coming when all that is in your house, and what your fathers have accumulated until this day, shall be carried to Babylon; nothing shall be left,' says the Lord" (2 Kings 20:16,17).

End of Time Prophecies

Isaiah prophesied that Judah and the inhabitants of Jerusalem would be captured and carried to Babylon. History records several attacks on Jerusalem by Babylon. The capture of young Daniel and his friends occurred in 605BC.

BC is the abbreviation for *Before Christ*. In AD532 the monk Dionysius Exiguus introduced a system of dating events. He began his calendar with the year that he believed Jesus Christ was born; this was set at AD1. AD or *anno Domini*, is Latin for "in the year of our Lord." There is no zero year. This will come into play as we calculate dates and determine time-lines. An alternative system in use today uses the same numbering method, but does not refer to Christ. It uses CE or *Common Era* for AD and BCE or *Before Common Era* for BC. This book will use BC and AD.

Daniel's Training

Daniel and his four friends are captured from Jerusalem and are selected for special training so that they will be able to serve in the palace of the Babylonian king.

"And the king spake unto Ashpenaz the master of his eunuchs, that he should bring [certain] of the children of Israel, and of the king's seed, and of the princes; ₄Children in whom [was] no blemish, but well favoured, and skillful in all wisdom, and cunning in knowledge, and understanding science, and such as [had] ability in them to stand in the king's palace, and whom they might teach the learning and the tongue of the Chaldeans. ₅And the king appointed them a daily provision of the king's meat, and of the wine which he drank: so nourishing them three years, that at the end thereof they might stand before the king. ₆Now among these were of the children of Judah, Daniel, Hananiah, Mishael, and Azariah: ₇Unto whom the prince of the eunuchs gave names: for he gave unto Daniel [the name] of Belteshazzar; and to Hananiah, of Shadrach; and to Mishael, of Meshach; and to Azariah, of Abed-nego" (Daniel 1:3-7 KJV).

The Hebrew Captives

Name the four Jewish captives and their new Chaldean names:

	Hebrew Name	Chaldean Name
1.	Daniel	(Belteshazzar)
2.	Hananiah	(Shadrach)
3.	Mishael	(Meshach)
4.	Azariah	(Abed-nego)

How long was their training to last?

3 years.

"But Daniel purposed in his heart that he would not defile himself with the portion of the king's meat, nor with the wine which he drank: therefore he requested of the prince of the eunuchs that he might not defile himself. 9Now God had brought Daniel into favour and tender love with the prince of the eunuchs. 10And the prince of the eunuchs said unto Daniel, I fear my lord the king, who hath appointed your meat and your drink: for why should he see your faces worse liking than the children which [are] of your sort? then shall ye make [me] endanger my head to the king. 11Then said Daniel to Melzar, whom the prince of the eunuchs had set over Daniel, Hananiah, Mishael, and Azariah, 12Prove thy servants, I beseech thee, ten days; and let them give us pulse to eat, and water to drink. 13Then let our countenances be looked upon before thee, and the countenance of the children that eat of the portion of the king's meat: and as thou seest, deal with thy servants. 14So he consented to them in this matter, and proved them ten days. 15And at the end of ten days their countenances appeared fairer and fatter in flesh than all the children which did eat the portion of the king's meat. 16Thus Melzar took away the portion of their meat, and the wine that they should drink; and gave them pulse. 17As for these four children, God gave them knowledge and skill in all learning and wisdom: and Daniel had understanding in all visions and dreams. 18 Now at the end of the days that the king had said he should bring them in, then the prince of the eunuchs brought them in before Nebuchadnezzar. 19And the king communed with them; and among them all was found none like Daniel, Hananiah, Mishael, and Azariah: therefore stood they before the king. 20And in all matters of wisdom [and] understanding, that the king inquired of them, he found them ten times better than all the magicians [and] astrologers that [were] in all his realm. 21And Daniel continued [even] unto the first year of king Cyrus" (Daniel 1:8-21 KJV).

End of Time Prophecies

Daniel and his three friends resolved to remain faithful to God. The king provided delicacies and food from his own table. But this food violated the dietary laws that God had ordained for man's health. Daniel and his friends did not want to break any of the strict Jewish dietary laws, believing that God's ideal for them was best. They approached the school's chief officer and respectfully asked for a simple diet. They proposed a ten day test.

What were the results of the 10-day test?

"And at the end of ten days their features appeared better and fatter in flesh than all the young men who ate the portion of the king's delicacies" (Verse 15).

List 2 ways Daniel and his friends could be defiled by the kings food:

1. Unclean food. This was forbidden in Leviticus.
2. The food could may have been offered to idols.

"This is the law of the animals and the birds and every living creature that moves in the waters, and of every creature that creeps on the earth, 47to distinguish between the unclean and the clean, and between the animal that may be eaten and the animal that may not be eaten" (Leviticus 11:46,47).

"But if anyone says to you, 'This was offered to idols,' do not eat it for the sake of the one who told you, and for conscience sake; for 'the earth is the LORD's, and all its fullness'" (1 Corinthians 10:28).

How did God bless Daniel and his friends?

"As for these four young men, God gave them knowledge and skill in all literature and wisdom; and Daniel had understanding in all visions and dreams" (Verse 17).

The Metal Statue
Daniel Chapter 2

The book of Daniel is God's tutorial on how to rightly interpret all prophecy. The dream revealed in this chapter is the easiest prophecy to decipher. Using this dream we discover and confirm the core concepts needed to properly interpret prophecy.

Our working guideline

1. We need God's guidance.
2. We must study the Bible to see if the answer or interpretation is revealed. If the answer is not revealed we cannot guess.
3. We cannot guess at interpretation, but must wait until history has passed and the prophecy is proved.

In Daniel 2 God does not reveal the complete interpretation—not yet at least. Later in Daniel's life more visions will be given to him. These visions will be used to unlock some of the secrets that are in this vision. We will use history to rightly interpret other parts of this dream and to confirm that God's interpretation was perfect.

The techniques used to properly decipher this vision will carry over to all future deciphering of prophecy. When we study the prophecies found in Revelation we will not have the hand holding that God provides to Daniel, but using the same techniques found in the study of Daniel, we can know that our interpretation of Revelation will be accurate and pure.

The King's Dream

"Now in the second year of Nebuchadnezzar's reign, Nebuchadnezzar had dreams; and his spirit was so troubled that his sleep left him." "Then the secret was revealed to Daniel in a night vision. So Daniel blessed the God of heaven" (Daniel 2:1,19).

End of Time Prophecies

When did King Nebuchadnezzar have his dream?

2nd year.

"And the king appointed them a daily provision of the king's meat, and of the wine which he drank: so nourishing them three years, that at the end thereof they might stand before the king" (Daniel 1:5 KJV).

Daniel and his friends trained for three years.

"As for these four young men, God gave them knowledge and skill in all literature and wisdom; and Daniel had understanding in all visions and dreams" (Daniel 1:17).

How would Daniel 2:1, 19 validate the statement from Daniel 1:17 that "Daniel had understanding in all visions and dreams?"

Daniel's test at the end of his schooling was three years after his captivity, but in year two he interpreted the King's dream.

"Then the king commanded to call the magicians, and the astrologers, and the sorcerers, and the Chaldeans, for to shew the king his dreams. So they came and stood before the king. ₃And the king said unto them, I have dreamed a dream, and my spirit was troubled to know the dream. ₄Then spake the Chaldeans to the king in Syriack, O king, live for ever: tell thy servants the dream, and we will shew the interpretation. ₅The king answered and said to the Chaldeans, The thing is gone from me: if ye will not make known unto me the dream, with the interpretation thereof, ye shall be cut in pieces, and your houses shall be made a dunghill. ₆But if ye shew the dream, and the interpretation thereof, ye shall receive of me gifts and rewards and great honour: therefore shew me the dream, and the interpretation thereof. ₇They answered again and said, Let the king tell his servants the dream, and we will shew the interpretation of it. ₈The king answered and said, I know of certainty that ye would gain the time, because ye see the thing is gone from me. ₉But if ye will not make known unto me the dream, [there is but] one decree for you: for ye have prepared lying and corrupt words to speak before me, till the time be changed: therefore tell me the dream, and I shall know that ye can shew me the interpretation thereof" (Daniel 2:2-9 KJV).

King Nebuchadnezzar woke up from a fitful dream. This dream troubled the king. He wanted to know the true meaning of this dream. He was not going to be satisfied with a guess at the meaning.

The Metal Statue

The king, in his wisdom, set up a test for his astrologers, magicians and wise men to prove if they could give him truth.

What did the king ask of his wise men?

"To tell the king his dreams" (Verse 2).

The wise men knew they were in trouble. They begged the king to tell them his dream and then they would create a plausible interpretation. This is a direct contradiction of the rules of prophecy. The wise men wanted to guess at the interpretation; we cannot guess at interpretations.

"The Chaldeans answered before the king, and said, There is not a man upon the earth that can shew the king's matter: therefore [there is] no king, lord, nor ruler, [that] asked such things at any magician, or astrologer, or Chaldean. 11And [it is] a rare thing that the king requireth, and there is none other that can shew it before the king, except the gods, whose dwelling is not with flesh. 12For this cause the king was angry and very furious, and commanded to destroy all the wise [men] of Babylon. 13And the decree went forth that the wise [men] should be slain; and they sought Daniel and his fellows to be slain" (Daniel 2:10-13 KJV).

What was the countenance of the king?

"For this reason the king was **angry** and **very furious**, and gave the command to destroy all the wise men of Babylon" (Verse 12).

"Then Daniel answered with counsel and wisdom to Arioch the captain of the king's guard, which was gone forth to slay the wise [men] of Babylon: 15He answered and said to Arioch the king's captain, Why [is] the decree [so] hasty from the king? Then Arioch made the thing known to Daniel. 16Then Daniel went in, and desired of the king that he would give him time, and that he would shew the king the interpretation. 17Then Daniel went to his house, and made the thing known to Hananiah, Mishael, and Azariah, his companions: 18That they would desire mercies of the God of heaven concerning this secret; that Daniel and his fellows should not perish with the rest of the wise [men] of Babylon" (Daniel 2:14-18 KJV).

Daniel and his three friends were in school to become part of the king's wise men. They were included in the death decree that King Nebuchadnezzar had just ordered.

How did Daniel confront the king's guard?

"Then **with counsel and wisdom** Daniel answered Arioch, the captain of the king's guard, who had gone out to kill the wise men of Babylon" (Verse 14).

"Then Daniel went to his house, and made the decision known to Hananiah, Mishael, and Azariah, his companions" (Verse 17).

Daniel followed **Rule 1:** *We Need God's Guidance.* He did not try to solve the problem alone but consulted his three companions and together they sought the mercies and grace of the one true God.

"Then was the secret revealed unto Daniel in a night vision. Then Daniel blessed the God of heaven. $_{20}$Daniel answered and said, Blessed be the name of God for ever and ever: for wisdom and might are his: $_{21}$And he changeth the times and the seasons: he removeth kings, and setteth up kings: he giveth wisdom unto the wise, and knowledge to them that know understanding: $_{22}$He revealeth the deep and secret things: he knoweth what [is] in the darkness, and the light dwelleth with him. $_{23}$I thank thee, and praise thee, O thou God of my fathers, who hast given me wisdom and might, and hast made known unto me now what we desired of thee: for thou hast [now] made known unto us the king's matter" (Daniel 2:19-23 KJV).

How was the secret revealed to Daniel?

"In a night vision" (Verse 19).

Daniel's Prayer of Thanks

"Therefore Daniel went in unto Arioch, whom the king had ordained to destroy the wise [men] of Babylon: he went and said thus unto him; Destroy not the wise [men] of Babylon: bring me in before the king, and I will shew unto the king the interpretation. $_{25}$Then Arioch brought in Daniel before the king in haste and said thus unto him, I have found a man of the captives of Judah, that will make known unto the king the interpretation. $_{26}$The king answered and said to Daniel, whose name [was] Belteshazzar, Art thou able to make known unto me the dream which I have seen, and the interpretation thereof? $_{27}$Daniel answered in the presence of the king, and said, The secret which the king hath demanded cannot the wise [men,] the astrologers, the magicians, the soothsayers, shew unto the king; $_{28}$But there is a God in heaven that revealeth secrets, and maketh known to the king Nebuchadnezzar what *shall be in the latter days. Thy dream, and the visions of thy head upon thy bed, are these;* ₂₉*As for thee, O king, thy thoughts came [into thy mind] upon thy bed, what should come to pass hereafter: and he that revealeth secrets maketh known to thee what shall come to pass.* ₃₀*But as for me, this secret is not revealed to me for [any] wisdom that I have more than any living, but for [their] sakes that shall make known the interpretation to the king, and that thou mightest know the thoughts of thy heart" (Daniel 2:24-30 KJV).*

Whom did Daniel give credit for revealing the secret to the king?

"But there is a **God** in heaven who reveals secrets," (Verse 28).

What was the purpose of the king's dream?

To reveal "what **would come to pass** after this" (Verse 29).

The Vision is Revealed

"Thou, O king, sawest, and behold a great image. This great image, whose brightness was excellent, stood before thee; and the form thereof [was] terrible. ₃₂*This image's head [was] of fine gold, his breast and his arms of silver, his belly and his thighs of brass,* ₂₃*His legs of iron, his feet part of iron and part of clay.* ₃₄*Thou sawest till that a stone was cut out without hands, which smote the image upon his feet [that were] of iron and clay, and brake them to pieces.* ₃₅*Then was the iron, the clay, the brass, the silver, and the gold, broken to pieces together, and became like the chaff of the summer threshingfloors; and the wind carried them away, that no place was found for them: and the stone that smote the image became a great mountain, and filled the whole earth" (Daniel 2:31-35 KJV).*

Describe the image that the king saw:

The king saw a great image (Verse 31).
The head was of fine gold (Verse 32).
The breast and arms of silver (Verse 32).
The belly and thighs of brass (Verse 32).
The legs of iron (Verse 33).
The feet part of iron and part clay (Verse 33).

What item struck the feet and broke them in pieces?

"A **stone** was cut out without hands" (Verse 34).

What happened to the metals of the image?

"And became like **chaff** from the summer threshing floors; the winds carried them away so that no trace of them was found" (Verse 35).

What did the Stone turn into?

"The stone turned into **a great mountain**" (Verse 35).

The Vision Interpreted

This dream had a purpose, it was to show *"what shall be in the later days" (Verse 28).* This is the first vision of many that will describe the events of the earth from Daniel's present day until the final coming of Jesus Christ. We will build upon this vision and learn the purpose, timing, and meaning of each item presented in this prophetic dream.

Currently in our study of this dream, we are only aware that a dream took place. We have a statue formed from many metals, and we know that someday a stone, one cut without hands, will strike the statue and destroy it completely, leaving behind no trace of the metals. We also know that this stone will turn itself into a huge mountain, one that will fill the whole earth.

We could guess at the meaning of the metals, the stone, and the mountain, but God is not one who works by guessing. As we continue our study of scripture we will perfectly know what every detail represents.

Our rules state that prophecy can only be understood if one of two conditions exist:
1. God reveals the answer, or
2. History has passed and proved the interpretation accurate.

God Reveals Part of the Interpretation

"This is the dream. Now we will tell the interpretation of it before the king. ₃₇You, O king, are a king of kings. For the God of heaven has given you a kingdom, power, strength, and glory; ₃₈and wherever the children of men dwell, or the beasts of the field and the birds of the heaven, He has given them into your hand, and has made you ruler over them all— you are this head of gold" (Daniel 2:36-38).

The head of gold has a perfect meaning:

God said, "You are this head of gold" (Verse 38).

Who is the "You"?

King Nebuchadnezzar.

No guessing was required! God said it and it is so.

The Other Kingdoms

"And after thee shall arise another kingdom inferior to thee, and another third kingdom of brass, which shall bear rule over all the earth. ₄₀And the fourth kingdom shall be strong as iron: forasmuch as iron breaketh in pieces and subdueth all [things:] and as iron that breaketh all these, shall it break in pieces and bruise. ₄₁And whereas thou sawest the feet and toes, part of potters' clay, and part of iron, the kingdom shall be divided; but there shall be in it of the strength of the iron, forasmuch as thou sawest the iron mixed with miry clay. ₄₂And [as] the toes of the feet [were] part of iron, and part of clay, so the kingdom shall be partly strong, and partly broken. ₄₃And whereas thou sawest iron mixed with miry clay, they shall mingle themselves with the seed of men: but they shall not cleave one to another, even as iron is not mixed with clay" (Daniel 2:39-43 KJV).

What do the metals represent?

Kingdoms.

The metals represent different occupying nations, kingdoms or world powers. We are not given the names of the succeeding kingdoms—yet, but we are given identifying characteristics of each. We could guess at the kingdoms to come, but God never wants us to guess at His Word. We must read on and study. Soon God will reveal the exact names of the kingdoms to follow, but these will not come until Daniel chapters 7 and 8.

The Stone Identified

"And in the days of these kings shall the God of heaven set up a kingdom, which shall never be destroyed: and the kingdom shall not be left to other people, [but] it shall break in pieces and consume all these kingdoms, and it shall stand for ever. ₄₅Forasmuch as thou sawest that the stone was cut out of the mountain without hands, and that it brake in pieces the iron, the brass, the clay, the silver, and the gold; the great God hath made known to the king what shall come to pass hereafter: and the dream is certain, and the interpretation thereof sure. ₄₆Then the king Nebuchadnezzar fell upon his face, and worshiped Daniel, and commanded that they should offer an oblation and sweet odours unto him. ₄₇The king answered unto Daniel, and said, Of a truth [it is,] that your God is a God of gods, and a Lord of kings, and a revealer of secrets, seeing thou couldst reveal this secret. ₄₈Then the king made Daniel a great man, and gave him many great gifts, and made him ruler over the whole province of Babylon, and chief of the governors over all the wise [men] of Babylon. ₄₉Then Daniel requested of the king, and he set Shadrach, Meshach, and Abed-nego, over the affairs of the province of Babylon: but Daniel [sat] in the gate of the king" (Daniel 2:44-49 KJV).

"**It shall break in pieces and consume all these kingdoms**" Here is a direct parallel to verses 34 and 35 *"broke them in pieces" "so that no trace of them was found."*

This stone, cut without hands, can be rightly deciphered. Using line upon line and precept upon precept the Scriptures will unlock its own mystery.

Who is the Rock?

> "He is the Rock, His work is perfect; For all His ways are justice, A God of truth and without injustice; Righteous and upright is He" (Deuteronomy 32:4).

> "The LORD is my rock and my fortress and my deliverer; My God, my strength, in whom I will trust; My shield and the horn of my salvation, my stronghold" (Psalm 18:2).

Jesus Christ, our Lord and Savior, is the Rock. Soon He will set up His kingdom. When God sets up His kingdom the earthly kingdoms will not exist, they will be scattered like chaff and will be found no more. God's kingdom will fill the entire earth and will be the only nation in existence.

What is the mountain called?

> "And he carried me away in the Spirit to a great and high mountain, and showed me the great city, the holy Jerusalem, descending out of heaven from God," (Revelation 21:10).

> "So you shall know that I am the LORD your God, Dwelling in Zion My holy mountain. Then Jerusalem shall be holy, And no aliens shall ever pass through her again" (Joel 3:17).

> The symbol of the mountain represents Zion, the holy Jerusalem.

God does not give us truth to be guessed at. Many interpreters of prophecy see the name Jerusalem and instantly look to the earthly city with the same name. Do not jump to conclusions without study. The Jerusalem mentioned, as turning from a stone into a great mountain, is the New Jerusalem (Revelation 21), the one that descends out of heaven from God.

Some popular interpretations of scriptural prophecy try to claim that God's kingdom will be set up while other earthly kingdoms exist. Some claim the Jewish nation will be revived or the nation of Israel will resume rule. Nevertheless, this dream clearly shows us that God's kingdom will occur only *after* all earthly kingdoms are removed and scattered like the chaff in the wind. There will not be the United States, or Israel, or Europe when God's kingdom is set up!

Here we leave Chapter 2 with all of the information that God chose to reveal to Daniel at this time. A lot of data has been revealed, and yet there is a lot of the interpretation that is unknown to us, as it was to Daniel. We know that this dream covered the entire span of history from the life of King Nebuchadnezzar through to the

End of Time Prophecies

End of Time when Jesus Christ will finally descend from the clouds above and bring with Him the New Jerusalem—His kingdom. This dream tells us that after Nebuchadnezzar's reign other earthly kingdoms will reign. Sometime, during the fourth kingdom, they will become intermingled.

The names of the kingdoms that followed Babylon are well known, but we are trying to learn how to properly interpret prophecy, as John or Daniel would have to do. So far, Daniel has no further revelations from God, nor has he lived long enough to prove from history what the succeeding kingdoms would be. For this reason we will leave the full interpretation of this vision to later, something Daniel had to do.

The Kingdoms of Daniel

Daniel 2	Daniel 7	Daniel 8	Daniel 11	Kingdom
Gold	◆	◆	◆	Babylon
Silver	◆	◆	◆	◆
Brass	◆	◆	◆	◆
Iron	◆	◆	◆	◆
Iron & Clay	◆	◆	◆	◆
Stone	◆	◆	◆	Jesus Christ

The Fiery Furnace
Daniel Chapter 3

This chapter does not contain any prophecy or vision. We will briefly touch on this chapter. King Nebuchadnezzar creates a larger than life statue representing the statue from his dream. A few key modifications are made; the most obvious is that the king's created statue is made from all gold—instead of just the head.

The king organizes a nationwide festival and invites everyone to bow down and worship the image that he created. What follows is the story of Shadrach, Meshach, Abed-nego and the fiery furnace.

"Nebuchadnezzar the king made an image of gold, whose height was sixty cubits and its width six cubits. He set it up in the plain of Dura, in the province of Babylon" (Daniel 3:1).

A *cubit* is the length of a man's forearm, from elbow to tip of his finger, conservatively set at 18 inches. A *score* means twenty. There are 12 *inches* to a *foot*.

How big was the statue?

Dimension	Cubit	Inches	Feet
Height:	60 cu.	1080 in.	90 ft.
Width:	6 cu.	108 in.	9 ft.

Forced to Worship the Image

"Then Nebuchadnezzar the king sent to gather together the princes, the governors, and the captains, the judges, the treasurers, the counselors, the sheriffs, and all the rulers of the provinces, to come to the dedication of the image which Nebuchadnezzar the king had set up. ₃Then the princes, the governors, and captains, the judges, the treasurers, the counselors, the sheriffs, and all the rulers of the provinces, were gathered together unto the dedication of the image that Nebuchadnezzar the king had set up; and they stood before the image that Nebuchadnezzar had set up. ₄Then an herald cried aloud, To you it is commanded, O people, nations, and languages, ₅[That] at what time ye hear the sound of the cornet, flute, harp, sackbut, psaltery, dulcimer, and all kinds of musick, ye fall down and worship the golden image that

End of Time Prophecies

Nebuchadnezzar the king hath set up: 6 And whoso falleth not down and worshippeth shall the same hour be cast into the midst of a burning fiery furnace. 7Therefore at that time, when all the people heard the sound of the cornet, flute, harp, sackbut, psaltery, and all kinds of musick, all the people, the nations, and the languages, fell down [and] worshiped the golden image that Nebuchadnezzar the king had set up. 8Wherefore at that time certain Chaldeans came near, and accused the Jews. 9They spake and said to the king Nebuchadnezzar, O king, live for ever. 10Thou, O king, hast made a decree, that every man that shall hear the sound of the cornet, flute, harp, sackbut, psaltery, and dulcimer, and all kinds of musick, shall fall down and worship the golden image: 11And whoso falleth not down and worshippeth, [that] he should be cast into the midst of a burning fiery furnace. 12There are certain Jews whom thou hast set over the affairs of the province of Babylon, Shadrach, Meshach, and Abed-nego; these men, O king, have not regarded thee: they serve not thy gods, nor worship the golden image which thou hast set up. 13Then Nebuchadnezzar in [his] rage and fury commanded to bring Shadrach, Meshach, and Abed-nego. Then they brought these men before the king. {3:14} 14Nebuchadnezzar spake and said unto them, [Is it] true, O Shadrach, Meshach, and Abed-nego, do not ye serve my gods, nor worship the golden image which I have set up? 15 Now if ye be ready that at what time ye hear the sound of the cornet, flute, harp, sackbut, psaltery, and dulcimer, and all kinds of musick, ye fall down and worship the image which I have made; [well:] but if ye worship not, ye shall be cast the same hour into the midst of a burning fiery furnace; and who [is] that God that shall deliver you out of my hands? 16Shadrach, Meshach, and Abed-nego, answered and said to the king, O Nebuchadnezzar, we [are] not careful to answer thee in this matter. 17If it be [so,] our God whom we serve is able to deliver us from the burning fiery furnace, and he will deliver [us] out of thine hand, O king. 18But if not, be it known unto thee, O king, that we will not serve thy gods, nor worship the golden image which thou hast set up" (Daniel 3:2-18 KJV).

What are two of the 10 Commandments (Exodus 20) that the king of Babylon asked the Jews to break:

1st - "You shall have no other gods before Me" (Verse 3).

2nd - "You shall not make for yourself a carved image" (Verse 4).

What punishment did the king have set up?

"Whoever does not fall down and worship shall be cast into the midst of a burning fiery furnace" (Verse 11).

The Fiery Furnace

"Then was Nebuchadnezzar full of fury, and the form of his visage was changed against Shadrach, Meshach, and Abed-nego: [therefore] he spake, and commanded that they should heat the furnace one seven times more than it was wont to be heated. 20And he commanded the most mighty men that [were] in his army to bind Shadrach, Meshach, and Abed-nego, [and] to cast [them] into the burning fiery furnace. 21Then these men were bound in their coats, their hosen, and their hats, and their [other] garments, and were cast into the midst of the burning fiery furnace. 22Therefore because the king's commandment was urgent, and the furnace exceeding hot, the flame of the fire slew those men that took up Shadrach, Meshach, and Abed-nego. 23And these three men, Shadrach, Meshach, and Abed-nego, fell down bound into the midst of the burning fiery furnace. 24Then Nebuchadnezzar the king was astonied, and rose up in haste, [and] spake, and said unto his counselors, Did not we cast three men bound into the midst of the fire? They answered and said unto the king, True, O king. 25He answered and said, Lo, I see four men loose, walking in the midst of the fire, and they have no hurt; and the form of the fourth is like the Son of God" (Daniel 3:19-25 KJV).

How many were thrown into the fiery furnace?

"Did we not cast three men bound into the midst of the fire?" (Verse 24).

How many were seen in the fiery furnace?

"I see four men loose, walking in the midst of the fire" (Verse 25).

What was the form of the fourth man?

"And the form of the fourth is like the Son of God" (Verse 25).

How did the king know what the Son of God looked like?

"But God has revealed them to us through His Spirit. For the Spirit searches all things, yes, the deep things of God. 11For what man knows the things of a man except the spirit of the man which is in him? Even so no one knows the things of God except the Spirit of God" (1 Corinthians 2:10,11).

"But sanctify the Lord God in your hearts, and always be ready to give a defense to everyone who asks you a reason for the hope that is in you, with meekness and fear; 16having a good conscience, that when they defame you as evildoers, those who revile your good conduct in Christ may be ashamed" (1 Peter 3:15,16).

The character of the three men had in daily life and other events always represented the truth of Christ. When asked for a reason of their faith, they plainly and simply uplifted Christ. The king, knowing their character, recognized the Son of God. God revealed it to the king that the fourth person was Jesus Christ, the Son of God.

> "Then Nebuchadnezzar came near to the mouth of the burning fiery furnace, [and] spake, and said, Shadrach, Meshach, and Abed-nego, ye servants of the most high God, come forth, and come [hither.] Then Shadrach, Meshach, and Abed-nego, came forth of the midst of the fire. 27And the princes, governors, and captains, and the king's counselors, being gathered together, saw these men, upon whose bodies the fire had no power, nor was an hair of their head singed, neither were their coats changed, nor the smell of fire had passed on them. 28[Then] Nebuchadnezzar spake, and said, Blessed [be] the God of Shadrach, Meshach, and Abed-nego, who hath sent his angel, and delivered his servants that trusted in him, and have changed the king's word, and yielded their bodies, that they might not serve nor worship any god, except their own God. 29Therefore I make a decree, That every people, nation, and language, which speak any thing amiss against the God of Shadrach, Meshach, and Abed-nego, shall be cut in pieces, and their houses shall be made a dunghill: because there is no other God that can deliver after this sort. 30Then the king promoted Shadrach, Meshach, and Abed-nego, in the province of Babylon" (Daniel 3:26-30 KJV).

I do not believe that they would have been spared if they were trying to gain glory of self. The king promoted the three Jews for standing up for their convictions and choosing to worship only the true God.

The topic of worship will be a major test during the End of Time. When we get into Revelation we will see that there will be a false worship required of men, like Nebuchadnezzar required of the Jews. Those who bow down to the image will receive the mark of the beast. Those who stand tall to the precepts of God will be sealed and will see the Son of God.

Nebuchadnezzar is Humbled
Daniel Chapter 4

This chapter introduces a new dream of King Nebuchadnezzar. This dream is a prophecy, but not one that describes the End of Time. This dream was meant for the King, showing him what would transpire in his life.

"Nebuchadnezzar the king, To all peoples, nations, and languages that dwell in all the earth: Peace be multiplied to you. 2I thought it good to declare the signs and wonders that the Most High God has worked for me. 3How great are His signs, And how mighty His wonders! His kingdom is an everlasting kingdom, And His dominion is from generation to generation" (Daniel 4:1-3).

The original authors did not write the chapters and verses that we have in the Bible today. Evidence of this is seen in these verses. "The Hebrew Bible makes the content of Daniel 4:1-3 the conclusion of chapter 3."[1] It is possible that the translators meant for these verses to be a foreshadowing of events found in chapter four, but these three verses may better fit as a conclusion to Chapter 3. These verses show the King proclaiming to the world that the fourth person in the fire is the Son of God, and He alone is the ruler of the universe.

The book of Daniel is God's tutor book for interpreting prophecy. Here is a warning for us to be careful of verse and chapter numbers and separations. Original Hebrew and Greek writings did not have any of the punctuation or separation of text that we now enjoy. The current arrangement of chapters and verses were added centuries after the completed canon of the Bible was compiled. The chapters and verses are a great aid in locating particular passages, but it can be confusing and misleading when we try to understand where ideas start and where they end. This issue becomes more visible as we study the prophecies in Revelation.

---

1   Stefanovic, Zdravko, *Daniel: Wisdom to the Wise*, (ID: Pacific Press Publishing Assoc., 2007), 149.

End of Time Prophecies

"I Nebuchadnezzar was at rest in mine house, and flourishing in my palace: 5I saw a dream which made me afraid, and the thoughts upon my bed and the visions of my head troubled me. 6Therefore made I a decree to bring in all the wise [men] of Babylon before me, that they might make known unto me the interpretation of the dream. 7Then came in the magicians, the astrologers, the Chaldeans, and the soothsayers: and I told the dream before them; but they did not make known unto me the interpretation thereof" (Daniel 4:4-7 KJV).

Did the king forget this dream?

No. He remembered this dream, and simply asked for his wise men, Daniel included, to present the interpretation of his dream.

Why didn't the king's wise men want to interpret this dream?

This dream took place after the dream of Daniel 2. The wise men knew that there was a true God of Heaven who knows all. They were aware that if they guessed at the meaning of this dream and if Daniel's interpretation differed from theirs they would be executed.

God does not design prophecy to be guessed at. We must wait for it to pass (history), or wait until God reveals the Truth. Those who guess at prophecy might discover that God will hold them to the same accountability that King Nebuchadnezzar held his wise men.

The King's Dream Revealed

"But at the last Daniel came in before me, whose name [was] Belteshazzar, according to the name of my god, and in whom is the spirit of the holy gods: and before him I told the dream, [saying,] 9O Belteshazzar, master of the magicians, because I know that the spirit of the holy gods [is] in thee, and no secret troubleth thee, tell me the visions of my dream that I have seen, and the interpretation thereof. 10Thus [were] the visions of mine head in my bed; I saw, and behold a tree in the midst of the earth, and the height thereof [was] great. 11The tree grew, and was strong, and the height thereof reached unto heaven, and the sight thereof to the end of all the earth: 12The leaves thereof [were] fair, and the fruit thereof much, and in it [was] meat for all: the beasts of the field had shadow under it, and the fowls of the heaven dwelt in the boughs thereof, and all flesh was fed of it. 13I saw in the visions of my head upon my bed, and, behold, a watcher and an holy one came down from heaven; 14He cried aloud, and said thus, Hew down the tree, and cut off his branches, shake off his leaves, and scatter his fruit: let the beasts get away from under it, and the fowls from his branches: 15Nevertheless leave the stump of his roots in the earth, even with

a band of iron and brass, in the tender grass of the field; and let it be wet with the dew of heaven, and [let] his portion [be] with the beasts in the grass of the earth: 16Let his heart be changed from man's, and let a beast's heart be given unto him; and let seven times pass over him. 17This matter [is] by the decree of the watchers, and the demand by the word of the holy ones: to the intent that the living may know that the most High ruleth in the kingdom of men, and giveth it to whomsoever he will, and setteth up over it the basest of men. 18This dream I king Nebuchadnezzar have seen. Now thou, O Belteshazzar, declare the interpretation thereof, forasmuch as all the wise [men] of my kingdom are not able to make known unto me the interpretation: but thou [art] able; for the spirit of the holy gods [is] in thee" (Daniel 4:8-18 KJV).

The king's vision is of a large fruitful tree. Its visibility extends to all the earth. The king saw a holy one come down and chop down the tree. In verse 16 there is a dream-like switch. The dream was talking about a tree, then the switch is flipped, and we are now talking about a man whose heart is changed into the heart of a beast. This beast like heart was to last for seven times.

The King's Dream is Interpreted

"Then Daniel, whose name [was] Belteshazzar, was astonied for one hour, and his thoughts troubled him. The king spake, and said, Belteshazzar, let not the dream, or the interpretation thereof, trouble thee. Belteshazzar answered and said, My lord, the dream [be] to them that hate thee, and the interpretation thereof to thine enemies. 20The tree that thou sawest, which grew, and was strong, whose height reached unto the heaven, and the sight thereof to all the earth; 21Whose leaves [were] fair, and the fruit thereof much, and in it [was] meat for all; under which the beasts of the field dwelt, and upon whose branches the fowls of the heaven had their habitation: 22It [is] thou, O king, that art grown and become strong: for thy greatness is grown, and reacheth unto heaven, and thy dominion to the end of the earth. 23And whereas the king saw a watcher and an holy one coming down from heaven, and saying, Hew the tree down, and destroy it; yet leave the stump of the roots thereof in the earth, even with a band of iron and brass, in the tender grass of the field; and let it be wet with the dew of heaven, and [let] his portion [be] with the beasts of the field, till seven times pass over him; 24This [is] the interpretation, O king, and this [is] the decree of the most High, which is come upon my lord the king: 25That they shall drive thee from men, and thy dwelling shall be with the beasts of the field, and they shall make thee to eat grass as oxen, and they shall wet thee with the dew of heaven, and seven times shall pass over thee, till thou know that the most High ruleth

in the kingdom of men, and giveth it to whomsoever he will. 26And whereas they commanded to leave the stump of the tree roots; thy kingdom shall be sure unto thee, after that thou shalt have known that the heavens do rule. 27Wherefore, O king, let my counsel be acceptable unto thee, and break off thy sins by righteousness, and thine iniquities by shewing mercy to the poor; if it may be a lengthening of thy tranquility" (Daniel 4:19-27 KJV).

Why was Daniel *"astonished for a time?"*

"It is you, O king, who have grown and become strong; for your greatness has grown and reaches to the heavens, and your dominion to the end of the earth" (Verse 22).

"They shall drive you from men, your dwelling shall be with the beasts of the field, and they shall make you eat grass like oxen. They shall wet you with the dew of heaven, and seven times shall pass over you, till you know that the Most High rules in the kingdom of men, and gives it to whomever He chooses" (Verse 25).

This prophecy bothered Daniel because the dream described events that would happen to the King. The kingdom of Babylon had become a world power, it was not the only kingdom in existence, but it was large enough to be known, seen, feared, and have influence over the entire earth. Something was about to happen to the king, he was going to be cut down and humiliated. The king was going to be driven from men and made to dwell in a field like a lowly beast. He would be given grass to eat like the oxen and would remain this way for seven times. At the end of this time, the king would understand that the Most High God is the ruler of all and He gives the kingdom of men to whomsoever He wills.

The Dream Becomes Reality

"All this came upon the king Nebuchadnezzar. 29At the end of twelve months he walked in the palace of the kingdom of Babylon. 30The king spake, and said, Is not this great Babylon, that I have built for the house of the kingdom by the might of my power, and for the honour of my majesty? 31While the word [was] in the king's mouth, there fell a voice from heaven, [saying,] O king Nebuchadnezzar, to thee it is spoken; The kingdom is departed from thee. 32And they shall drive thee from men, and thy dwelling [shall be] with the beasts of the field: they shall make thee to eat grass as oxen, and seven times shall pass over thee, until thou know that the most High ruleth in the kingdom of men, and giveth it to

Nebuchadnezzar is Humbled

whomsoever he will. 33The same hour was the thing fulfilled upon Nebuchadnezzar: and he was driven from men, and did eat grass as oxen, and his body was wet with the dew of heaven, till his hairs were grown like eagles [feathers,] and his nails like birds' [claws.] 34And at the end of the days I Nebuchadnezzar lifted up mine eyes unto heaven, and mine understanding returned unto me, and I blessed the most High, and I praised and honoured him that liveth for ever, whose dominion [is] an everlasting dominion, and his kingdom [is] from generation to generation: 35And all the inhabitants of the earth [are] reputed as nothing: and he doeth according to his will in the army of heaven, and [among] the inhabitants of the earth: and none can stay his hand, or say unto him, What doest thou? 36At the same time my reason returned unto me; and for the glory of my kingdom, mine honour and brightness returned unto me; and my counselors and my lords sought unto me; and I was established in my kingdom, and excellent majesty was added unto me. 37 Now I Nebuchadnezzar praise and extol and honour the King of heaven, all whose works [are] truth, and his ways judgment: and those that walk in pride he is able to abase" (Daniel 4:28-37 KJV).

How long after the dream before it came true?

At the end of twelve months.

This dream was prophetic. This dream has a perfect interpretation only because the events came to pass exactly as foretold; history had passed. Daniel writes, *"All this came upon King Nebuchadnezzar."*

This dream is recorded in the book of Daniel only after the prophecy came true. The prophecy was recorded in verses 4-18, and the historical proof was the last part of the chapter verses 19-37.

This vision holds no interpretation for future events. This vision would only affect this king; there is no connection to End of Time events. I believe this vision was included in God's tutorial of interpretation for two reasons; the first being that not all prophecy must point to the End of Time; and the second is for us to understand that words can be symbolic; specifically the word *times*.

The term *"seven times"* is one that we will see again as we study prophecy. The use of this term in this dream told how long the King was to remain a beast. History and other studies show us that the King was a beast for 7 years; thus the term *"seven times"* is the same as seven years.

Times = 1 year. (Further study is found in "Prophetic Timings").

End of Time Prophecies

Counterfeit Prophecy Warning

The Jehovah's Witness interpret this recorded dream as one that foretells the future events of the earth, similar to the dream from Daniel 2. This book and our study of scripture does not support this interpretation.

The alternative interpretation labels the great tree as Jesus Christ's earthly kingdom, spreading its branches over the entire earth. They see the Israelites who escaped Egypt as the time when the tree flourished. This tree was chopped down and banded when they were captured in 607BC by the Chaldeans. They calculate a time when the tree will be restored and the nation of Israel will be reestablished as God's singular nation. Seven years is calculated to represent 2520 literal years. (They use one *day* = one "year", a proper tool supported by scriptures, and will be discussed later in the chapter "Prophetic Timings"). They claim that from 607BC and adding 2520 years (accounting for no zero year) lands at AD1914.

According to this alternative interpretation, Christ's kingdom was then, in AD1914, reestablished on the earth.

The alternative interpretation sounds fascinating, but it is not what Daniel nor God declared.

This alternative interpretation fails on several key items most notably it goes against God's clear word that says this prophecy came true with King Nebuchadnezzar. If this chopped down tree was in fact Christ's kingdom, it would contradict the metal statue vision. Daniel 2 clearly states that Christ's new kingdom will come and exist only when all other kingdoms are like the chaff in the wind, blown away so that no place is found for them. Christ's earthly kingdom will not coexist with any other human nation. Moreover, the clearest evidence is that God's Kingdom does not now exist. Do not be tricked. *"For false christs and false prophets will rise and show great signs and wonders to deceive, if possible, even the elect" (Matthew 24:24).*

Prophetic Timings
A Day for a Year Concept

Prophecy includes a lot of symbolic language. There are terms such as years, days, times, and seasons that appear to have a double meaning. The dream in Daniel 4 spoke of the term *"seven times."* We saw briefly that this was seven years. How did we know this? Did we guess? No! The Bible, with study and prayerful guidance, will reveal its answers.

Cows Represent Years

"Then Pharaoh said to Joseph: "Behold, in my dream I stood on the bank of the river. ₁₈Suddenly seven cows came up out of the river, fine looking and fat; and they fed in the meadow. ₁₉Then behold, seven other cows came up after them, poor and very ugly and gaunt, such ugliness as I have never seen in all the land of Egypt. ₂₀And the gaunt and ugly cows ate up the first seven, the fat cows. ₂₁When they had eaten them up, no one would have known that they had eaten them, for they were just as ugly as at the beginning. So I awoke. ₂₂Also I saw in my dream, and suddenly seven heads came up on one stalk, full and good. ₂₃Then behold, seven heads, withered, thin, and blighted by the east wind, sprang up after them. ₂₄And the thin heads devoured the seven good heads. So I told this to the magicians, but there was no one who could explain it to me." ₂₅Then Joseph said to Pharaoh, "The dreams of Pharaoh are one; God has shown Pharaoh what He is about to do: ₂₆The seven good cows are seven years, and the seven good heads are seven years; the dreams are one. ₂₇And the seven thin and ugly cows which came up after them are seven years, and the seven empty heads blighted by the east wind are seven years of famine" (Genesis 41:17-27).

What did the seven fat cows represent?

"The seven good cows are seven years" (Verse 26).

What did the seven poor and ugly cows represent?

"And the seven thin and ugly cows which came up after them are seven years" (Verse 27).

End of Time Prophecies

Items can represent time periods. The prophetic dream in Daniel 4 tells us that the king was to be like a beast *"till his hair had grown like eagles' feathers and his nails like birds' claws" (Verse 33).* This would not be a very short time. It would take time for his appearance to get to this state. Seven years would be an appropriate time.

The word *times* is translated from the original word *'iddan* an Aramaic word meaning "a season, period." This same word has the meaning of a "year" in Daniel 7:25 and 12:7, and is confirmed in Revelation.

Prophetic Calendars

Prophecy uses a different calendar system then our current Gregorian calendar when computing time. Prophecy uses the Jewish reckoning of days and months.

Our modern calendar denotes a year as being 365 ¼ days, the four quarters add up to an extra day every four years, giving us leap year. The Jewish calendar, the calendar that prophecy uses, is based on a 360-day calendar. There are 12 months of exactly 30 days in length. Feasts were added yearly and every 40 years to balance out the calendar. The feasts are not discussed when calculating time in prophecy.

The Jewish system does not have to be guessed at, but can be seen in the story of the Genesis flood.

"Then God remembered Noah, and every living thing, and all the animals that were with him in the ark. And God made a wind to pass over the earth, and the waters subsided. ₂The fountains of the deep and the windows of heaven were also stopped, and the rain from heaven was restrained. ₃And the waters receded continually from the earth. At the end of the hundred and fifty days the waters decreased. ₄Then the ark rested in the seventh month, the seventeenth day of the month, on the mountains of Ararat" (Genesis 8:1-4).

How long was the ark floating on the waters?

"At the end of the hundred and fifty days the waters decreased" (Verse 3).

Genesis chapter 8 gives us the exact day that the ark rested on the mountains of Ararat:

The 17th day of the 7th month.

Genesis chapter 7 gives us the exact day that the flood began.

"In the six hundredth year of Noah's life, in the second month, the seventeenth day of the month, on that day all the fountains of the great deep were broken up, and the windows of heaven were opened" (Genesis 7:11).

What month and day did the flood begin?

Seventeenth Day of the Second Month.

Counting from the 2nd month, 17th day until the 7th month, 17th day is exactly 5 months, to the day.

Genesis 8:3 says that the ark floated for exactly 150 days.

150÷5 = 30 days exactly. Here is mathematical and biblical evidence to support that a prophetic month is 30 days.

Day for a Year

"According to the number of the days in which you spied out the land, forty days, for each day you shall bear your guilt one year, namely forty years, and you shall know My rejection" (Numbers 14:34).

"And when you have completed them, lie again on your right side; then you shall bear the iniquity of the house of Judah forty days. I have laid on you a day for each year" (Ezekiel 4:6).

Here are two texts that give us a conversion table for prophetic time.

How long is a day to represent?

One day in prophecy may represent one literal year.

This conversion is used throughout prophecy and has been proven accurate through the process of history. Prophecies include many symbols and symbols of time such as this one day for a year. The best course of action when reading the Bible and prophecy is to try and read it with a literal interpretation. If a literal reading is obviously silly or errant, such as a lion with wings, then search for a proper symbol or timing from Scripture. Beasts with horns that have their own eyes and speak (Daniel 7) are clearly symbols and cannot be taken literally.

Strength in Numbers

Isaiah 28:10 shows us that line upon line and precept upon precept is a proper way to study scriptures. There is another concept that helps us rightly interpret scriptures.

"One witness shall not rise against a man concerning any iniquity or any sin that he commits; by the mouth of two or three witnesses the matter shall be established" (Deuteronomy 19:15).

The mouth or words of a single text do not carry the weight that two or more texts, speaking on the same topic, do. Often there are texts within Scripture that appear to contradict each other. When this contradiction appears, compare other parallel texts and see where the weight of the evidence lies. This is not a guaranteed answer, but will help guide you in the right direction.

Numbers and Ezekiel confirm each other, stating that one day can be a symbol for one literal year.

Prophetic Timings Key

1 prophetic year = 360 days

1 prophetic month = 30 days

1 prophetic day = 1 year

A Prophetic Time = 1 prophetic year = 360 prophetic days = 360 literal years.

The Fall of Babylon
Daniel Chapter 5

This is a new chapter in the life of Daniel, a new king is now ruling the kingdom—Belshazzar an heir of the great Nebuchadnezzar.

There is a prophecy in this chapter, but like the tree in Daniel 4, it has no bearing on the End of Time other than to prove who the next kingdom was which would follow the Chaldeans. This prophecy, its revealing, interpretation and fulfillment, all occur in the span of a single evening.

"Belshazzar the king made a great feast to a thousand of his lords, and drank wine before the thousand. 2Belshazzar, whiles he tasted the wine, commanded to bring the golden and silver vessels which his father Nebuchadnezzar had taken out of the temple which [was] in Jerusalem; that the king, and his princes, his wives, and his concubines, might drink therein. 3Then they brought the golden vessels that were taken out of the temple of the house of God which [was] at Jerusalem; and the king, and his princes, his wives, and his concubines, drank in them. 4They drank wine, and praised the gods of gold, and of silver, of brass, of iron, of wood, and of stone" (Daniel 5:1-4 KJV).

Where did the gold and silver vessels come from?

"The gold and silver vessels which his father Nebuchadnezzar had taken from the temple which had been in Jerusalem" (Verse 2).

"In the same hour the fingers of a man's hand appeared and wrote opposite the lampstand on the plaster of the wall of the king's palace; and the king saw the part of the hand that wrote. 6Then the king's countenance changed, and his thoughts troubled him, so that the joints of his hips were loosened and his knees knocked against each other. 7The king cried aloud to bring in the astrologers, the Chaldeans, and the soothsayers. The king spoke, saying to the wise men of Babylon, "Whoever reads this writing, and tells me its interpretation, shall be clothed with purple and have a chain of gold around his neck; and he shall be the third ruler in the kingdom." 8Now all the king's wise men came, but they could not read the writing, or make known to the king its interpretation. 9Then King Belshazzar was greatly troubled, his countenance was changed, and his lords were astonished" (Daniel 5:5-9).

End of Time Prophecies

How fearful was King Belshazzar of this mysterious writing?
"The joints of his hips were loosened and his knees knocked against each other" (Verse 6).

"[Now] the queen, by reason of the words of the king and his lords, came into the banquet house: [and] the queen spake and said, O king, live for ever: let not thy thoughts trouble thee, nor let thy countenance be changed: 11There is a man in thy kingdom, in whom [is] the spirit of the holy gods; and in the days of thy father light and understanding and wisdom, like the wisdom of the gods, was found in him; whom the king Nebuchadnezzar thy father, the king, [I say,] thy father, made master of the magicians, astrologers, Chaldeans, [and] soothsayers; 12Forasmuch as an excellent spirit, and knowledge, and understanding, interpreting of dreams, and shewing of hard sentences, and dissolving of doubts, were found in the same Daniel, whom the king named Belteshazzar: now let Daniel be called, and he will shew the interpretation. 13Then was Daniel brought in before the king. [And] the king spake and said unto Daniel, [Art] thou that Daniel, which [art] of the children of the captivity of Judah, whom the king my father brought out of Jewry? 14I have even heard of thee, that the spirit of the gods [is] in thee, and [that] light and understanding and excellent wisdom is found in thee. 15And now the wise [men,] the astrologers, have been brought in before me, that they should read this writing, and make known unto me the interpretation thereof: but they could not shew the interpretation of the thing: 16And I have heard of thee, that thou canst make interpretations, and dissolve doubts: now if thou canst read the writing, and make known to me the interpretation thereof, thou shalt be clothed with scarlet, and [have] a chain of gold about thy neck, and shalt be the third ruler in the kingdom" (Daniel 5:10-16 KJV).

Belshazzar, the current king of Babylon, had strayed from the wisdom of his fathers. He no longer respected his grandfathers decrees, especially in regards to giving honor to the most High God (Daniel 3:29). He had updated his cabinet members with individuals who had forgotten the accurate interpretations of prophecy that were delivered through Daniel in the past. Now the king was forced to call upon God's true servant Daniel, a Jewish captive. The Jews were the same group that the king was now ridiculing through drunken revelry, and now a Jew was asked to interpret the writing on the wall.

The Fall of Babylon

"Then Daniel answered and said before the king, Let thy gifts be to thyself, and give thy rewards to another; yet I will read the writing unto the king, and make known to him the interpretation. 18O thou king, the most high God gave Nebuchadnezzar thy father a kingdom, and majesty, and glory, and honour: 19And for the majesty that he gave him, all people, nations, and languages, trembled and feared before him: whom he would he slew; and whom he would he kept alive; and whom he would he set up; and whom he would he put down. 20But when his heart was lifted up, and his mind hardened in pride, he was deposed from his kingly throne, and they took his glory from him: 21And he was driven from the sons of men; and his heart was made like the beasts, and his dwelling [was] with the wild asses: they fed him with grass like oxen, and his body was wet with the dew of heaven; till he knew that the most high God ruled in the kingdom of men, and [that] he appointeth over it whomsoever he will. 22And thou his son, O Belshazzar, hast not humbled thine heart, though thou knewest all this; 23But hast lifted up thyself against the Lord of heaven; and they have brought the vessels of his house before thee, and thou, and thy lords, thy wives, and thy concubines, have drunk wine in them; and thou hast praised the gods of silver, and gold, of brass, iron, wood, and stone, which see not, nor hear, nor know: and the God in whose hand thy breath [is,] and whose [are] all thy ways, hast thou not glorified:" (Daniel 5:17-23 KJV).

Daniel calmly recites the history of the Belshazzar's grandfather and how Nebuchadnezzar was forced to live as a beast for seven years. Daniel recites the story of the fiery furnace and the appearance of the fourth person—the Son of God. Daniel tells stories that remind the king of just how far he has fallen from the graces of God.

The Writing Interpreted

"Then the fingers of the hand were sent from Him, and this writing was written. 25"And this is the inscription that was written: MENE, MENE, TEKEL, UPHARSIN. 26This is the interpretation of each word. MENE: God has numbered your kingdom, and finished it; 27TEKEL: You have been weighed in the balances, and found wanting; 28PERES: Your kingdom has been divided, and given to the Medes and Persians." 29Then Belshazzar gave the command, and they clothed Daniel with purple and put a chain of gold around his neck, and made a proclamation concerning him that he should be the third ruler in the kingdom" (Daniel 5:24-29).

End of Time Prophecies

> **MENE:** God has numbered your kingdom, and finished it;
>
> **TEKEL:** You have been weighed in the balances, and found wanting;
>
> **PERES:** Your kingdom has been divided, and given to the Medes and Persians.

"That very night Belshazzar, king of the Chaldeans, was slain. 31 And Darius the Mede received the kingdom, being about sixty-two years old" (Daniel 5:30, 31).

What joint kingdom conquered Babylon?

The Medes and Persians.

Babylon, the capital of the Chaldean nation was captured by the Medes and Persians in 539BC. The actual capture of the city was directed by Cyrus, a Persian, who was the nephew of King Darius, a Mede. Out of respect for Darius, all of Cyrus' conquests were done in the name and honor of Darius. Two years later Darius would die leaving Cyrus the Persian leader of the entire empire.

The process of this capture was amazing. The Median-Persian army dug a drainage trench to divert the Euphrates river which ran through central Babylon. On the night of the invasion the water was diverted until the river became knee deep. Soldiers waded through the lowered river and discovered the river gates had not been secured. They gained access to the streets, slew the unsuspecting guards and opened the city from the inside.

This method of drying up the waters under Babylon will be revisited when we get into Revelation and speak about spiritual Babylon.

This chapter of Daniel provides a definite answer for the next kingdom from Daniel 2. History has passed sufficiently to prove that the next ruling kingdom, the arms and chest of silver would be the Medes and Persians. We have confirmation of the next kingdom!

Daniel and the Lion's Den
Daniel Chapter 6

This chapter contains one of the best-known stories in the entire Bible, that of Daniel and the lion's den. There is no prophetic language in this chapter, and thus not much time will be spent in its study. This story is one of comfort and deliverance for those who trust in God. The God of heaven who delivered Daniel from the lion's den still lives today to rescue us from the perplexities of life.

"It pleased Darius to set over the kingdom an hundred and twenty princes, which should be over the whole kingdom; 2And over these three presidents; of whom Daniel [was] first: that the princes might give accounts unto them, and the king should have no damage. 3Then this Daniel was preferred above the presidents and princes, because an excellent spirit [was] in him; and the king thought to set him over the whole realm" (Daniel 6:1-3 KJV).

Why was Daniel promoted?

"Because an excellent spirit was in him" (Verse 3).

"Then the presidents and princes sought to find occasion against Daniel concerning the kingdom; but they could find none occasion nor fault; forasmuch as he [was] faithful, neither was there any error or fault found in him. 5Then said these men, We shall not find any occasion against this Daniel, except we find [it] against him concerning the law of his God. 6Then these presidents and princes assembled together to the king, and said thus unto him, King Darius, live for ever. 7All the presidents of the kingdom, the governors, and the princes, the counselors, and the captains, have consulted together to establish a royal statute, and to make a firm decree, that whosoever shall ask a petition of any God or man for thirty days, save of thee, O king, he shall be cast into the den of lions. 8Now, O king, establish the decree, and sign the writing, that it be not changed, according to the law of the Medes and Persians, which altereth not. 9Wherefore king Darius signed the writing and the decree" (Daniel 6:4-9 KJV).

The presidents and princes could not find any fault in Daniel, so they created a new law, one that would restrict his religion and his worship of the one true God.

End of Time Prophecies

Daniel's predicament is no different from the predicament that will soon be placed upon the earth when the demand is made to worship a system that is counterfeit to God's order of worship. We visit this in more detail when we get to Revelation chapter 13. Daniel was not allowed to worship the one true God, the God of creation. Daniel was forced to worship only the king—the king of Babylon. This same scenario will be repeated on a global level before the return of Jesus Christ. Perhaps Daniel's story will bring you hope and encouragement in following God and His method of worship.

Daniel's Choice

"Now when Daniel knew that the writing was signed, he went home. And in his upper room, with his windows open toward Jerusalem, he knelt down on his knees three times that day, and prayed and gave thanks before his God, as was his custom since early days" (Daniel 6:10).

Why do you think Daniel did not hide during his prayers to heaven?

"You shall not bear false witness against your neighbor" (Exodus 20:16).

"Let your light so shine before men, that they may see your good works and glorify your Father in heaven" (Matthew 5:16).

Daniel was not ashamed of his God. He was not going to pretend to obey the king's law. Hiding your religion is like hiding a light under a basket, it does no one any good.

Daniel in the Lion's Den

"Then these men assembled, and found Daniel praying and making supplication before his God. 12Then they came near, and spake before the king concerning the king's decree; Hast thou not signed a decree, that every man that shall ask [a petition] of any God or man within thirty days, save of thee, O king, shall be cast into the den of lions? The king answered and said, The thing is true, according to the law of the Medes and Persians, which altereth not. 13Then answered they and said before the king, That Daniel, which [is] of the children of the captivity of Judah, regardeth not thee, O king, nor the decree that thou hast signed, but maketh his petition three times a day. 14Then the king, when he heard [these] words, was sore displeased with himself, and set [his] heart on Daniel to deliver him: and he laboured till the going down of

Daniel and the Lion's Den

the sun to deliver him. 15Then these men assembled unto the king, and said unto the king, Know, O king, that the law of the Medes and Persians [is,] That no decree nor statute which the king establisheth may be changed. 16Then the king commanded, and they brought Daniel, and cast [him] into the den of lions. [Now] the king spake and said unto Daniel, Thy God whom thou servest continually, he will deliver thee. 17And a stone was brought and laid upon the mouth of the den; and the king sealed it with his own signet, and with the signet of his lords; that the purpose might not be changed concerning Daniel. 18Then the king went to his palace, and passed the night fasting: neither were instruments of musick brought before him: and his sleep went from him. 19Then the king arose very early in the morning, and went in haste unto the den of lions. 20And when he came to the den, he cried with a lamentable voice unto Daniel: [and] the king spake and said to Daniel, O Daniel, servant of the living God, is thy God, whom thou servest continually, able to deliver thee from the lions? 21Then said Daniel unto the king, O king, live for ever. 22My God hath sent his angel, and hath shut the lions mouths, that they have not hurt me: forasmuch as before him innocency was found in me; and also before thee, O king, have I done no hurt. 23Then was the king exceeding glad for him, and commanded that they should take Daniel up out of the den. So Daniel was taken up out of the den, and no manner of hurt was found upon him, because he believed in his God" (Daniel 6:11-23 KJV).

How do we know King Darius had faith in Daniel's God?

"But the king spoke, saying to Daniel, "Your God, whom you serve continually, He will deliver you" (Verse 16).

Your Sins Will Find You Out

"And the king commanded, and they brought those men which had accused Daniel, and they cast [them] into the den of lions, them, their children, and their wives; and the lions had the mastery of them, and brake all their bones in pieces or ever they came at the bottom of the den. 25Then king Darius wrote unto all people, nations, and languages, that dwell in all the earth; Peace be multiplied unto you. 26I make a decree, That in every dominion of my kingdom men tremble and fear before the God of Daniel: for he is the living God, and stedfast for ever, and his kingdom [that] which shall not be destroyed, and his dominion [shall be even] unto the end. 27He delivereth and rescueth, and he worketh signs and wonders in heaven and in earth, who hath delivered Daniel from the power of the lions. 28So this Daniel prospered in the reign of Darius, and in the reign of Cyrus the Persian" (Daniel 6:24-28 KJV).

End of Time Prophecies

The historian Josephus[1] records this same story but adds some interesting details that are not included in the Bible. After Daniel's safe return, the wise men, presidents and princes attributed Daniel's safety to the fact that the lions had been over fed by the king, and thus were not hungry enough to attack Daniel. They tried to justify away God's miracle. The king knew this was not the case. To prove his point, the king, in front of his wise men, fed the lions until they were full and would not eat anymore. Then the king summoned that all of the princes, wise men and their families be thrown into the lion's den. The lions *"broke all their bones in pieces before they ever came to the bottom of the den"* (Verse 24).

---

1   Whiston, William, *The Works of Josephus: Complete and Unabridged*, (MA: Hendrickson Publishers, 1987), 284.

Cartoon Beasts
Daniel Chapter 7

"In the first year of Belshazzar king of Babylon, Daniel had a dream and visions of his head while on his bed. Then he wrote down the dream, telling the main facts" (Daniel 7:1).

We begin this chapter with a specific date. Belshazzar was the king from chapter 5, the same king who saw the writing on the wall and that same evening was defeated and killed. This chapter should be placed before both chapters 5 and 6.

Why is it here?

One possibility for this arrangement may be that whoever compiled the book of Daniel attempted to lighten up the heavy text of symbols, beasts and mysterious prophecies with stories of hope and encouragement. Daniel fainted several times and was weighed down by some of the visions he witnessed. Stories like the fiery furnace (Daniel 3) and the lion's den (Daniel 6) give hope and relief from the heavy visions of times, horns, kingdoms and more. This type of organization is seen in Revelation and may be used to comfort John during the many visions that he was given about the End of Time.

Another possibility for placing this chapter out of chronological order is that God planned to use the writings of Daniel to teach us how to unlock prophecy. Daniel is God's tutorial to interpreting prophecy. We see that prophetic writing is not always arranged chronologically or in order of events. This is a very important fact, especially when we dive into Revelation. End of Time prophecies are not meant to be read one after another. Many of the visions relating to the End of Time are designed to be read simultaneously, meaning side by side, each vision adding more information to the ones beside or before it.

End of Time Prophecies

The Vision Revealed

"Daniel spake and said, I saw in my vision by night, and, behold, the four winds of the heaven strove upon the great sea. ₃And four great beasts came up from the sea, diverse one from another. ₄The first [was] like a lion, and had eagle's wings: I beheld till the wings thereof were plucked, and it was lifted up from the earth, and made stand upon the feet as a man, and a man's heart was given to it. ₅And behold another beast, a second, like to a bear, and it raised up itself on one side, and [it had] three ribs in the mouth of it between the teeth of it: and they said thus unto it, Arise, devour much flesh. ₆After this I beheld, and lo another, like a leopard, which had upon the back of it four wings of a fowl; the beast had also four heads; and dominion was given to it. ₇After this I saw in the night visions, and behold a fourth beast, dreadful and terrible, and strong exceedingly; and it had great iron teeth: it devoured and brake in pieces, and stamped the residue with the feet of it: and it [was] diverse from all the beasts that [were] before it; and it had ten horns" (Daniel 7:2-7 KJV).

How many beasts are listed?

"Those great beasts, which are four, are four kings which arise out of the earth" (Daniel 7:17).

What does a beast represent?

From verse 17 we see that the beasts represent four kings which arise out of the earth.

How many solid metal kingdoms from Daniel 2 are described (not including the mixed kingdoms of iron and clay)?

4 Kingdoms[1]: 1) Gold, 2) Silver, 3) Brass, 4) Iron.

Daniel 2 and Daniel 7 are parallel in nature and content. The vision of the cartoon beasts and the vision of the metal statue are speaking of the same set of events. The four beasts are the same four numbered kingdoms from Daniel 2.

---

1   The iron and clay portion of the statue was not a new numbered kingdom. It was simply parts of the fourth kingdom (Daniel 2:41).

Looking to the end of Daniel 7 we notice that this vision ends at the same event found in Daniel 2.

"Then the kingdom and dominion, And the greatness of the kingdoms under the whole heaven, Shall be given to the people, the saints of the Most High. His kingdom is an everlasting kingdom, And all dominions shall serve and obey Him" (Daniel 7:27).

The events of this vision continue until all of the kingdoms under the whole heaven—in the whole earth, are given to the people, the saints of the Most High. This is the same event described in Daniel 2 with the stone that became a great mountain covering the whole earth. God's kingdom will not appear alongside any human run kingdom or nation.

The Cartoon-like Beasts

Each cartoon beast describes unique characteristics of the kingdom that it represents. God is being sure that students of history will have enough information to rightly define the name of each successive kingdom.

Beast 1

Describe the first beast (Verse 4).

> Like a lion.
> Had eagle's wings.
> The wings were plucked off.
> The beast had a man's heart given to it.

Who is this beast?

> This beast is the first kingdom: Babylonians under the Chaldeans.

"Israel is like scattered sheep; The lions have driven him away. First the king of Assyria devoured him; Now at last this Nebuchadnezzar king of Babylon has broken his bones" (Jeremiah 50:17).

"For indeed I am raising up the Chaldeans, A bitter and hasty nation Which marches through the breadth of the earth, To possess dwelling places that are

End of Time Prophecies

not theirs. ₇They are terrible and dreadful; Their judgment and their dignity proceed from themselves. ₈Their horses also are swifter than leopards, And more fierce than evening wolves. Their chargers charge ahead; Their cavalry comes from afar; They fly as the eagle that hastens to eat" (Habakkuk 1:6-8).

"And they shall drive you from men, and your dwelling shall be with the beasts of the field. They shall make you eat grass like oxen; and seven times shall pass over you, until you know that the Most High rules in the kingdom of men, and gives it to whomever He chooses" (Daniel 4:32).

The first beast is a perfect description of the Chaldean's or the Babylonians under King Nebuchadnezzar. Prophecy is perfect. No guessing is ever required to interpret prophecy. Archaeologists and visitors to the ruins of Babylon can still see carvings of lions on the walls and large stone lions crouching over archways. Clay tablets have been unearthed speaking of King Nebuchadnezzar, his dreams, his riches and even descriptions of his seven years of madness. History supports the Bible.

The Chaldeans ruled from 607BC until 539BC.

Beast 2

Describe the second beast (Verse 5).

   Like a bear.
   One side is raised up.
   Three ribs in its mouth.

Who is this beast?

   This beast is the second kingdom: The Medes and Persians who ruled jointly.

We did not have to guess at the names, because we have the vision in Chapter 5 of the fall of Babylon to the Medes. There is another vision, in chapter 8, which has an animal with two horns, one raised higher than the other. The name given to this animal is the Medes and Persians.

"Then I lifted my eyes and saw, and there, standing beside the river, was a ram which had two horns, and the two horns were high; but one was higher than the other, and the higher one came up last" (Daniel 8:3).

This imagery is similar to the description of a bear that has one side raised up higher than the other.

"The ram which you saw, having the two horns— they are the kings of Media and Persia" (Daniel 8:20).

God, in Daniel 8, reveals exactly who the ram kingdom represents, the Medes and Persians.

All of these parallels give us enough evidence that the visions of Daniel 2, 7 and even 8 are speaking of the same events.

Horns of Prophecy

No guessing is ever required to rightly interpret prophecy. We did not have to guess at the meaning of the second beast, history would reveal it to Daniel, and God would later confirm it.

Chapter 7 reveals more symbols and thus more information than the simple metal symbols of chapter 2. One of these added symbols is the symbol of a horn.

"The ten horns are ten kings Who shall arise from this kingdom. And another shall rise after them; He shall be different from the first ones, And shall subdue three kings" (Daniel 7:24).

"The ram which you saw, having the two horns— they are the kings of Media and Persia" (Daniel 8:20).

What does a horn represent?

> A horn, according to Daniel 7:24 represents a kingdom.
> Ten horns, ten kingdoms.

History reveals that the Medes were early rulers but soon joined alliances with the Persians. The Persians would attain higher eminence than the Medes, thus accurately fitting the description of one side or one horn (Daniel 8) being higher than the other. The three ribs in the Bear's mouth represent three powers that were eaten up or oppressed by the Median-Persian empire. Babylon, Lydia and Egypt were the three super powers of the day that were oppressed by this dual empire.

The Median-Persian empire ruled from 539BC until 331BC.

Beast 3

Describe the third beast (Verse 6).

> Like a leopard.
> With four wings.
> With four heads.
> And dominion was given to it.

Following the example of the previous beasts, this one represents the third kingdom, the kingdom of brass that would follow the kingdoms of silver and gold.

Before we turn to Daniel 8:21 and find the name of this kingdom, let us practice the role of interpretation using history.

We know that this is the third beast, the third metal, the third kingdom to rule after Nebuchadnezzar.

History tells us that the Babylonians were swift conquerors. Recalling the cartoon description of Babylon we see that the lion had a set of eagles wings. The cartoon of the third beast depicts a leopard, faster than a lion, with four wings; two more than the lion's. This kingdom must have some characteristic of speed that is greater than the Chaldeans.

This kingdom has four heads, four leaders.

Dominion is given to this kingdom, something neither beast before it obtained.

Pick up a history book and it will tell you that the next ruling kingdom, after the Persians, was Greece. Alexander the Great and his style of leading aroused the admiration of the world. Beginning almost from scratch he united contentious Greek communities, conquered mighty Persia and in twelve lightening years ruled all of civilization, obtaining total dominion. His military feats were swifter than swift. Tragically on June 13, 323 BC Alexander the Great, at the prime of his life—32 years old, died of a fever. His kingdom was ripped into four parts headed by his four generals (301 BC).

History proves that Greece is the third kingdom, the third metal, the third beast.

God will now grade our interpretation.

"And the male goat is the kingdom of Greece. The large horn that is between its eyes is the first king" (Daniel 8:21).

Though we have not fully studied Daniel 8, we will see that it is a vision that also corresponds to the same set of events found in Daniel 2 and Daniel 7.

Greece is the third Kingdom.

Greece ruled from 331 BC until 31 BC.

Beast 4

Describe the fourth beast (Verse 7).

> It is dreadful and terrible and strong.
> It has iron teeth.
> It devoured and broke into pieces and trampled the residue with its feet.
> It was different from all the beasts before it.
> It had ten horns.

Nowhere in scripture is the name of this beast mentioned by name. We will have to rely on history instead of direct revelation from God to rightly interpret this beast. But God is a Master Teacher. He has shown us how to interpret history correctly. Throughout Daniel and Revelation there are more descriptions for this fourth beast than any of the other kingdoms. God does not want us to guess and has provided so many specific characteristics of this kingdom and its change that it only fits one kingdom in all of history.

The fourth beast is Rome. A study of history will reveal this. Further descriptions of this fourth kingdom will be revisited throughout our study of End of Time prophecies.

Rome ruled from 31bc until ad476.

God's Court is Convened

"I considered the horns, and, behold, there came up among them another little horn, before whom there were three of the first horns plucked up by the roots: and, behold, in this horn [were] eyes like the eyes of man, and a mouth speaking great things" (Daniel 7:8 KJV).

There is much to be said about this little horn that develops inside of the Roman Empire. Daniel is both fascinated and concerned about understanding this little horn. There are more descriptions about this one symbol than any other prophetic symbol in the scriptures, except those which point to Jesus Christ. God wants us to be sure that we know who or what this little horn represents. More will be revealed in the chapter: "The Little Horn of Prophecy."

"I beheld till the thrones were cast down, and the Ancient of days did sit, whose garment [was] white as snow, and the hair of his head like the pure wool: his throne [was like] the fiery flame, [and] his wheels [as] burning fire. 10A fiery stream issued and came forth from before him: thousand thousands ministered unto him, and ten thousand times ten thousand stood before him: the judgment was set, and the books were opened" (Daniel 7:9,10 KJV).

This event follows the emergence of the little horn. This event is one of a courtroom, a place of judgment, with thousands and tens of thousands of beings looking on.

Who is the Ancient of Days?

God the Father.

The Ancient of Days is either Jesus Christ or God the Father, but in verse 13 we see one like the Son of Man approach the Ancient of Days.

Daniel 7 gives us insight into heaven, specifically a time when a court is convened and books are opened. "*The court*" is a translation of the

Aramaic word *din* meaning "judgment, or place of judgment." The scene that is set before Daniel is the judgment seat of God.

Judgment is not a single act. It is composed of several separate acts. The first is a trial: is there enough evidence to convict or exonerate the defendant? If convicted, then a sentence is announced. There is usually an opportunity for an appeal, checking of the records to prove the decisions made; afterwards the sentence is executed whether it is serving time, paying a fine, or the death penalty. God's judgment works the same way.

Daniel sees the events of the investigative judgment: the trial. He watches as the courtroom in heaven is set up. Court is convened and the books are opened. The heavenly court compares the life record of everyone who has ever lived on earth against the laws of God's universe.

"I beheld then because of the voice of the great words which the horn spake: I beheld [even] till the beast was slain, and his body destroyed, and given to the burning flame. 12As concerning the rest of the beasts, they had their dominion taken away: yet their lives were prolonged for a season and time" (Daniel 7:11,12 KJV).

After the court is set, and this judgment is complete, Daniel watches the destruction of the fourth beast— specifically the little horn, in a lake of fire. This is also described by John in Revelation 19:19,20.

The End of Time Events

"I saw in the night visions, and, behold, [one] like the Son of man came with the clouds of heaven, and came to the Ancient of days, and they brought him near before him. 14And there was given him dominion, and glory, and a kingdom, that all people, nations, and languages, should serve him: his dominion [is] an everlasting dominion, which shall not pass away, and his kingdom [that] which shall not be destroyed" (Daniel 7:13,14 KJV).

Notice carefully the order of events in Daniel 7. The little horn develops out of the fourth beast— Rome. Judgment is set in heaven. The little horn is destroyed after the judgment occurs. Then, and only then does Jesus Christ, the Son of Man, receive His kingdom. Only after Jesus receives His kingdom does He then return

End of Time Prophecies

in the clouds above to receive His saints (1 Corinthians 15:51,52; 1 Thessalonians 4:14-18; Revelation 19:6-16).

There is a lot more information and verses to discuss in this chapter, but we will leave it for now.

"I, Daniel, was grieved in my spirit within my body, and the visions of my head troubled me" (Daniel 7:15).

"This is the end of the account. As for me, Daniel, my thoughts greatly troubled me, and my countenance changed; but I kept the matter in my heart" (Daniel 7:28).

The many symbols of horns, courts, Ancient of Days, dominions and kingdoms confused and troubled Daniel. God would clear up some of this confusion through more visions.

The Kingdoms of Daniel

Daniel 2	Daniel 7	Daniel 8	Daniel 11	Kingdom
Gold	Lion with wings	♦	♦	Babylon
Silver	Bear stronger on one side	♦	♦	Medes & Persians
Brass	Leopard with four heads	♦	♦	Greeks
Iron	Terrible beast	♦	♦	Romans
Iron & Clay	♦	♦	♦	Divided Nations
Stone	Thrones set in place	♦	♦	Jesus Christ

Translations of the Bible
Why are there so many?

Why are there so many translations of the Bible? Which translation is more accurate? These questions appear to be important and must be addressed if we are to trust that the Scriptures are the inspired Word of God.

"All Scripture is given by inspiration of God, and is profitable for doctrine, for reproof, for correction, for instruction in righteousness, 17that the man of God may be complete, thoroughly equipped for every good work" (2 Timothy 3:16, 17).

All scripture is inspired by God, this includes the many translations that we have today. They are inspired by God and are profitable for growth and learning about who God is and what He expects of us in faith and belief.

Canonization of the Bible

The canonization of the Bible means simply that a list of authoritative books or writings are now bound together in a single book. The process of choosing which ancient writings to include has a Biblical foundation.

"For prophecy never came by the will of man, but holy men of God spoke as they were moved by the Holy Spirit" (2 Peter 1:21).

The Holy Spirit, God Himself, assisted the organization of His word. God did not leave His word to chance, He gave a set of instructions that could be used to test if a particular document or book was truly inspired by Him.

Here are two tests for proving if a document was inspired by God.

"But the prophet who presumes to speak a word in My name, which I have not commanded him to speak, or who speaks in the name of other gods, that prophet shall die.' 21And if you say in your heart, "How shall we know the word which the LORD has not spoken?'— 22when a prophet speaks in the name of the LORD, if the thing does not happen or come to pass, that is the thing which the LORD has not spoken; the prophet has spoken it presumptuously; you shall not be afraid of him" (Deuteronomy 18:20-22).

End of Time Prophecies

Tests of Inspiration

The first is a Test of Doctrine. Verse 20 says that those who speak in the name of other gods or speak contrary to what God commanded are not prophets of the Lord. The standard for evaluating any writing is the Law of God as revealed to Adam, Abraham and recorded by Moses. If a self-proclaimed prophet taught or wrote something that disagreed with what the Lord had revealed to Moses, he was a false prophet, his writings were not to be used, and he was to be stoned.

The second test is Fulfillment. Verses 21 & 22 tell us that the way to know whether a prophet was from God was to see if what he predicted came true.

Writings that passed both tests were recognized to be the words of God. Those that failed one test or the other were removed.

Men who experienced God wrote the Scriptures. They were eyewitnesses to the events recorded in the Bible.

"For we did not follow cunningly devised fables when we made known to you the power and coming of our Lord Jesus Christ, but were eyewitnesses of His majesty." "And so we have the prophetic word confirmed, which you do well to heed as a light that shines in a dark place, until the day dawns and the morning star rises in your hearts; 20knowing this first, that no prophecy of Scripture is of any private interpretation, 21for prophecy never came by the will of man, but holy men of God spoke as they were moved by the Holy Spirit" (2 Peter 1:16,19-21).

The writings that became our Bible, composed of 66 books, were public domain before they were canonized. This allowed the test of living witnesses to prove or disprove their accuracy. The letters of Paul, Peter, James and John were circulated among the early churches and their members. These people lived, witnessed and could personally attest to the ministry of Christ and the early church. If any of the writings were false they would not have been believed or treated with respect.

The Old Testament became a solid unit of 39 books sometime around 150 – 100BC. BC time counts down to 1BC, and AD counts up from AD1. The *Septuagint* was an early Greek translation of these 39 Hebrew writings.

The New Testament writings began around AD35 with James and concluded around AD96 with John's book of Revelation. The complete and formal Bible, with its 39 OT and 27 NT books, could be dated to AD383-405, with Jerome's Latin translation called the *Vulgate*. This became the standard Bible for over a thousand years.

In 1526, William Tyndale "Father of the English Bible" translated the New Testament into English which ultimately led to his execution. In 1604, King James I of England commissioned a new English translation. It was published in 1611 as the King James Version.

Today there are more than 3000 original Hebrew manuscripts of the Old Testament, and over 5500 ancient Greek manuscripts in existence today that contain part or all of the Scriptures. These are more than any other writings from the same periods. One of the most famous examples is the dead sea scrolls of Qumran found in AD1947 that contained copies of Biblical books such as Isaiah that date back to 150BC or later.

Problems in Translating

Most of the Old Testament was written in Hebrew. The New Testament was mostly written in Greek, specifically *koine*, or common Greek. Translating from Hebrew into Greek or into another language, say English, presents a few problems.

One of the problems is the simple task of communicating the author's intent. For example, the word *gay* to you or me (implying homosexual) takes on a different meaning than it did the in the 1950's (implying happy). This is a span of less than a century. What about a span of several hundred centuries?

Another problem is how to convert words that carry subtle nuances of a concept into a language that uses a word void of these nuances. I like to use the example of the English word *love*. We *love* our mothers, we *love* our cars, and we *love* our spouse; but we do not *love* all three in the same manner. The Greek language has four verbs that can mean *love*, each with a nuance of its own (*phileo, agapao, eros, thelo*).

The study of translations and textual criticism is a science unto itself, one that is unbelievably difficult and complex. Realizing that translations vary depending on their target audiences is important. A study of the various translations reveals that they differ mainly in emphasis, style, and nuance, and do not present radically different pictures of God, Jesus or Christianity. Some are better for personal reading, while others lend themselves to formal usage such as public readings.

Today we have English translations that are actually more accurate than Jerome's Vulgate, Tyndale's English, or the King James Version of the Bible. The New King James, and the English Standard Version both update the language to fit our day and time better than translations that use old and outdated English. Furthermore these modern translations compared a wider variety of the original manuscripts than were available to the translators of the 1500 and 1600's.

You can trust that God's word is true. You do not need to understand Greek and Hebrew to hear the Word of God. If you are doing a study, read several versions. Each version will bring out a nuance within the passages at study. Begin each study in prayer, asking God's Spirit to enlighten and guide your reading of His Word.

Studying and interpreting prophecy requires that we realize that a single translation may accidentally hide or define a word or phrase that is key to a deeper understanding. Evidence of this will be seen in our study of both Daniel and Revelation. (Cf. Daniel 8:12; the word "sacrifice" is added by translators and is not in the original text.) These additions or omissions do not alter the gospel of God's Word, written by humans.

Rams and Goats
Daniel Chapter 8

God revealed the future to Daniel. We do not have the actual video of his vision, but we are left with simple words that attempt to explain what Daniel saw. We do know that what Daniel saw troubled him.

"In the third year of the reign of King Belshazzar a vision appeared to me— to me, Daniel— after the one that appeared to me the first time" (Daniel 8:1).

How many years had passed between the vision in Daniel 8 and the vision in Daniel 7?

Two years. The vision in Daniel 7 was during King Belshazzar's first year.

If you recall from the end of the last vision, Daniel was troubled and confused by the many symbols found within the vision. This vision would help Daniel understand some of the symbols.

The Two Horned Ram

"And I saw in a vision; and it came to pass, when I saw, that I [was] at Shushan [in] the palace, which [is] in the province of Elam; and I saw in a vision, and I was by the river of Ulai. ₃Then I lifted up mine eyes, and saw, and, behold, there stood before the river a ram which had [two] horns: and the [two] horns [were] high; but one [was] higher than the other, and the higher came up last. ₄I saw the ram pushing westward, and northward, and southward; so that no beasts might stand before him, neither [was there any] that could deliver out of his hand; but he did according to his will, and became great" (Daniel 8:2-4 KJV).

Daniel sees a ram with two horns. We know this is a symbol for the joint kingdom of the Medes and Persians. God proves this interpretation.

"The ram which you saw, having the two horns— they are the kings of Media and Persia" (Daniel 8:20).

End of Time Prophecies

The Goat

"And as I was considering, behold, an he goat came from the west on the face of the whole earth, and touched not the ground: and the goat [had] a notable horn between his eyes. ₆And he came to the ram that had [two] horns, which I had seen standing before the river, and ran unto him in the fury of his power. ₇And I saw him come close unto the ram, and he was moved with choler against him, and smote the ram, and brake his two horns: and there was no power in the ram to stand before him, but he cast him down to the ground, and stamped upon him: and there was none that could deliver the ram out of his hand. ₈Therefore the he goat waxed very great: and when he was strong, the great horn was broken; and for it came up four notable ones toward the four winds of heaven" (Daniel 8:5-8 KJV).

The goat with the notable horn is Alexander the Great, the leader of the Greek nation. Again we do not have to guess as God reveals this answer to us.

"And the male goat is the kingdom of Greece. The large horn that is between its eyes is the first king" (Daniel 8:21).

These descriptions of the two kingdoms fit perfectly with their historic characteristics. The speed of Greece is noted in the scriptures as a goat that *"touched not the ground."* The death of Alexander is noted with precision in verse 8 *"and when he was strong, the great horn was broken."* The four notable horns that came to power are the four generals of Alexander's army:

Cassander controlled Macedonia and Greece;
Lysimachus took Thrace and much of Asia Minor;
Ptolemy retained Egypt, Cyrenaica and Palestine; and
Selecus retained Syria and the rest of Asia.

The Little Horn Appears

"And out of one of them came forth a little horn, which waxed exceeding great, toward the south, and toward the east, and toward the pleasant [land.] ₁₀And it waxed great, [even] to the host of heaven; and it cast down [some] of the host and of the stars to the ground, and stamped upon them. ₁₁Yea, he magnified [himself] even to the prince of the host, and by him the daily [sacrifice] was taken away, and the place of his sanctuary was cast down. ₁₂And an host was given [him] against the daily [sacrifice] by reason of transgression, and it cast down the truth to the ground; and it practised, and prospered" (Daniel 8:9-12 KJV).

The Little Horn of Prophecy
Daniel 7 & 8

We skipped over a lot of the symbols and verses in Chapters 7 and 8. This was to help identify the process of interpretation, and to keep you, the reader, from being overwhelmed as Daniel was when he experienced these visions.

"Then I wished to know the truth about the fourth beast, which was different from all the others, exceedingly dreadful, with its teeth of iron and its nails of bronze, which devoured, broke in pieces, and trampled the residue with its feet; 20and the ten horns that were on its head, and the other horn which came up, before which three fell, namely, that horn which had eyes and a mouth which spoke pompous words, whose appearance was greater than his fellows" (Daniel 7:19,20).

What symbol or beast did Daniel desire to understand?

He wanted to know the truth about the fourth beast, namely the little horn.

"After this I saw in the night visions, and behold, a fourth beast, dreadful and terrible, exceedingly strong. It had huge iron teeth; it was devouring, breaking in pieces, and trampling the residue with its feet. It was different from all the beasts that were before it, and it had ten horns. 8I was considering the horns, and there was another horn, a little one, coming up among them, before whom three of the first horns were plucked out by the roots. And there, in this horn, were eyes like the eyes of a man, and a mouth speaking pompous words" (Daniel 7:7,8).

"Thus he said: "The fourth beast shall be A fourth kingdom on earth, Which shall be different from all other kingdoms, And shall devour the whole earth, Trample it and break it in pieces. 24The ten horns are ten kings Who shall arise from this kingdom. And another shall rise after them; He shall be different from the first ones, And shall subdue three kings. 25He shall speak pompous words against the Most High, Shall persecute the saints of the Most High, And shall intend to change times and law. Then the saints shall be given into his hand For a time and times and half a time. 26"But the court shall be seated, And they shall take away his dominion, To consume and destroy it forever" (Daniel 7:23-26).

What name does History give to this fourth beast?

Rome. It is the fourth metal, the kingdom that followed Greece.

The fourth beast, the fourth kingdom to rule the earth, would follow Greece, but this fourth beast would be different from all the beasts before it. The uniqueness of this beast is important for End of Time prophecy. God provides more details about this fourth beast and its changes than any other beast. God wants us to be sure and perfect in our understanding of this beast.

The fourth beast began as the Roman Empire, but would grow into a different type of ruling power. These changes are well documented in scripture and history.

The legs of iron, in the metal statue, represent Rome. Just as there are two legs, Rome would, early in the 4th century AD, be split into two kingdoms: Eastern Rome and Western Rome. (It's fascinating to see that the chest and two arms represented the two nations of Media and Persia who would be a joint kingdom).

Rome is also labeled as a dreadful and terrible beast with 10 horns.

What does a horn represent?

Kingdom, ruler, nation, or power (Daniel 7:24).

The 10 horns represent ten kingdoms that would one day make up the Roman Empire. Rome began to break apart in AD351 and by AD476 the last emperor of Rome (Romulus Augustulus), was overthrown by a Germanic tribe– the Huns led by Odoacer. At this time Rome was completely divided into ten separate kingdoms: Huns, Ostrogoths, Visigoths, Franks, Vandals, Suevi (or Suebi, of which the Alemanni belonged), Burgundians, Heruli, Anglo-Saxons, and Lombards.

Rome or pagan Rome at this time looked very much like the kingdoms before it, but when the empire divided and began to crumble a new power developed within Rome that would be different from all the powers before it. This power would be the little horn power.

The Little Horn Power

Who is the Little Horn Power?

> The Scriptures will reveal who this power is. There are more descriptions given to this little horn power then given to any of the aforementioned kingdoms.

This little horn is a very important player in the events of the End of Time. The Bible gives us more characteristics about this little horn power than any other symbol in prophecy. God wants us to be sure that we know who or what this little horn represents.

Scriptures Define the Little Horn Power

"*I was considering the horns, and there was another horn, a little one, coming up among them, before whom three of the first horns were plucked out by the roots. And there, in this horn, were eyes like the eyes of a man, and a mouth speaking pompous words*" (Daniel 7:8).

"*I watched then because of the sound of the pompous words which the horn was speaking; I watched till the beast was slain, and its body destroyed and given to the burning flame*" (Daniel 7:11).

"*And the ten horns that were on its head, and the other horn which came up, before which three fell, namely, that horn which had eyes and a mouth which spoke pompous words, whose appearance was greater than his fellows. '21I was watching; and the same horn was making war against the saints, and prevailing against them, 22until the Ancient of Days came, and a judgment was made in favor of the saints of the Most High, and the time came for the saints to possess the kingdom'*" (Daniel 7:20-22).

"*The ten horns are ten kings Who shall arise from this kingdom. And another shall rise after them; He shall be different from the first ones, And shall subdue three kings. 25He shall speak pompous words against the Most High, Shall persecute the saints of the Most High, And shall intend to change times and law. Then the saints shall be given into his hand For a time and times and half a time*" (Daniel 7:24,25).

"*And out of one of them came a little horn which grew exceedingly great toward the south, toward the east, and toward the Glorious Land. 10And it grew up to the host of heaven; and it cast down some of the host and some of the stars to the ground, and trampled them. 11He even exalted himself as high as the Prince of the host; and by him the daily sacrifices were taken away,*

End of Time Prophecies

and the place of His sanctuary was cast down. ₁₂Because of transgression, an army was given over to the horn to oppose the daily sacrifices; and he cast truth down to the ground. He did all this and prospered. ₁₃Then I heard a holy one speaking; and another holy one said to that certain one who was speaking, 'How long will the vision be, concerning the daily sacrifices and the transgression of desolation, the giving of both the sanctuary and the host to be trampled underfoot?' ₁₄And he said to me, 'For two thousand three hundred days; then the sanctuary shall be cleansed'" (Daniel 8:9-14).

"*And in the latter time of their kingdom, When the transgressors have reached their fullness, A king shall arise, Having fierce features, Who understands sinister schemes. ₂₄His power shall be mighty, but not by his own power; He shall destroy fearfully, And shall prosper and thrive; He shall destroy the mighty, and also the holy people. ₂₅Through his cunning He shall cause deceit to prosper under his rule; And he shall exalt himself in his heart. He shall destroy many in their prosperity. He shall even rise against the Prince of princes; But he shall be broken without human means" (Daniel 8:23-25).*

"*And after the league is made with him he shall act deceitfully, for he shall come up and become strong with a small number of people. ₂₄He shall enter peaceably, even into the richest places of the province; and he shall do what his fathers have not done, nor his forefathers: he shall disperse among them the plunder, spoil, and riches; and he shall devise his plans against the strongholds, but only for a time. ₂₅He shall stir up his power and his courage against the king of the South with a great army. And the king of the South shall be stirred up to battle with a very great and mighty army; but he shall not stand, for they shall devise plans against him" (Daniel 11:23-25).*

"*And he was given a mouth speaking great things and blasphemies, and he was given authority to continue for fortytwo months. ₆Then he opened his mouth in blasphemy against God, to blaspheme His name, His tabernacle, and those who dwell in heaven. ₇It was granted to him to make war with the saints and to overcome them. And authority was given him over every tribe, tongue, and nation. ₈All who dwell on the earth will worship him, whose names have not been written in the Book of Life of the Lamb slain from the foundation of the world" (Revelation 13:5-8).*

ಐಲ

The Little Horn of Prophecy

All of these characteristics fit only one power in all of the earth's history.

This Little Horn Power...

- Uproots or removes three of the ten powers (Daniel 7:8).
- Has eyes like the eyes of a man (Daniel 7:8).
- Speaks pompous or blasphemous words against the God of heaven and creation (Daniel 7:8,11,25; Revelation 13).
- Will be slain, at the End of Time, and will be thrown into a lake of fire (Daniel 7:11; Revelation 19:20).
- Has an appearance that is greater than the kingdoms and rulers around it (Daniel 7:20).
- Makes war with the saints, destroying them for 1260 days, 42 months, or 3 ½ years. (A literal 1260 years.)(Daniel 7:21,25; Dan. 8:10,24; Dan.12:7; Revelation 11:2; Rev. 12:6; Rev. 13:5,7).
- Will exist until the saints possess the kingdom of Jesus Christ (Daniel 7:22).
- Will rule the whole earth (Daniel 7:23).
- Will make the whole earth, except for the saints, to worship and follow after it (Revelation 13:7,8).
- Shall think to change God's law— the 10 Commandments. Specifically the one that has time associated to it— the fourth Commandment (Daniel 7:25).
- Exalts himself to be equal or above the Prince of the Host— Jesus Christ (Daniel 8:11,25).
- Will be powerful and strong but not through its own power or army (Daniel 8:24; Revelation 13).
- Will cause deception to prosper, and will uplift traditions of men above the clear Word of God (Daniel 8:25).

The Little Horn Defined

The little horn is the system of Roman Catholicism or the papal system or the papacy. Every characteristic given in God's Word can accurately be given to this system, and only to this system.

The Roman empire began to splinter apart in the fourth century AD. Emperor Constantine inaugurated New Rome or Constantinople to be a new capital of the Roman Christian Empire on May 11, AD330. Rome was divided like two legs: Western and Eastern Rome.

Western Rome would disappear as a single power in AD476, but from its rubble the system of popes would be created and the power of the Roman Catholic Church would be consolidated.

Justinian, ruler of the fragment that was left of Western Rome wanted to consolidate his support and influence. Before embarking on a military campaign he issued a decree that would officially make the head bishop in Rome (Western Rome) the head or papa or pope of all the churches. Furthermore, his decree declared that the archbishop of Constantinople (Eastern Rome) would hold a rank below the pope in Rome. All of the churches, in both Eastern and Western Rome, gave their consent to this decree. By AD508, support for this decree was nearly unanimous among the many divisions of the Roman Empire. It was in this year that Clovis, king of the Franks (French) converted to Catholicism supporting the decree that the pope in Rome was the head of the church. Thirty years later in AD538, all resistance to this decree had been removed and the bishop of Rome began to consolidate power and influence that would be felt throughout the world. Over the next 1260 years, this influence would be powerful enough to control, setup and remove kings, kingdoms and powers.

A popular story highlights the power that was seen in the popes and the Roman Catholic Church during this time. Pope Gregory VII was the first pope to depose a crowned ruler, Emperor Henry IV. Pope Gregory declared Henry excommunicated and deposed, and he released Henry's subjects from their vows of loyalty. Pope Gregory's actions emboldened the opposition to Henry among the nobility, which agreed to meet, with Gregory in attendance, to decide Henry's fate. In one of the most dramatic events of the Middle Ages, Henry journeyed to meet pope Gregory at Canossa in the winter of 1077 and stood barefoot in the snow seeking forgiveness as a penitent sinner from the pope.

The little horn power is a diverse power not like the powers or kingdoms that appeared before it. Beginning in AD538 the system of Catholic popes influenced rule over Europe and much of the world. For 1260 years the popes held sway over these nations until AD1798 when it received a *"deadly wound"* (Revelation 13:3) and lost its influence and power over the nations. End of Time prophecies point to a time when this little horn power will regain influence and rule in the world.

"And I saw one of his heads as if it had been mortally wounded, and his deadly wound was healed. And all the world marveled and followed the beast [the little horn]" (Revelation 13:3).

Historical Evidence for The Little Horn as Papal Rome

The little horn plucked up three horns (kingdoms) before it. Daniel 7:8, 20, 24; 8:23; Revelation 13:1-8.

Historical Evidence: The papacy plucked up three of the ruling kingdoms that opposed its system of beliefs and traditions. Justinian, who gave the pope his power, conquered the last of these three, the Ostrogoths in AD538. The other two were the Heruli, AD493 and the Vandals, AD534.

It will have eyes like a man, looking greater than the kings around him, and be diverse from the other kingdoms. Daniel 7:8,20,24.

Historical evidence: The papacy would be cultivated and would rule with reason, in contrast to the barbaric natures of the other ruling kingdoms. This power would be diverse from the other kingdoms in that its power would be of a spiritual nature more than a political one.

It will have a mouth that will speak pompous words.

It will speak words against the Most High—that is God.

The little horn will think to change times and laws and by his power will magnify himself even to the Prince of Hosts—that is Jesus Christ.

Through his power and deceit he shall cause his craft and his lies to prosper (Daniel 7:8,20,25; 8:11,25).

Deceits and Errors Created by the Papacy

"For all have sinned and fall short of the glory of God," (Romans 3:23).

"If we say that we have not sinned, we make Him a liar, and His word is not in us" (1 John 1:10).

The popes have claimed *infallibility*; that is they and the church, can do no wrong. This belongs only to God.

"For the wages of sin is death, but the gift of God is eternal life in Christ Jesus our Lord" (Romans 6:23).

In the papal practice of giving *indulgences*— "the act of paying for the forgiveness of sins", they are usurping God's position, power and law. If we could pay for our own sins, then Jesus Christ would not have had to die for our salvation.

The papacy thought to *change* Gods Law (Exodus 20). They combined the first and second laws making them one and divided the tenth into two, making the ninth forbid the coveting of a neighbor's wife and the tenth that of coveting a neighbor's property. They have removed the words from the fourth commandment telling what day God set aside for His worship—the seventh-day Sabbath. The Catholic changing of God's law is superficial and in error. God's law cannot change, if it could be changed then Jesus Christ would not have needed to die for us.

The papacy transferred the religious celebration of the seventh-day *Sabbath to Sunday* (Council of Trent). Furthermore, the papacy holds that anyone who worships on Sunday does so because they are paying homage to the Roman Catholic Church, who, in their eyes, is able to change God's law.

The pope is called the vicar of Christ, which means he is Christ on earth. The pope magnifies himself to be equal in power and prestige with that of Jesus Christ.

By peace, the little horn will destroy many (Daniel 7:21, 25; 8:24, 25).

Historical Evidence: The Church of Rome has shed more innocent blood than any other institution that has ever existed among mankind. Any Protestant who has a complete knowledge of history will not question this fact. No power of imagination today can adequately realize the sufferings the saints felt at the hands of the papal church. Research the inquisitions by the Catholic Church, the French Huguenots, the Counter Reformation; read *Foxxes Book of Martyrs* for descriptions of the atrocities committed by the papacy in the name of religion.

Roman emperor Justinian, in AD533, wanted to obtain the influence of the bishop of Rome and the Catholic party. He issued a decree that constituted the head bishop in Rome as the head pope (father) of all the churches. The decree went into full effect in AD538.

The saints were prophesied to be given into the power of the little horn for 1260 years. (See the chapter: "Time-lines of Prophecy" for more details). 1260 years began in AD538 and continued until AD1798. In AD1798 General Berthier, with a French army, entered Rome, proclaimed a republic, took the pope prisoner and issued a deadly wound (Revelation 13:3) to the power of the papacy. (This wound would later be healed).

But he shall be broken without human means. Daniel 8:25.

Historical Evidence: Here is a direct reference to the stone in Daniel 2. The little horn will exist until the stone, the kingdom of Jesus Christ, strikes the earth and becomes the Great Kingdom. This prophecy is yet future. There is evidence that the papacy is growing. It has been revived, healed, and will continue to regain the status it once held until the day that Jesus Christ appears in the clouds above.

Conclusion

No other power, kingdom or entity perfectly fits these descriptions. The papal system of Roman Catholicism is the little horn power. It is the power that sprang up among the ten horns of Rome. It is the power that came after imperial Rome. Throughout the scriptures other names and symbols are given to describe this same system including: The beast from the sea (Revelation 13), the antichrist, man of sin, son of perdition (2 Thessalonians 2:3), Babylon, the mother of harlots (Revelation 17). Each of these titles will be discussed in time.

The little horn describes the *system* of Roman Catholicism, and does not necessarily refer to those who currently worship under this system. There are real God fearing Christians within this system who are serving God according to the best light they have. Studying the End of Time prophecies reveals that God will soon cause rays of light to penetrate the dense darkness that surrounds this system. All will have the opportunity to accept truth as it is revealed in the Scriptures and was seen in the life of Jesus Christ. Many at the End of Time will take their stand with truth and will come out of Babylon, out of this system, and will keep the commandments of God, having the faith of Jesus Christ.

The Seventy Week Prophecy
Daniel Chapter 9

This chapter begins with Daniel expecting something from God.

"In the first year of Darius the son of Ahasuerus, of the lineage of the Medes, who was made king over the realm of the Chaldeans— 2in the first year of his reign I, Daniel, understood by the books the number of the years specified by the word of the LORD through Jeremiah the prophet, that He would accomplish seventy years in the desolations of Jerusalem" (Daniel 9:1,2).

What was Daniel expecting God to accomplish within seventy years?

"For thus says the LORD: After seventy years are completed at Babylon, I will visit you and perform My good word toward you, and cause you to return to this place. 11For I know the thoughts that I think toward you, says the LORD, thoughts of peace and not of evil, to give you a future and a hope" (Jeremiah 29:10,11).

The prophet Jeremiah had prophesied that the nation of Judah would be taken captive by Babylon, and would be in captivity for seventy years. Daniel and his friends were captives in Babylon. Daniel now sought his freedom promised by God.

Historians claim that during the first year of Darius, Daniel would have been a captive in Babylon for over 60 years. Daniel was nearing the 70 years of captivity that Jeremiah had prophesied. He was looking forward to his people being set free, but something in his last vision, of Daniel 8, worried him.

"And he said unto me, Unto two thousand and three hundred days; then shall the sanctuary be cleansed" (Daniel 8:14 KJV).

Was God changing Jeremiah's time-line? Would Daniel and his people remain captives in Babylon for a longer period of time?

In the last vision there was a time-line that stretched for 2300 days. Daniel understood this to represent years. Which prophecy was accurate? His revelation from the angel or Jeremiah's? Daniel went to the only one in the universe that could answer his questions. Daniel knelt in prayer.

End of Time Prophecies

"Then I set my face toward the Lord God to make request by prayer and supplications, with fasting, sackcloth, and ashes. 4And I prayed to the LORD my God," (Daniel 9:3,4).

When did Daniel pray this prayer?

In the first year of Darius.

Recall that the book of Daniel is not written in chronological order. This prayer occurred during the first year of King Darius, this is also the same year that Daniel was thrown into the lion's den because he continued to pray to God in contradiction to the new law of the land. It is possible that this prayer was the one prayed by Daniel during these events.

The full prayer is found in Daniel 9:3-23. Much can be learned from this prayer that goes beyond prophecy, compare it with David's prayer in Psalm 51.

"And whiles I [was] speaking, and praying, and confessing my sin and the sin of my people Israel, and presenting my supplication before the LORD my God for the holy mountain of my God; 21Yea, whiles I [was] speaking in prayer, even the man Gabriel, whom I had seen in the vision at the beginning, being caused to fly swiftly, touched me about the time of the evening oblation. 22And he informed [me,] and talked with me, and said, O Daniel, I am now come forth to give thee skill and understanding. 23At the beginning of thy supplications the commandment came forth, and I am come to shew [thee;] for thou [art] greatly beloved: therefore understand the matter, and consider the vision" (Daniel 9:20-23 KJV).

Who visited Daniel?

The angel Gabriel visited Daniel.

What was the angel's purpose in visiting Daniel?

"To consider the matter, and understand the vision" (Verse 23).

Which vision confused Daniel?

The visions of Daniel 7 and 8 confused Daniel.

The Seventy Week Prophecy

The vision of the metal statue was simple to understand. It showed the span of time from Daniel until the End of Time. The vision of the beasts in chapters 7 and 8 were easy to understand. The item that really confused Daniel was the time of 2300 days and the description of the little horn.

2300 days would be a little over six years. If this was a literal length of time then the six years were nearly up, and Daniel's captivity should be nearing its close. However, if this was a prophetic timing, and represented 2300 years, then Daniel was more confused than ever. Daniel did not try to guess at the confusing time-lines. Daniel sought God.

70 Weeks Explained

God sent His angel Gabriel to give Daniel understanding and comfort. Gabriel was going to break down some of the prophetic time-lines.

"Seventy weeks are determined For your people and for your holy city, To finish the transgression, To make an end of sins, To make reconciliation for iniquity, To bring in everlasting righteousness, To seal up vision and prophecy, And to anoint the Most Holy" (Daniel 9:24).

"*Determined*" can mean cut off. Gabriel is showing Daniel that the 70 weeks would be cut off from the 2300 days. The 70 weeks would be determined, or set aside for his people.

Who are Daniel's people?

The Jews or the nation of Israel.

What was the purpose of the 70 weeks?

To make reconciliation for iniquity.

Daniel's people (God's people) were in captivity because they did not obey God. Captivity was a time for the Jewish nation to repent and return to God. God would give His nation another chance at reconciliation.

End of Time Prophecies

Using prophetic timings— a day represents a year (Ezekiel 4:6; Numbers 14:34), 70 prophetic weeks = 7 days x 70 weeks = 490 days or 490 literal years.

Daniel understood that this time-line would cover 490 years. All that he was missing was a start date.

> "Know therefore and understand, That from the going forth of the command to restore and build Jerusalem Until Messiah the Prince, There shall be seven weeks and sixty-two weeks; The street shall be built again, and the wall, Even in troublesome times" (Daniel 9:25).

What event is set to start the time-line?

> That from the going forth of the command to restore and build Jerusalem.

The 70 week time-line begins at the commandment to restore and rebuild Jerusalem. Here was good news to Daniel, the time-lines of 2300 years and 1260 years have nothing to do with his people's freedom or with Jeremiah's prophecy. These time-lines are for other key events in the history of the earth. Further hope was given to Daniel realizing that soon a command would be given that would allow his people to return to Jerusalem and freedom.

Four different commands were given to the Jewish captive's regarding a return to Jerusalem. Only one decree was issued that fully commissioned and even funded the Jews to both rebuild the tabernacle and to rebuild their nation allowing them to set up laws, magistrates and govern themselves. The Persian emperor Artaxerxes Longimanus in 457BC issued this decree. The decree can be read in Ezra 6 and 7.

Other Events

Gabriel continues to describe the events that would occur within the 490 years.

> "And after the sixty-two weeks Messiah shall be cut off, but not for Himself; And the people of the prince who is to come Shall destroy the city and the sanctuary. The end of it shall be with a flood, And till the end of the war desolations are determined. 27Then he shall confirm a covenant with many

The Seventy Week Prophecy

for one week; But in the middle of the week He shall bring an end to sacrifice and offering. And on the wing of abominations shall be one who makes desolate, Even until the consummation, which is determined, Is poured out on the desolate" (Daniel 9:26,27).

Within the 70 weeks (490 years) are three distinct time periods.

a) Seven weeks,
b) Threescore and two weeks, (62 weeks),
c) The last week.

Adding up all three time periods gives us the complete time of 70 weeks.

7 + 62 + 1 = 70 weeks.
7 weeks = 49 days = 49 literal years.
62 weeks = 434 days = 434 literal years.
1 week = 7 days = 7 literal years.

7 Weeks

The decree to rebuild Jerusalem was issued in 457BC. Adding 49 years to this date (subtracting, as BC counts down to zero), takes us to 408BC. This date marks the completion of the rebuild in Jerusalem. Read Nehemiah 13 for a description of the dedication service.

62 Weeks

Moving 434 years (62 prophetic weeks) from 408BC takes us to AD27. (The year zero is not used in calculating times).

AD27 is the recorded baptism of Jesus Christ, marking the beginning of the Messiah's ministry on earth (Matthew 3).

The Last Week

So far we have moved 69 weeks of the 70 weeks. Some attempt to interpret that the Messiah appeared during this 69th week and was cut off, or crucified during this same week. Verse 26 clearly shows us that this is impossible. *"And after the sixty-two weeks Messiah shall be cut off."* This verse says *after* the 62 weeks (including the 7 weeks, means *after* the 69th week) then the messiah shall be cut off. The messiah must be cut off sometime during the 70th week.

The First 3½ Days of Week 70

"Then he shall confirm a covenant with many for one week; But in the middle of the week He shall bring an end to sacrifice and offering" (Daniel 9:27).

Here is support that the Messiah was to enter the worldly scene during the 70th week. This began in AD27 at His baptism. During the middle of the week, that is after 3½ years (sometime in AD31), He would be cut off or crucified. It was at His crucifixion that the end to the sacrificial system and offerings were done away with, and the perfect penalty for sin would be paid once and for all. This was evidenced by the ripping of the tabernacle curtain from the top to the bottom (Matthew 27:51).

The Last 3½ Days of Week 70

The 70 weeks, 490 years, were given to Daniel's people. They were to finish the transgression, make an end of sins, and make reconciliation for iniquity. God warned the nation of Israel that if they continued to walk contrary to Him He would turn away from them. Three and a half years after the nation of Israel (the Jews), crucified Christ they were still persecuting His disciples. It was in AD34 that the Jewish leadership confirmed its rebellion against God. It was in that year that the Sanhedrim—the highest governing body of the Jews, officially stoned Stephen. In the killing of Jesus Christ, the Jewish leaders had persuaded the Romans to commit the murder for them. In the killing Stephen, they threw the rocks with their own hands. Saul, who later became Paul through a Damascus road conversion (Acts 9), was present at this stoning of Stephen. Later Paul, the converted Roman Jew, and Peter, (Acts 10) the disciple of Christ, would be the first to take the Gospel of Christ outside of the Jewish nation of Israel and present it to the whole world, and to the gentiles. The floodgates of Christianity were opened.

The Seventy Week Prophecy

The Fall of Israel

The Jews rejected the Savior, but the Savior did not fully reject the Jews or anyone else.

"What then? Israel has not obtained what it seeks; but the elect have obtained it, and the rest were blinded. ₈Just as it is written: 'God has given them a spirit of stupor, Eyes that they should not see And ears that they should not hear, To this very day.' ₉And David says: 'Let their table become a snare and a trap, A stumbling block and a recompense to them. ₁₀Let their eyes be darkened, so that they do not see, And bow down their back always.' ₁₁I say then, have they stumbled that they should fall? Certainly not! But through their fall, to provoke them to jealousy, salvation has come to the Gentiles. ₁₂Now if their fall is riches for the world, and their failure riches for the Gentiles, how much more their fullness! ₁₃For I speak to you Gentiles; inasmuch as I am an apostle to the Gentiles, I magnify my ministry," (Romans 11:7-13).

Though the Jewish nation rejected the Messiah, the Jews have a path to heaven, it is through grace, by faith in Jesus Christ, which is open to all, including the Gentiles, non-Jews and those who believe and make Jesus Christ Lord of their lives.

Let's check our math

```
    7 weeks, 49 years, to rebuild Jerusalem
  + 62 weeks, 434 years, until the Messiah would begin His earthly ministry
  + 1 week, 7 years, Christ would be cut off mid-week (3 ½ yrs) into His ministry
  = 70 total weeks, 490 years
```

457BC + 49 years	= 408BC	The dedication of Jerusalem
408BC + 434 years	= AD27	The baptism of Jesus Christ
AD27 + 3 ½ years	= AD31	The Crucifixion of Jesus Christ
AD31 + 3 ½ years	= AD34	The gospel was first preached to the Gentiles.

The 70 week prophecy is exact.

The Accuracy of these Dates with Modern History

Some scholars use 458BC as the date of Artaxerxes Command (Ezra 7); but they also change the date of Christ's baptism to AD26 to maintain the 70 weeks.

Anchoring Biblical events with pinpoint accuracy to our modern calendar is nearly impossible due to the many unique calendars, forms and methods of recording specific dates in the ancient world.

The Canon of Ptolemy, a notable reference for dates, uses 457BC. History and other prophecies confirm the use of 457BC as the starting date.

Pinpointing AD27 and AD31 to the baptism and crucifixion of Christ is met with the same challenges. By using scripture and fulfilled prophecies to confirm and anchor history, we can be sure that our dates are accurate.

A Disjointed 70 Weeks

There is an attempt among mainstream religions today to assume that the last week of this prophecy has not yet occurred. They accept the 69 weeks as introducing the Messiah, but they hold out that the last week, or last half of the week has not yet occurred but will in fact occur at some random time in the future. Nowhere does scripture ever support a scenario like this.

The 70 weeks are complete, contiguous and unbroken. There is no prophetic week floating around that will be enacted at some time future. The End of Time is upon us. Our study of Revelation and the rest of Daniel will show that we are living in the last days.

The 70 Weeks Anchors the 2300 Year Time-Line

The 70 weeks (490 years) are cut off from the beginning of the 2300 days (years) mentioned in Daniel 8:14.

Events not included within the 70 Weeks

The Destruction of Jerusalem in AD70.

The 70 Weeks concluded when the *"transgression was sealed;"* when the Jews were given one last chance *"to make an end of sins,"* and *"to make reconciliation for iniquity."* This was in AD34. After the conclusion of the 70 weeks there was a reference to another event that would transpire, but no specific time-line or date was given for this event.

"Then he shall confirm a covenant with many for one week; But in the middle of the week He shall bring an end to sacrifice and offering. And on the wing of abominations shall be one who makes desolate, Even until the consummation, which is determined, Is poured out on the desolate" (Daniel 9:27).

On the wing of abominations shall be one who makes desolate. Here is the hint to an event that would occur after the 70 weeks (490 years) had expired. When it would happen is not given exactly.

The words: *"Abominations"* and *"Desolate"* or *"Desolation"* exist in this combination only in the prophecies of Daniel 9:27; 11:31; 12:11, Matthew 24:15; (repeated in Mark 13:14 and Luke 16:15), and Revelation 17:4,5. Here are parallel passages that require investigation.

"Therefore when you see the 'abomination of desolation,' spoken of by Daniel the prophet, standing in the holy place (whoever reads, let him understand)," (Matthew 24:15).

Christ is speaking to His disciples as they are staring at the temple in Jerusalem. The time is somewhere between AD27 and AD31. Christ warns his disciples that one day destruction would come upon this temple so that no stone would be left standing upon another (Mathew 24:3).

Jesus does not give them a time-line but tells them to watch out for signs of the *"abomination of desolation"* standing in the *"holy place."*

The 70 week time-line said that destruction would appear *"on the wing of abominations."* This destruction is told to occur after the events of abominations; these including the crucifixion of the Messiah and the end of transgressions for the Jewish nation. No

End of Time Prophecies

time-line is revealed beyond the 70 weeks. The prophecy simply declares that at some time destruction would occur.

The 70 week prophecy ended in AD34. By this date the fate of the Jewish nation as a whole would be decided. If they chose to accept Jesus Christ, they would be accepted as a nation of God and would continue to receive the blessings promised in the scriptures. But the Jewish nation rejected the Savior. They persecuted all who believed in Jesus Christ and declared to the world that they were not followers of Jesus Christ.

Though the time-line of the 70 week prophecy was complete, the events foretold were not finished. When Jesus spoke to His disciples He was giving them another warning about this future destruction.

The destruction of the temple happened in AD70. The events of this destruction were perfectly foretold. All who heeded the warnings were spared destruction. Prior to AD70 the Romans under Cestius surrounded Jerusalem. Here was the *"abomination"* surrounding the Holy City. Unexpectedly the Romans abandoned the siege. A way of escape was made. Every Christian who believed the words of Jesus Christ and followed His commands fled the city, escaping to the mountains. Later, led by Titus, Rome returned to the city, laid siege to it and ultimately destroyed the city.

"And Jesus said to them, 'Do you not see all these things? Assuredly, I say to you, not one stone shall be left here upon another, that shall not be thrown down'" (Matthew 24:2).

Titus did not intend to destroy the Temple, but the Word of God never fails. A fire was accidentally started in the Temple, it became so hot that the gold melted and dripped down between the stones. The soldiers, trying to access the gold, ripped away stone upon stone fulfilling the prophecy perfectly.

The Seventy Week Prophecy

Events after the Time-lines

The 70 week prophecy, ending in AD34, shows us that other events were to follow after the 490 years (70 weeks), notably the destruction of Jerusalem. These events would not be determined by an exact time or date, but would require looking for signs to come.

These sequences of events will be repeated at the End of Time.

The last given time-line of prophecy ended in AD1844 marking the completion of the 2300 years. There are no more time-lines to be watching for. There would be other events after AD1844, but these would not be revealed by some date or time. These events require a watchful eye and knowledge of the signs.

5 Wise and 5 Foolish Virgins

The story of the wise and foolish virgins is a parable warning us to be ready for the return of Jesus Christ.

> *"Then the kingdom of heaven shall be likened to ten virgins who took their lamps and went out to meet the bridegroom. 2Now five of them were wise, and five were foolish. 3Those who were foolish took their lamps and took no oil with them, 4but the wise took oil in their vessels with their lamps. 5But while the bridegroom was delayed, they all slumbered and slept. 6And at midnight a cry was heard: 'Behold, the bridegroom is coming; go out to meet him!' 7Then all those virgins arose and trimmed their lamps. 8And the foolish said to the wise, 'Give us some of your oil, for our lamps are going out.' 9But the wise answered, saying, 'No, lest there should not be enough for us and you; but go rather to those who sell, and buy for yourselves.' 10And while they went to buy, the bridegroom came, and those who were ready went in with him to the wedding; and the door was shut. 11Afterward the other virgins came also, saying, 'Lord, Lord, open to us!' 12But he answered and said, 'Assuredly, I say to you, I do not know you.' 13Watch therefore, for you know neither the day nor the hour in which the Son of Man is coming"* (Matthew 25:1-13).

Wise virgins (Christians) know the signs of the End of Time, and will stand prepared in heart and soul to meet these events and our Judge and Savior Jesus Christ. Foolish virgins (Christians too!) are unprepared and will come up short when the End of Time comes.

End of Time Prophecies

The rest of this book will help outline the events that will transpire after the 2300 days (AD1844) but prior to the Second Coming of Jesus Christ. Becoming aware of these signs will help you to escape the destruction, the lies and the deceptions that are promised to envelop the entire world.

The Cleansing of the Sanctuary
Daniel 8:14

"And he [the angel] said to me [Daniel], 'For two thousand three hundred days; then the sanctuary shall be cleansed'" (Daniel 8:14).

The 2300 days is a time-line. Studying Daniel 9 we saw that this time-line was anchored in 457BC when king Artaxerxes issued a command to the Jews that they could return to Jerusalem, rebuild it and set up a ruler. The first 70 weeks or 490 literal years, of the 2300 years, gave us the starting time of Christ's earthly ministry beginning with His baptism in AD27. It told us that the Messiah would be cut off or crucified three and a half years into His ministry. It showed us that the Gospel of Christ would then be preached to the gentiles and to the world as a whole.

When does this time-line end?

2300 years from 457BC is AD1844.

According to Daniel 8:14 the sanctuary was to be cleansed in AD1844 at the end of the 2300 years.

What is the cleansing of the sanctuary?

Several *cleansings* were involved in the sanctuary system. Individual people, places and things required cleansing when they became unclean or defiled (spiritually and physically). Another cleansing involved the sanctuary and the sins of the people. This cleansing took place once a year on the Day of Atonement (Leviticus 16 and 23). It is this Day of Atonement which Daniel 8:14 and the 2300 days references.

The earthly sanctuary and its services met its fulfillment and end with the crucifixion of Christ (Matthew 27:51). Therefore, AD1844 could not be a reference to this earthly sanctuary.

Is there another sanctuary?

"And after that I looked, and, behold, the temple of the tabernacle of the testimony in heaven was opened:" (Revelation 15:5 KJV).

The earthly sanctuary was patterned after the sanctuary in heaven (see Exodus 25:8,9; Hebrews 8:5; 10:1). The earthly sanctuary and its services were given as a visual guide to the workings of God and the process of salvation and redemption.

The earthly tabernacle system with its sacrifices was never designed to take away sin or to redeem sinners. The system simply pointed the sinner forward to Jesus Christ- the Son of God, who would die on the cross for all sins. Today baptism and the communion service point us back to the amazing love and sacrifice of Jesus dying for our sins.

Does the heavenly sanctuary need cleansing?

Yes, and no.

No, there is not sin, dirt or filth in heaven; but *yes*, there is a record of our sins, evils, and imperfect lives. These are recorded in books that currently exist in heaven.

To clarify this answer it is important that we fully understand the atonement process outlined in the earthly sanctuary and its services.

Atonement: A Two Part System

What does atonement mean?

Atonement is the act of wiping something clean.

Entrance into heaven (salvation) is impossible without the process of atonement. No sin or sinner will remain in heaven, unless we can be wiped clean of our sins.

Sin is not something that God can wink at. God cannot ignore sin. The law of God states simply that all sin— no matter how big or small, requires death from the one who sinned. No other option exists. If God could excuse sin, then Jesus Christ would not have had to die, and God would be a liar for saying that the wages of sin is death (Romans 6:23).

This is where the beauty of Christianity shines: *"In Him [Jesus Christ] we have redemption through His blood, the forgiveness of sins, according to the riches of His grace" (Ephesians 1:7).*

Jesus lived a perfect life as a human— similar in nature to Adam before he sinned (Philippians 2:5-11). Jesus did not deserve death, but He gave up His life so that His perfect life could atone or pay for our sinful life. Jesus Christ shed His life for ours so that through faith in Him we can claim that our debt to sin has been paid.

The Daily Sacrifices

Part one of the atonement process is seen through the Old Testament system of sacrifices and sin offerings.

If someone sinned, they were to select a perfect lamb to sacrifice. This lamb was to be a visual representation of the future Messiah (Leviticus 1:3).

"And he shall bring the bullock unto the door of the tabernacle of the congregation before the LORD; and shall lay his hand upon the bullock's head, and kill the bullock before the LORD" (Leviticus 4:4 KJV).

The sinner would confess his sins and with a repentant heart, lay his hands on the head of the sacrifice implying a transfer of sins from the sinner to the sacrifice. Upon slaying the animal the priest would catch its blood.

"Then the anointed priest shall take some of the bull's blood and bring it to the tabernacle of meeting. 6The priest shall dip his finger in the blood and sprinkle some of the blood seven times before the LORD, in front of the veil of the sanctuary. 7And the priest shall put some of the blood on the horns of the altar of sweet incense before the LORD, which is in the tabernacle of meeting; and he shall pour the remaining blood of the bull at the base of the altar of the burnt offering, which is at the door of the tabernacle of meeting" (Leviticus 4:5-7).

End of Time Prophecies

When the priest dipped his finger into the lamb's blood, he, symbolically, took on the sins of the sinner. When the priest transferred the blood, to the altar and by sprinkling on the tabernacle veil, the sins of the sinner were now transferred to the tabernacle.

Symbolically the sinner was forgiven. The sins of the sinner no longer rested on the sinner. But now the sins had been transferred to the priest and the tabernacle.

Today when you sin, and with a repentant heart turn away from your sin and ask Jesus Christ to forgive you for your sins, your sins, by faith, are removed from you and placed on Jesus Christ.

Your sins have not yet been reconciled before God. They have simply been transferred and rest upon our perfect High Priest— Jesus Christ. The process of reconciliation or the cleansing of your sins from off of Jesus Christ is explained in the second half of the atonement process.

The Yearly Cleansing of Sins

The earthly sanctuary is a teaching tool given to us by God, showing us the process of salvation. The confessed sins of the people sat on the tabernacle by the literal sprinkling of blood. This blood represents the books and records that are in heaven. These books and records will be used to determine or judge who is a saint and who is not (Revelation 3:5; Malachi 3:16-18; Revelation 20:12; Psalm 56:8; Revelation 3:8; Philippians 4:3; Nehemiah 13:14; Ecclesiastes 12:14).

Once a year, at the end of the sanctuary cycle, there was a cleansing— an atonement, for the sins of the people.

"Also on the tenth [day] of this seventh month [there shall be] a day of atonement: it shall be an holy convocation unto you; and ye shall afflict your souls, and offer an offering made by fire unto the LORD" (Leviticus 23:27 KJV).

"And he [the high priest] shall make an atonement for the holy [place,] because of the uncleanness of the children of Israel, and because of their transgressions in all their sins: and so shall he do for the tabernacle of the congregation, that remaineth among them in the midst of their uncleanness. 17And there shall be no man in the tabernacle of the congregation when he

The Cleansing of the Sanctuary

goeth in to make an atonement in the holy [place,] until he come out, and have made an atonement for himself, and for his household, and for all the congregation of Israel" (Leviticus 16:16,17 KJV).

The camp of Israel was to prepare themselves for this process. It was a day of judgment. The high priest, and only the high priest, would enter into the most holy place and stand before the Shechinah Glory— the Presence of God. Here the high priest was to offer the blood of a sacrifice symbolizing that the penalty of death had been paid for all sins. If God accepted the blood sacrifice, the high priest would live, the tabernacle and all who participated by faith and action in the sacrificial system that year would be forever cleansed of their sins.

Leaving the presence of God, the high priest would symbolically place all of the forgiven sins of the camp onto the head of a waiting sacrifice or scape goat. This sacrifice was then led into the deep wilderness and banished forever. Here is the symbol of our sins being removed forever from the universe, mind, and actions of God.

This process is a visual guide to the removal of our sins from us and from God's books.

Jesus Christ is our High Priest.

"For Christ is not entered into the holy places made with hands, [which are] the figures of the true; but into heaven itself, now to appear in the presence of God for us:" (Hebrews 9:24 KJV).

Jesus, on the heavenly Day of Atonement or cleansing, entered into the most holy place to stand before God for us. Daniel saw this scene when he wrote that the thrones were set up and the court set (Daniel 7:10,26).

We are now standing in the day of judgment. That there should be a judgment is not strange.

"Because He has appointed a day on which He will judge the world in righteousness by the Man whom He has ordained. He has given assurance of this to all by raising Him from the dead" (Acts 17:31).

Were God alone concerned, there would be no need of an investigation of the life records of men in this judgment, for God is all knowing (omniscient). Even before the creation of the world He knew man would sin and that man would need a Savior. Moreover, as Sovereign God, He also knows just who will accept and who will reject His great salvation (Hebrews 2:3). The purpose of judgment is not to teach God anything that He doesn't already know, for He knows everything. The purpose of this *investigative judgment* is to ensure that everybody knows exactly why God has judged the way He has. The saved and lost, among both humans and angels, will have an opportunity to understand God's love for His creation as well as the justice of His law.

Instead of literal blood sprinkled upon a veil, Christ and God are reviewing the opened books.

The Opened Books

The book of life records all who have ever claimed faith in Jesus (Philippians 4:3).

The book of remembrance records the good deeds done by those who fear the Lord (Malachi 3:16-18).

There are other books that record every deed whether for good or not (Psalm 56:8; Revelation 3:8).

The atonement process began in AD1844. Beginning with Abel (the first to die), the names of everyone who have died and have claimed faith in Jesus Christ are having their lives reviewed before the judgment seats in the heavenly court. If they have confessed the name of Christ (Matthew 10:32; Romans 10:9); if they ran the race (Hebrews 12:1,2); or if they, by grace, overcame (1 John 2:13) and are called a friend of God (James 2:23), then they will not be blotted from the Lamb's book of life (Revelation 3:5). But if any turned away from faith in Christ (Ezekiel 18:24-32; 2 Timothy 3:5); walked their own path (Proverbs 3:5; Proverbs 4:19), or failed to develop a relationship with Christ, then Christ will have to blot that name out of His book (Exodus 32:33), and will have to exclaim *"depart from Me"*, *"I never knew you"* (Matthew 7:21-23).

The judgment of the living follows this same procedure: comparing the names in the Lamb's book of life to their confession of faith. But, since the life of the living is not yet complete there must be some test whereby creation (angels, humans and other beings) can see which side of the great controversy the living choose. This test of loyalty will simply be *worship*. Adam and Eve had a simple test, do not eat of a unique tree. At the End of Time God's test for determining His people will be to *worship* Him as He asks. When we get into Revelation, we will see that the little horn, also called the beast, will have an image, an idea, that can be worshiped. This will be contrary to the true style and day of worship that God, the Creator, set up from the beginning of time. We have not yet had our names presented before the thrones in heaven, because we are living. Soon there will come a time when worship of the beast and his image will be forced. It will be at this time that the mark of the beast (worship contrary to God's ordained day) is set up. Those who continue to worship contrary to God's Sabbath will receive the mark, and will be blotted from the book of life.

Soon Christ will stand up from His work as our High Priest and will put on His kingly attire. He will then appear in the clouds gathering His saints home. Amen.

Time-Lines of Prophecy
Important Dates in History

There is a purpose for every word found within the Bible. Numbers, dates, and time-lines are no exception. Daniel records the following time-lines: 2300 days (Daniel 8:14), 1335 days (Daniel 12:12), 1290 days (Daniel 12:11), 1260 days— also counted as 42 months, 3 ½ years, and *Time, Times, and half a Time* (Daniel 7:25; 12:7; Revelation 11:2,3; 12:6,14; 13:5).

How do these time-lines relate?

These time-lines are given so that when they are combined together they tell the history of the earth for the next 2,300 years. All of these time-lines are needed to be able to pinpoint key events in history. Remove one of these time-lines and the Scriptures would lose its accuracy in revealing the future.

The following chart reveals how seamlessly and perfectly the time-lines relate to each other. Each turn in the time-line anchors both an important date in history and the start or end of a relevant time-line.

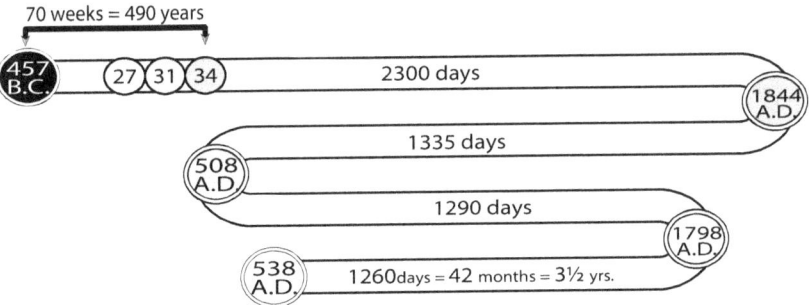

"Then I heard a holy one speaking; and another holy one said to that certain one who was speaking, 'How long will the vision be, concerning the daily sacrifices and the transgression of desolation, the giving of both the sanctuary and the host to be trampled underfoot?' ₁₄*And he said to me, 'For two thousand three hundred days; then the sanctuary shall be cleansed'"* (Daniel 8:13,14).

The time-line of 2300 days is to include events such as a host being trampled underfoot, a vision of daily sacrifices, some transgression of desolation and more. These key words point us to other time-lines throughout both Daniel and Revelation. The 2300 days, are years; within these 2300 years all of the time-lines must fit. Knowing the length, all that is missing is a start date.

The Beginning of the 2300 years

"And he informed me, and talked with me, and said, "O Daniel, I have now come forth to give you skill to understand. 23At the beginning of your supplications the command went out, and I have come to tell you, for you are greatly beloved; therefore consider the matter, and understand the vision:" (Daniel 9:22,23).

Daniel was asking to *"understand the vision."*

Which vision was Daniel trying to understand?

> It would be the last vision prior to Daniel 9. It was the vision of Daniel 8 which included the 2300 year time-line.

The angel Gabriel was sent to help Daniel understand the many time-lines. A key part of this understanding would be the starting point for the 2300 year prophecy.

"Know therefore and understand, That from the going forth of the command To restore and build Jerusalem Until Messiah the Prince" (Daniel 9:25).

What event started the 2300 years?

> The command to restore and build Jerusalem.

Recall that Daniel and his people, the Jews, were captives in Babylon. There were several commands issued from Babylon allowing portions of the captives to return to Jerusalem, but there was only one command that gave the power to rebuild Jerusalem, the tabernacle, and allowed them to set up laws, magistrates, and a system of governance. This command was issued by King Artaxerxes in 457BC. You can read about it in Ezra 7.

Time-Lines of Prophecy

End of the 2300 years

"And he said to me, 'For two thousand three hundred days; then the sanctuary shall be cleansed'" (Daniel 8:14).

What event concludes the 2300 year time-line?

Cleansing of the heavenly sanctuary. The Day of Atonement.

Moving 2300 years beginning with 457BC takes us to AD1844.

BC counts down to year 1BC, then jumps to AD1. There is no zero year. Moving 457 years from 457BC takes us to AD1. Subtracting the 457 years from 2300 years leaves us with 1843 years. But since we are now at AD1, adding 1843 years to 1 takes us to AD1844.

The day of cleansing the sanctuary began sometime in AD1844.

The First 70 weeks

Anchoring the 2300 year time-line was a prophecy of 70 weeks or 490 years. We discussed this in detail in the chapter: "The Seventy Week Prophecy."

457BC The command to restore rule and build Jerusalem is given.

408BC The temple is dedicated in Jerusalem. 7 weeks = 49 years.

AD27 Jesus begins his ministry. Plus 62 weeks = 434 years.

AD31 Jesus is cut off— crucified. Mid week = 3 ½ years.

AD34 The Jews reject Christianity. End of last week = 3 ½ years.

The 1335 year Time-line

"And from the time that the daily sacrifice is taken away, and the abomination of desolation is set up, there shall be one thousand two hundred and ninety days. 12Blessed is he who waits, and comes to the one thousand three hundred and thirty-five days. 13But you, go your way till the end; for you shall rest, and will arise to your inheritance at the end of the days" (Daniel 12:11-13).

End of Time Prophecies

Several clues help anchor this 1335 day prophecy:
1. It is mentioned in connection to the 1290 year period,
2. It occurs during the 2300 days period,
3. It concludes when Daniel "*stands in his lot*" (KJV) or when he "*will arise to your inheritance at the end of the days*" (NKJV).

Daniel is told to "*go your way till the end,*" this end would be the end of the 2300 days. It would be then, at the Day of Atonement, that Daniel's inheritance would be determined.

"But the land shall be divided by lot; they shall inherit according to the names of the tribes of their fathers. 56According to the lot their inheritance shall be divided between the larger and the smaller" (Numbers 26:55,56).

The Promised Land, Canaan, was to be divided by lots. This was the inheritance given to the children of Israel- the nation of believers in God. This division of lots occurred before the land was fully conquered.

At the end of the 2300 days Daniel would stand in his lot. It would be during the atonement process that Daniel and others who have died will have their lives judged, determining eternal life or eternal death.

The 1335 year time-line ends at AD1844.

Counting backwards from 1844 lands us in the year AD508. Simply subtracting 1335 from 1844 gives us the length of time that separates events. The event would have occurred before the 1335 years begins, or at the zero point.

The 1335 year time-line begins in the year AD508.

AD508

Prior to AD508 there were divisions within the Roman empire which sought to tear it apart. One division centered around the concept of Arianism. This belief included the idea that Jesus Christ was a created being and not truly God. The powers that believed in this concept also opposed the centralization of the church under the banner of Catholicism.

Clovis, the king of the Franks converted to the Catholic faith in AD496. In AD507 Clovis kills Alaric, the leader of the Visigoths who was a staunch believer in the Arian belief. One year later, AD508, Clovis would create a peace treaty with Theodoric the Ostrogoth pacifying the region for a time and allowing Catholicism to grow in peace.

Here marked the beginning of the little horn's growth to power. This act set the scene for the consolidation of power and control under the banner of Roman Catholicism headed by the system of popes and fulfills the language of Daniel 12:11 declaring that the "*abomination of desolation is set up.*"

The 1290 year Time-line

This time-line extends 1290 years from the moment that the "*abomination of desolation is set up*" (Daniel 12:11). This was the time when the papal system was first set up. This began in AD508, the same year the 1335 time-line began.

Moving 1290 years from AD508 lands us in the year AD1798.

"And I saw one of his heads as if it had been mortally wounded, and his deadly wound was healed. And all the world marveled and followed the beast" (Revelation 13:3).

The little horn received a deadly wound in AD1798. General Berthier, with a French army, entered Rome, proclaimed a republic, took the pope prisoner and issued the "*deadly wound.*" Scripture reveals that before the End of Time this wound would be healed, and the entire world would marvel and follow the beast, the little horn, the papal system.

End of Time Prophecies

The 1260 year Time-line

This time-line goes by several names: 1260 days, 42 months, 3 ½ years, and *Time, Times, and half a Time* (Daniel 7:25; 12:7; Revelation 11:2; 12:6,14). All of these names refer to the exact same period in earth's history. This is important. Some try to combine the 3 ½ years together showing that this is the missing week from Daniel's 70 week prophecy in Daniel chapter 9. We saw that this is not what the scripture revealed.

3 ½ years is 42 months is 1260 days, they are the same.

Reading each reference of this time-line reveals that the little horn (called the beast in Revelation), would rule for 1260 years. During this time it would trample on the saints, persecute them and kill many. This time-line speaks of the dark ages in earth's history; a time when a religious power controlled civil agencies and destroyed all who dared to contradict its beliefs and traditions.

The beast lost it's power in AD1798. Counting backwards 1260 years gives us the year AD538.

AD538

The Roman Emperor Justinian, in an attempt to consolidate power, issued a decree that the bishop of Rome be made the head of all churches throughout the empire. Dissenting factions within the Roman sphere of influence hampered this decree for a time. Daniel 7:8 declares that three powers (horns) would be uprooted by the little horn. The last of these powers were removed in AD538. The little horn— Roman Catholicism, now had full power, control and influence over the entire Roman Empire.

The little horn (Catholicism) ruled for 1260 years claiming open war on the saints, and anyone else who would not bow to its form of religious rule. This period was full of torture and destruction. The Church of Rome shed more innocent blood than any other institution that has ever existed. Read *Foxxes' Book of Martyrs*, research the inquisitions by the Catholic Church, study the French Huguenots and the French revolution. The reign of terror that extended over this 1260 year period was not perpetrated by some obscure power, but was inflicted by a triumphant Roman church with deliberation.

God's Promises

The time-lines fit together like a perfect puzzle. Each length is needed to move us to important anchor points in history. It is because of this accuracy that I write this book. It is because of this accuracy with dates, times, and numbers that I find added comfort in God's word to be true, perfect and accurate. These time-lines give me hope that if the promises attached to these prophecies came true, perfectly, then the future promises of mansions in heaven, of salvation through faith and obedience to Jesus Christ, and of a loving God will also hold true.

Daniel Mourns Three Full Weeks
Daniel Chapter 10

The last three chapters of Daniel are not separate events but describe a single event in Daniel's life. This is his last recorded vision.

This last vision gives more specific details about history than any of Daniel's other visions with the exception of the 70 week prophecy.

God has not revealed the exact interpretation of this vision, therefore we must rely on history to prove the evidence found in this last vision. Looking back at history, we will see that it confirms the Word of God perfectly.

The level of detail given in this vision requires that we rightly determine the correct words recorded by Daniel. Here is where the many translations of the Bible come into play. Recall that each translation is an interpretation from Hebrew into English using the best information available at that time. The King James Bible was translated in AD1611. The translators did the best they could with the amount of history that had transpired. They did not have the four hundred plus years of history that we have today.

Here is Daniel 10:1 from the New King James Version:

"In the third year of Cyrus king of Persia a message was revealed to Daniel, whose name was called Belteshazzar. The message was true, but the appointed time was long; and he understood the message, and had understanding of the vision" (Daniel 10:1).

And now from a Literal Translation:[1]

"In the third year of Cyrus king of Persia, a thing was revealed to Daniel, whose name was called Belteshazzar. And the thing was true, and a great conflict. And he understood the thing, and had understanding of the vision" (Daniel 10:1).

---

1   Green, Sr., Jay P., *The Interlinear Bible*, (MA: Hendrickson Publishers, Inc., 2013)

Notice the words *"a great conflict"* are totally absent from the New King James Bible. The translators did their best to convey the meaning of this verse, as they understood it, but what if this understanding has changed because more of history has been played?

Personally, I believe that the words *"a great conflict"* strengthen the interpretation of this last vision. This great conflict is the essence of the vision. This great conflict is between the king of the North and the king of the South, and is important in the End of Time.

Daniel was seeking understanding about the little horn, the power that would enter the world stage, speak blasphemous words against the Most High, and would persecute the saints.

Before we dive into the study of this last vision it must be reminded that when we don't have a direct *thus saith the Lord* for an interpretation and have to rely on history to show us the exact answer, then every word, every item of the prophecy must fit to the interpretation given. If we say that one symbols represents a nation, then that nation must fit every description attached to the symbol, if not, then we cannot trust our interpretation.

Most scholars of Daniel are united in their interpretation of this last vision to a point. All interpretations tend to agree up through Daniel 11:13. After verse thirteen, there are a few branches or categories of interpretation that scholars tend to follow.

There is only one interpretation that is perfect. Testing history against scripture will prove the perfect interpretation. The outline of this interpretation became truth in recent years when the other branches of interpretation did not occur as they predicted they would. Now that history has developed, the final meanings and interpretations of Daniel have been unlocked.

Why Daniel Mourned

"In the third year of Cyrus king of Persia a thing was revealed unto Daniel, whose name was called Belteshazzar; and the thing [was] true, but the time appointed [was] long: and he understood the thing, and had understanding of the vision. ₂In those days I Daniel was mourning three full weeks. ₃I ate

no pleasant bread, neither came flesh nor wine in my mouth, neither did I anoint myself at all, till three whole weeks were fulfilled. ₄And in the four and twentieth day of the first month, as I was by the side of the great river, which [is] Hiddekel; ₅Then I lifted up mine eyes, and looked, and behold a certain man clothed in linen, whose loins [were] girded with fine gold of Uphaz: ₆His body also [was] like the beryl, and his face as the appearance of lightning, and his eyes as lamps of fire, and his arms and his feet like in colour to polished brass, and the voice of his words like the voice of a multitude. ₇And I Daniel alone saw the vision: for the men that were with me saw not the vision; but a great quaking fell upon them, so that they fled to hide themselves. ₈Therefore I was left alone, and saw this great vision, and there remained no strength in me: for my comeliness was turned in me into corruption, and I retained no strength. ₉Yet heard I the voice of his words: and when I heard the voice of his words, then was I in a deep sleep on my face, and my face toward the ground" (Daniel 10:1-9 KJV).

What understanding was Daniel seeking?

"Now I have come to make you understand what will happen to your people in the latter days, for the vision refers to many days yet to come" (Daniel 10:14).

Daniel was mourning. He ate no food, and did not even anoint himself (bath?) for three full weeks. Clearly, Daniel was still confused about the visions that had long periods of time. Daniel desired understanding and comfort.

God sent comfort to Daniel.

"And, behold, an hand touched me, which set me upon my knees and [upon] the palms of my hands. ₁₁And he said unto me, O Daniel, a man greatly beloved, understand the words that I speak unto thee, and stand upright: for unto thee am I now sent. And when he had spoken this word unto me, I stood trembling. ₁₂Then said he unto me, Fear not, Daniel: for from the first day that thou didst set thine heart to understand, and to chasten thyself before thy God, thy words were heard, and I am come for thy words. ₁₃But the prince of the kingdom of Persia withstood me one and twenty days: but, lo, Michael, one of the chief princes, came to help me; and I remained there with the kings of Persia. ₁₄ Now I am come to make thee understand what shall befall thy people in the latter days: for yet the vision [is] for [many] days. ₁₅And when he had spoken such words unto me, I set my face toward the ground, and I became dumb. ₁₆And, behold, [one] like the similitude of the sons of men touched my

End of Time Prophecies

lips: then I opened my mouth, and spake, and said unto him that stood before me, O my lord, by the vision my sorrows are turned upon me, and I have retained no strength. ₁₇For how can the servant of this my lord talk with this my lord? for as for me, straightway there remained no strength in me, neither is there breath left in me. ₁₈Then there came again and touched me [one] like the appearance of a man, and he strengthened me, ₁₉And said, O man greatly beloved, fear not: peace [be] unto thee, be strong, yea, be strong. And when he had spoken unto me, I was strengthened, and said, Let my lord speak; for thou hast strengthened me. ₂₀Then said he, Knowest thou wherefore I come unto thee? and now will I return to fight with the prince of Persia: and when I am gone forth, lo, the prince of Grecia shall come" (Daniel 10:10-20 KJV).

How many weeks was Daniel mourning?

Three full weeks, or twenty-one days (Verse 2).

How many days was the angelic being restrained by the prince of the kingdom of Persia?

Twenty-one days (Verse 13).

Here is a wonderful peek into the spiritual realm.

"For we do not wrestle against flesh and blood, but against principalities, against powers, against the rulers of the darkness of this age, against spiritual hosts of wickedness in the heavenly places" (Ephesians 6:12).

Daniel began his prayer, his mourning and crying out to God, exactly twenty-one days before his comfort arrived through the angelic being. Daniel was in no eminent danger, and so God could allow delay for His comfort and answer. How often do we fret and worry when God does not answer us immediately? Perhaps God has answered us but knows that our faith will survive and in the process through tribulation, our character will be improved. Trust God, lean not on your own understanding!

"But I will tell you what is noted in the Scripture of Truth. No one upholds me against these, except Michael your prince" (Daniel 10:21).

And with this introduction the angel spends the next 45 verses, found in chapter 11, detailing the events that were to come to pass in the future of the earth and the End of Time.

Daniel's Last Vision
Daniel Chapter 11

This chapter is the revelation that angel Gabriel gives Daniel explaining the vision in chapter 8. Specifically Daniel learns about the little horn, how it would come to power, and what would transpire when it did come into power. This prophecy consists of more literal language than the visions of chapters 2, 7 and 8.

"And now I will tell you the truth: Behold, three more kings will arise in Persia, and the fourth shall be far richer than them all; by his strength, through his riches, he shall stir up all against the realm of Greece" (Daniel 11:2).

Who were the next three kings to arise in Persia?

    Cambyses (reigned 530 – 522 BC)

    Gaumata "false Bardiya", "Smerdis" (522 BC)

    Darius I "Hystaspes" (522-486 BC)

The fourth king was Xerxes (486-465 BC) who stirred up Greece by invading it, only to be defeated at the Battle of Salamis (480 BC).

"Then a mighty king shall arise, who shall rule with great dominion, and do according to his will" (Daniel 11:3).

Who is this mighty king?

Is he Median-Persian or is he Greek?

"And when he has arisen, his kingdom shall be broken up and divided toward the four winds of heaven, but not among his posterity nor according to his dominion with which he ruled; for his kingdom shall be uprooted, even for others besides these" (Daniel 11:4).

Here is accurate information to identify which king was mentioned in verse 3. He is mighty, able to do his will, but will die young and his kingdom will be split into four winds, or four parts.

"And the male goat is the kingdom of Greece. The large horn that is between its eyes is the first king. 22As for the broken horn and the four that stood up

End of Time Prophecies

in its place, four kingdoms shall arise out of that nation, but not with its power" (Daniel 8:21,22).

Here is a direct parallel passage to Daniel 11:3,4. This king is Grecian. He is Alexander the Great who ruled from 336-323BC and died at a young age after conquering the world. His kingdom was divided into four parts by his four generals.

The Key to Unlock Daniel 11

Notice that Daniel 11 skipped 129 years. The focus switched from Darius I the Persian king (486BC), to Alexander the Grecian king (336BC). Daniel switched focus the moment a decisive battle took place and the ruling power (Persia) lost to the next future power (Greece).

This is key to unlocking the rest of this vision. Power moves to the next ruling power whenever the current ruling power challenges the former and the former completely loses. Focus will shift to the new power even though the old one may continue to rule and reign for some time.

Xerxes (Persia) lost to Greece in 480BC, and it is then that Daniel 11:3 switches focus from Media-Persia to Greece. There were other Persian kings, but for the purpose of this vision they did not matter. Greece would be the focus until a new power entered the scene.

Four Points of a Compass

"Also the king of the South shall become strong, as well as one of his princes; and he shall gain power over him and have dominion. His dominion shall be a great dominion" (Daniel 11:5).

Here is the first introduction of a power in relation to a direction—the South. This method of describing kings or powers by a compass direction will continue throughout this vision.

The South of what?

The Bible supports, and historians agree, that the reckoning of direction in this prophecy is from Jerusalem—the city at the heart of the Jewish nation. Thus, a king of the South will be one who enters, attacks, or dwells south of Jerusalem. North, East, and West must enter, attack or dwell from their proper designations.

We do not have to take the word of men for this evidence. The Bible uses these same references.

"Who walk to go down to Egypt, And have not asked My advice, To strengthen themselves in the strength of Pharaoh, And to trust in the shadow of Egypt!" "The burden against the beasts of the South" (Isaiah 30:2, 6).

"For thus says the Lord GOD: 'Behold, I will bring against Tyre from the north Nebuchadnezzar king of Babylon'" (Ezekiel 26:7).

The Kingdom of Greece

Alexander's kingdom was split into 4 pieces:

King of the South: Ptolemy I Soter (305-285BC), ruled Egypt to the South of Jerusalem.

King of the East: Seleucus I Nicator (305-281BC), ruled Babylon to the East. Interestingly Seleucus (King of the East) was forced to flee his city of Babylon in 316BC. He sought protection under Ptolemy (South) for a time, but in 312BC he returned to Babylon and reconquered it. He continued to conquer Syria and Media, and become stronger that Ptolemy I (South).

King of the West: Cassander (305-297BC), ruled Greece.

King of the North: Lysimachus (305-281BC), ruled Asia Minor.

These four generals were the four horns of the *"he goat"* in Daniel 8, the four heads of the leopard in Daniel 7, and the four winds of Daniel 11.

Joining Forces

The successors of Cassander (West) were soon conquered by Lysimachus (North). Seleucus (East) later conquered Lysimachus (North) and became the sole King of the North.

"And at the end of some years they shall join forces, for the daughter of the king of the South shall go to the king of the North to make an agreement; but she shall not retain the power of her authority, and neither he nor his

authority shall stand; but she shall be given up, with those who brought her, and with him who begot her, and with him who strengthened her in those times" (Daniel 11:6).

Ptolemy II Philadelphus (285-246BC) (South) made an alliance with Antiochus II Theos (261-246BC) (North), by giving his daughter Berenice in marriage to the king of the North. Antiochus' current wife Laodice did not like this arrangement and poisoned the couple.

"But from a branch of her roots one shall arise in his place, who shall come with an army, enter the fortress of the king of the North, and deal with them and prevail. 8And he shall also carry their gods captive to Egypt, with their princes and their precious articles of silver and gold; and he shall continue more years than the king of the North" (Daniel 11:7,8).

Berenice's brother, Ptolemy III Evergetes (246-221BC) ruled in Egypt (South). He invaded the Seleucid (North) kingdom, conquered its capital Antioch, and took spoils of war back to Egypt.

"Also the king of the North shall come to the kingdom of the king of the South, but shall return to his own land" (Daniel 11:9).

Seleucus II Callinicus (246-225BC) (North) tried, but failed to get revenge for the invasion of Ptolemy III (South).

"However his sons shall stir up strife, and assemble a multitude of great forces; and one shall certainly come and overwhelm and pass through; then he shall return to his fortress and stir up strife" (Daniel 11:10).

"His sons" These are the sons of Seleucus II (North).

His sons were Seleucus III Ceraunus (226-223BC) and Antiochus III later called "The Great" (223-187BC). Both continued skirmishes with the Ptolemies (South).

Seleucus III (North) was murdered but his brother Antiochus III (North) reestablished control over most of the huge Northern Kingdom.

"Between 212 and 206BC he reasserted Seleucid [North] sway over huge areas of Asia" and gained control of the eastern Mediterranean sea ports including Antioch. By 218BC he held Lebanon (Coele Syria), Palestine, and Phoenicia.[1]

"And the king of the South shall be moved with rage, and go out and fight with him, with the king of the North, who shall muster a great multitude; but the multitude shall be given into the hand of his enemy. 12 When he has taken away the multitude, his heart will be lifted up; and he will cast down tens of thousands, but he will not prevail" (Daniel 11:11,12).

The "*he*" and "*his*" gets a little confusing in these two verses. It helps to understand a common form of writing used by Hebrew authors called *chiasm*. This word is based on the Greek letter X, pronounced "kai" a hard "ch" sound.

Chiasm describes a way of thinking and writing that was quite typical of Hebrew people, but is foreign to us today. For example, a typical outline today would move from A to B to C. In a chiastic outline you go from A to B to C back to B' then to A', but the second B' and the second A' are enhanced from the first ones. Think of it as ascending a mountain. You start at the base A, climb up the side B and reach the top C. On the way down you go down the other side B' and reach the base A' from the other side. In the process you have learned and experienced something new about the mountain or topic at hand.[2]

With this concept in mind, allow me to paraphrase verses 11 and 12.

Verse 11 The king of the South fights the king of the North. The king of the North musters a great army but shall be given into the hands of the king of the South.

Verse 12 The king of the South takes away the multitude of the North's army. The Southern kings heart will be lifted up in pride and he will cast down tens of thousands but he will not prevail.

---

1 Dudley, Donald R., *The Civilization of Rome*, (NY: New American Library, 1960), 59.
2 Paulien, Jon, *The Deep Things of God*, (MD: Review and Herald Publishing Assoc., 2004), 119.

South versus North

The king of the South is Ptolemy IV (221-205BC).

The king of the North is Antiochus III.

In 217BC, Antiochus III (North) musters a large army numbering over 62,000 infantry, 6,000 cavalry, and 102 elephants. Ptolemy IV's (South) army number 75,000. The two meet at Raphia, the southern most city in Syria. The battle is given into his- the king of the South's hand (Ptolemy IV).[3]

Ptolemy IV (South) did not pursue Antiochus III (North), but made peace so that he would have time to indulge his selfish passions. He was known for his sensuality, feasting, and debauchery. His pride, his heart, was "*lifted up*" and he did not strengthen his nation but was sufficient to ruin it. He died in 205BC leaving his five year old son Ptolemy V Epiphanes (r. 205-180BC) to rule.

"For the king of the North will return and muster a multitude greater than the former, and shall certainly come at the end of some years with a great army and much equipment" (Daniel 11:13).

After the loss to Ptolemy IV (South) Antiochus III (North) let the peace stand for about four years before he began an eastward campaign in 212BC. He pressed forward as far as India, setting up alliances, and vassal states. Antiochus III now adopted the title "Great King" or "The Great" comparing him to Alexander the Great.

Seeing the throne of the South now ruled by a child (Ptolemy V), Antiochus III (North) re-invaded Palestine in 201BC.

The Little Horn Introduced

"Now in those times many shall rise up against the king of the South. Also, violent men of your people shall exalt themselves in fulfillment of the vision, but they shall fall" (Daniel 11:14).

---

[3] Egypt, Ancient, *Encyclopedia Britannica Deluxe*, (India: Magic Software, 2010)

Daniel's Last Vision

During the next several decades, the king of the South faced many challengers, including Rhodes, Pergamum, Achaean & Aetolian leagues. One of these challenges included the emerging power of Rome. At this time Rome actually protects the infant king Ptolemy V (South) thwarting the plans of Philip, king of Macedonia and Antiochus III, king of Syria (North).

"Also" This is a parenthesis—a side note. Here is the introduction of a new power— *"the violent men of thy people."*

Who are "thy people?"

> It must be Daniel's people—the Jewish nation, out of which the Christian church developed.

"The violent men" This has also been translated as "The robbers" in different translations. The literal Hebrew words have the meaning "the sons," or "the people of the violent ones." Whatever group is mentioned here they *"shall exalt themselves to establish the vision."*

What is "the vision?"

We found this answer in chapter 10. Daniel received this last vision so that he would have a clearer understanding of the little horn. We have seen that the little horn is the system of the papacy that controls the civil powers of the earth. The little horn began as pagan or political Rome, but transformed itself into the religious entity of the papacy ruling the nations.

The little horn is the focus of this vision, it is this power that would establish the vision. Rome, in all its parts, is *"the violent men of thy people."*

"But they shall fall" Here is a booster to Daniel's faith; he saw that one day, when the stone cut without hands appeared, it would crush the statue (Daniel 2:34) and this power would fall. (See Daniel 11:45; Revelation 19:20; 20:10).

Rome, out of which the little horn would develop, was watching all that was occurring and even sent ambassadors to Ptolemy V (South), but could not lend him any serious assistance.

"So the king of the North shall come and build a siege mound, and take a fortified city; and the forces of the South shall not withstand him. Even his choice troops shall have no strength to resist" (Daniel 11:15).

North Invades South

After the parenthetical remark about Rome the vision completes Antiochus III's (North) invasion of the South.

"Fenced cities" This is most likely a reference to Gaza and/or Sidon.

"Egypt [South] was not able to sustain the role of world power. In the reign of Ptolemy V Epiphanes [South] she lost all of her possessions outside Africa except Cyprus, and entered a period of decline marked by weak rulers and dynastic quarrels."[4]

"But he who comes against him shall do according to his own will, and no one shall stand against him. He shall stand in the Glorious Land with destruction in his power" (Daniel 11:16).

"He who comes" Here is Rome entering the vision with force.

Sometime in 192 BC Antiochus III (North) was asked to help liberate the Aetolians from the power of Rome. In 191 BC Rome cut of Antiochus III's (North) advances and chased him until 189 BC at the battle of Magnesia near mount Sipylus. Here Antiochus III (North) was decisively defeated by the Romans. "No ruler of comparable stature occupied the Syrian (North) throne after the death of Antiochus the Great."[5]

Rome became the king of the North.

Between 189 BC and 129 BC Rome acquired power throughout the known world becoming the fourth beast of Daniel 7:7 and the fourth kingdom of iron in Daniel 2:33.

Rome now stood in the *"glorious land."*

---

[4]   Dudley, *The Civilization of Rome*, 57.
[5]   Dudley, *The Civilization of Rome*, 61.

Daniel's Last Vision

Some interpreters of prophecy attempt to relate the rest of Daniel 11 to the rule of Antiochus IV Epiphanes (r. 175-163BC) the son of Antiochus III, but this does not fit. According to the first sixteen verses, when a ruling power lost a major battle to the next ruling power then focus switched to the new ruling power.

Rome clearly defeated Antiochus III in 180BC, and thus assumed the power of the North. Unlike Ptolemy IV, who did not follow up, Rome ruled.

History gives evidence that Antiochus IV Epiphanes was a hostage to Rome and subservient to her wishes. There is a story that highlights this fact. Antiochus IV Epiphanes was planning on invading Egypt but was forced to meekly and instantly abandon his plans at the bidding of Rome. A Roman envoy simply drew a circle in the dirt around Antiochus IV Epiphanes with a stick and said "Answer me yes or no before you step out of that circle" as to the invasion. Clearly Rome was in control.[6]

"He shall also set his face to enter with the strength of his whole kingdom, and upright ones with him; thus shall he do. And he shall give him the daughter of women to destroy it; but she shall not stand with him, or be for him. 18After this he shall turn his face to the coastlands, and shall take many. But a ruler shall bring the reproach against them to an end; and with the reproach removed, he shall turn back on him. 19Then he shall turn his face toward the fortress of his own land; but he shall stumble and fall, and not be found" (Daniel 11:17-19).

"He" This is Rome, the king of the North.

"Whole kingdom" Rome takes the final steps to consolidate control over the entire world fulfilling the visions of Daniel 2, the legs of iron and Daniel 7, the terrible beast.

"Upright ones" and **"something morally straight"** Both are references to the Jews who assisted Rome during this period, even providing an army under Antipater the Idumean.

---

6   Dudley, *The Civilization of Rome*, 61.

"The daughter of women" Cleopatra VII is the last of the Greek Ptolemaic dynasty to rule in Egypt (South). She was ambitious to rule the world and realized she would have to conquer Rome. Her path lay through marriage with whoever held power. The surviving portraits show that she was no great beauty; nonetheless she charmed Julius Caesar bearing him a son.

Caesar rose to power in Rome and soon declared himself dictator for life in 44BC. He *"stumbled"* and fell and was *"not found"* when he was murdered on March 15, 44BC.

Cleopatra turned her charm to Marcus Antonius (Mark Antony) and produced him a set of twins. Antony shared in power with Caius Octavius (Octavian), the nephew of Caesar. Conflict arose between these two leaders culminating in the naval battle of Actium in 31BC. Octavian was the victor. One year later, after losing a battle on Egyptian soil, Mark Antony committed suicide. Cleopatra followed him a few days later, some accounts say after an attempt to seduce Octavian failed.

The last kingdom of Alexander's successors fell to Rome.

Rome rules the "Whole Kingdom."

"There shall arise in his place one who imposes taxes on the glorious kingdom; but within a few days he shall be destroyed, but not in anger or in battle" (Daniel 11:20).

Octavius- given the title Caesar Augustus, succeeded his uncle Julius Caesar. He was emphatically a raiser of taxes. *"And it came to pass in those days that a decree went out from Caesar Augustus that all the world should be registered [to be taxed]" (Luke 2:1).*

Rome reached the pinnacle of its greatness and power during this Augustan age. Augustus died peacefully in his bed, in AD14.

"And in his place shall arise a vile person, to whom they will not give the honor of royalty; but he shall come in peaceably, and seize the kingdom by intrigue" (Daniel 11:21).

"It is recorded that as Augustus was about to nominate his successor, his wife, Livia, besought him to nominate Tiberius, her son by a former husband. But the emperor said, 'Your son is too vile to wear the purple of Rome!' The nomination went to Agrippa, a much respected Roman citizen. Nevertheless, the prophecy said a '*vile person*' would succeed Augustus. Agrippa died. Livia renewed her intercessions for Tiberius. Augustus weakened by age and sickness succumbed to her 'flatteries' and appointed Tiberius."[7]

"With the force of a flood they shall be swept away from before him and be broken, and also the prince of the covenant" (Daniel 11:22).

"**The prince of the covenant**" is a direct reference to Jesus Christ.

The Little Horn Becomes Strong

"And after the league is made with him he shall act deceitfully, for he shall come up and become strong with a small number of people" (Daniel 11:23).

Here is the literal version of this verse: *"And after they join themselves to him, he shall practice deceit. For he shall come and be strong with a few people"* (Daniel 11:23).[8]

This verse shows the transition in the type of power that the king of the North was to become. Remember that this vision was given to Daniel to explain the little horn power.

Who joined themselves to him?

How did he become strong with a few people?

A lot of history transpired from *"the prince of the covenant"*—Jesus Christ in AD31, until the change in the Roman world. During this time Pagan Rome would be transformed from a terrible and fierce beast into the little horn power. Review the chapter titled: "The Little Horn of Prophecy" to read about the characteristics it would carry.

---

[7] Smith, Uriah, *Daniel and the Revelation*, (MD: Review and Herald Publishing Assoc., 1972), 255.
[8] Green, *The Interlinear Bible*.

End of Time Prophecies

The king of the North is still Rome, but it has now changed into the little horn Rome— or the papacy that controls nations.

A little background history, not provided in this vision, will be useful to prove that the change from political Rome to papal Rome is here mentioned.

"After this I saw in the night visions, and behold, a fourth beast, dreadful and terrible, exceedingly strong. It had huge iron teeth; it was devouring, breaking in pieces, and trampling the residue with its feet. It was different from all the beasts that were before it, and it had ten horns. 8 I was considering the horns, and there was another horn, a little one, coming up among them, before whom three of the first horns were plucked out by the roots. And there, in this horn, were eyes like the eyes of a man, and a mouth speaking pompous words" (Daniel 7:7,8).

Reading Daniel 7:7,8 we know that the little horn appears from among the ten horns that would compose the dreadful and terrible fourth beast, that is the fourth metal kingdom of Daniel 2, the one that rules after Greece.

The terrible beast, Rome proper, gained full control of the world in 31bc when Egypt relinquished its power to Rome. For the next 360 years the Roman empire stood united.

During this time, the bishops of each local Christian church led their congregations as they saw fit. The city of Rome was the largest, richest and most powerful city in the world. Over time the bishops in Rome felt that they deserved respect, honor and power that was proportionate to the rank of the city in which they resided. The other cities yielded up this honor and power. Soon the Roman church took this honor a step further believing that it should be the mother of all Christian churches. This elitist attitude would later add to contentions in the empire.

Emperor Constantine moved the capital of the empire from Rome to Istanbul renaming it New Rome or Constantinople in AD330. (Some see reference to a "time" in Daniel 11:24 as this 360 year (1 prophetic year or time) as this period of unified rule from 31bc to AD330. But the Aramaic word in Daniel 11:24 for time is *adeth*, this is different from *iddanin* the word used in Daniel 4:16 and 7:25 when time was used as a prophetic year).

Under Constantine, Rome split into its two legs of iron: Western Rome and Eastern Rome.

Ten Horns

The visions tell of Rome being divided into ten kingdoms. Between AD351 and AD476 Western Rome broke apart and was overrun by barbarian nations. The ten kingdoms that maintained power and control were: Huns, Ostrogoths, Visigoths, Franks, Vandals, Suevi (or Suebi, of which the Alemanni belonged), Burgundians, Heruli, Anglo-Saxons, and Lombards.

Three Horns Plucked Up

Daniel 7: 7, 8 shows that the little horn would rise in power after the ten kingdoms were in place. Furthermore, during the rise of the little horn it would pluck up or remove three of the ten kingdoms. The three kingdoms that would later be removed were the Heruli, Vandals, and Ostrogoths.

Many of the barbarian kingdoms were pagan or non-religious in their leadership, but some of them held to a form of Christianity called Arianism. This belief was started by Arius, a priest of Alexandria, who claimed that Jesus Christ was a created being, therefore inferior to the Father both in nature and dignity. Constantine called together a council at Nicaea in AD325 to consider the claims made by Arius. The council condemned Arius' ideas and banished him.

The Arian nations opposed any rule or power of the Roman Catholic Church. The Heruli were the first of the barbarian tribes to rule over the city of Rome. The Herulian leader, Odoacer, took the city of Rome in AD476. He was hated in Italy. Emperor Zeno of the Eastern Empire persuaded Theodoric of the Ostrogoths to invade Rome and depose Odoacer and the Heruli. This was finalized in AD493. The first kingdom was plucked up. However, the Catholic Church was no better than before, as Theodoric and the Ostrogoths also opposed the Roman Church and followed after Arius' teachings.

Meanwhile the Vandals led by Genseric, who had previously captured Rome in June AD455, settled in North Africa and were intolerant of Catholic believers who opposed their Arian ideas.

In AD533, the Byzantines (Eastern Roman Empire) under Belisarius invaded North Africa and in one campaigning season the Vandal kingdom was destroyed. Rome again ruled the area and restored the churches to the Roman Catholics. The Vandals played no further role in history, a second kingdom was plucked up.

The Roman Catholic Church received a huge swing in the balance of power throughout the world when Clovis the king of the Franks (French), became baptized into the Roman Catholic faith in the year AD496. A pagan nation now supported the Catholic religion. Eleven years later, AD507, Clovis kills Alaric the ruler of the Visigoths, another believer in the Arian belief. One year later Clovis would receive honorary titles and dignity from the Eastern Emperor Anastasius. In this year Clovis, then a Catholic, made a peace treaty with Theodoric the Ostrogoth of Arian beliefs. After years of peace, Theodoric would die in AD526. Then a period of instability ensued in the ruling dynasty that would eventually provoke the Byzantine emperor Justinian to declare war on the Ostrogoths in AD534 in an effort to wrest Italy from their grasp. The Ostrogoths were removed from Rome in AD538, and thereafter they had no national existence.

The Roman Catholic Church Unites

"Clovis was the first to unite all the elements from which the new social order was formed, namely, the barbarians, whom he established in power; the Roman civilization, to which he rendered homage by receiving the insignia of patrician and of consul from the Emperor Anastasius; and finally, the Catholic Church, with which he formed that fruitful alliance which was continued by his successors."[9]

---

9   Durvy, Victor, *The History of the Middle Ages*, (NY: Henry

AD508 was the turning point for the Roman Catholic Church. The influence of the church was beginning to be felt throughout the entire Western and Eastern Empire. This date anchors two timelines within Daniel: The 1290 years, and the 1335 years. The 1290 years begins in AD508 when the little horn begins its rise to power and culminates when this power receives a deadly wound in AD1798. The 1335 years, also begins in AD508, but extends until Daniel stands in his lot, that is at the judgment proceedings called the cleansing of the sanctuary, in AD1844.

The final steps leading up to the full power and influence of the little horn power began when Justinian became emperor of Eastern Rome. He sought to help the cause of the Catholics in the world while bolstering his political presence. He sent his general Belisarius to remove the Vandals of North Africa. This was accomplished by AD534. Just prior to this military campaign Justinian wished to secure the influence of the bishop of Rome, who had then attained a position in which his opinion had great weight throughout a large part of Christendom. Justinian, in a letter written in AD533, declared that the archbishop of Rome should be the head of all the churches, and should increase in honor and authority. Justinian would later codify his desires declaring in law "We therefore decree that the most holy pope of the elder Rome is the first of all the priesthood, and that the most blessed Archbishop of Constantinople, the New Rome, shall hold the second rank after the holy Apostolic chair of the elder Rome."[10]

The 1260 year Time-Line Begins

The pope was fully established by AD538 when Belisarius ran the Ostrogoths out of Rome. This date marks the beginning of the 1260 years of the little horn power.

AD538 marks the beginning of the Papacy in power. The entire empire, both West and East now viewed the pope—the bishop of

---

Hold and Co., 1891), 35.
10   Smith, *Daniel and the Revelation*, 276.

End of Time Prophecies

Rome, as the new head of all the churches in the empire. They had *"joined themselves to him."*

The papacy became *"strong with a few people."*

"He shall enter peaceably, even into the richest places of the province; and he shall do what his fathers have not done, nor his forefathers: he shall disperse among them the plunder, spoil, and riches; and he shall devise his plans against the strongholds, but only for a time" (Daniel 11:24).

"But for a time" Here is designated a period of time. The length is not discussed here and it does not need to be. Daniel had been given the exact length of time that the little horn—the papal power, would rule, 1260 prophetic days, or 1260 literal years. This time is also recorded as *42 months* or *3 ½ years* or *Time, Times and Half a Time* (Daniel 7:24-26; 8:9-14; 12:11-13; Revelation 11:3-6; 12:14).

The Little Horn versus The King of the South

"He shall stir up his power and his courage against the king of the South with a great army. And the king of the South shall be stirred up to battle with a very great and mighty army; but he shall not stand, for they shall devise plans against him" (Daniel 11:25).

Who was the last king of the South?

It was Cleopatra VII, as recorded in verse 17.

Egypt, the king of the South, became a part of the king of the North in AD31 at the hands of Octavius.

Egypt is not the king of the South in verse 25!

Islam Emerges

So who is this king of the South?

History plainly reveals the answers. Between AD610 and AD642 a new power was being organized. Muhammad, according to tradition, received his first vision and call in AD610. The next thirty years he spent organizing a religion, culture and community to a single focus. "To accomplish his main task and unite a population torn asunder by dissension, Muhammad needed cooperation of Muhājirūn—a king of local bodyguard. This required economic independence. In these circumstances, Muhammad had no other choice but to ensure this independence by raids on Meccan caravans. These raids weighed on the conscience of the members of his community, but were finally accepted as proper after the logic of necessity and the conscious break from paganism had made its full impact. This logic was confirmed in a 'revelation' which said the offense of the Meccan's in their disbelief was graver than the sin of disturbing the peace [of raiding the caravans]."[11]

With this logic secure, the expanse of Islam into the world was quick.

AD629 Muhammad's forces venture into Byzantine (Eastern Rome) territory.

AD630 Muhammad conquers Mecca.

AD632 Muhammad dies of a fever but not before setting up plans to invade southern Palestine and east Jordan.

AD633 Islam conquers Palestine.

AD635 Damascus surrenders to Islamic forces.

AD637 Jerusalem is taken.

AD639 Egypt is entered.

AD642 Byzantine control of Egypt is given to Islam.

Islam now becomes the king of the South.

---

11   Grunebaum, G.E. von, *Classical Islam*, (Aldine Publishing Company, 1970), 36.

End of Time Prophecies

The Crusades

"He [the king of the North—the papacy] shall stir up his power and his courage against the king of the South [Islam]" *(Daniel 11:25).*

The crusades were almost exclusively initiated by western leadership—the pope of Rome, the king of the North.

AD1095 pope Urban II at the council of Clermont called for the first crusade in an attempt to counter the growth of Islam and to reinstate its control.

"Yes, those who eat of the portion of his delicacies shall destroy him; his army shall be swept away, and many shall fall down slain. 27Both these kings' hearts shall be bent on evil, and they shall speak lies at the same table; but it shall not prosper, for the end will still be at the appointed time. 28While returning to his land with great riches, his heart shall be moved against the holy covenant; so he shall do damage and return to his own land" (Daniel 11:26-28).

There were at least nine formal crusades approved by the papacy, with many minor ones not always sanctioned. Many were slain. Both sides, Roman Catholicism and Islam, lied, cheated, stole and were responsible for atrocities too graphic to discuss here. The loot from the crusades led to many relics and artifacts being taken back to Western Europe—the seat of the papacy.

"At the appointed time he shall return and go toward the south; but it shall not be like the former or the latter" (Daniel 11:29).

"Former" This is the first of three time periods mentioned in this verse. These periods refer to the conflicts between the kings of the North (little horn) and the South (Islam). The former times includes the crusades and other skirmishes between these two kings (powers). During the *"former"* time the king of the North would retain the upper hand. This period includes the period of time in Revelation 9:1-11 called *"the first woe"*, of trumpet five.

During this *"former"* time, the Ottoman Turks (Muslims) fought with the remnant of the Roman Empire, but never conquered them. Revelation 9:10 gives us details about the last *"five months"* or 150 years of this *"former"* time. The last one hundred fifty years began on July 27, 1299 when Othman (Atman) fought Muzalo, the Roman army commander, in a battle near Nicomedia, the capital of Bithynia and won. One hundred and fifty years later in AD1449 Constantine XI Palaeologus is crowned emperor of Rome, but would not ascend to the throne without consent from the Turkish (Islamic) sultan. Essentially Rome allowed its authority to be checked by the Islamic state. This marked the beginning of the second woe (Revelation 9:13-21).

Constantine XI Palaeologus, the last Byzantine Emperor (Eastern Rome), is killed in the final defense of Constantinople against the Ottoman Turks in AD1453. During the three centuries to follow Muslims held more land in Europe than the Christians did in the east.

"Latter" This is the last, or the third period of time which defines major conflicts between the little horn (North) and Islam (South). Daniel 11:40 begins to discuss this *"latter"* period of time. Like the *"former"* this period is marked by the little horn retaining the upper hand.

Between the *"former"* and the *"latter"* occurs a period where the king of the South (Islam) has the upper hand in its conflicts with the king of the North (little horn). Revelation 9:13-21 describes this period of time calling it the *"second woe"* or the sixth trumpet. Studying the sixth trumpet, there is a prophecy which allows us to date this period of time.

"So the four angels, who had been prepared for the hour and day and month and year, were released to kill a third of mankind" (Revelation 9:15).

Adding up the prophetic hour, day, month and year and applying the prophetic conversion of a day for a year makes a total of 391 years and 15 days. This is the period of time that Islam (South) would have the upper hand on the Roman Empire (North). According to Revelation, the first woe (*"former"*) concluded on July 27, 1449 when the next emperor for the Byzantine (Eastern Roman) Empire would not ascend to the throne without the permission of the Ottoman Turks (Islam).

End of Time Prophecies

The 391 years and 15 days of Islamic influence began on July 27, 1449. Josiah Litch, a minister and student of prophecy, predicted in 1838, that a major blow would be struck to the Ottoman Empire (Islam) on August 11, 1840. This is exactly 391 years and 15 days from July 27, 1449. His interpretation of prophecy was proven accurate, down to the exact day! The chapter "The Seven Trumpets" discusses these dates in more detail.

On a historical note, the Ottoman Empire (Islam) surrendered its power to the ruler of Egypt (Christian) on August 11, 1840, and in AD1922 Turkey would officially abolish the Ottoman Empire.

"For ships from Cyprus shall come against him; therefore he shall be grieved, and return in rage against the holy covenant, and do damage. 'So he shall return and show regard for those who forsake the holy covenant'" (Daniel 11:30).

"**Ships from Cyprus**" The Ottoman empire (Islam—the king of the South) had naval victories against "*him*" the king of the North—the little horn power. These victories led to decades of Islamic naval control (AD1538 – 1560).

"**He shall be grieved**" The "*he*" is the king of the South. Pope Pius V (AD1571) organizes a fleet of forces from Spain, Venice and Italy, and almost destroys the Ottoman fleet at the Battle of Lepanto.

The Abomination of Desolation

"And arms shall stand on his part, and they shall pollute the sanctuary of strength, and shall take away the daily [sacrifice,] and they shall place the abomination that maketh desolate. ₃₂And such as do wickedly against the covenant shall he corrupt by flatteries: but the people that do know their God shall be strong, and do [exploits.] ₃₃And they that understand among the people shall instruct many: yet they shall fall by the sword, and by flame, by captivity, and by spoil, [many] days. ₃₄Now when they shall fall, they shall be holpen with a little help: but many shall cleave to them with flatteries. ₃₅And [some] of them of understanding shall fall, to try them, and to purge, and to make [them] white, [even] to the time of the end: because [it is] yet for a time appointed. ₃₆And the king shall do according to his will; and he shall exalt himself, and magnify himself above every god, and shall speak marvellous things against the God of gods, and shall prosper till the indignation be accomplished: for that that is determined shall be done.

Daniel's Last Vision

₃₇Neither shall he regard the God of his fathers, nor the desire of women, nor regard any god: for he shall magnify himself above all. ₃₈But in his estate shall he honour the God of forces: and a god whom his fathers knew not shall he honour with gold, and silver, and with precious stones, and pleasant things. ₃₉Thus shall he do in the most strong holds with a strange god, whom he shall acknowledge [and] increase with glory: and he shall cause them to rule over many, and shall divide the land for gain" (Daniel 11:31-39 KJV).

This language is similar to Daniel 8:11-13. The little horn expands its control of Christianity attempting to change God's times and laws. The Roman Catholic Church created traditions and doctrines that are contrary to the plain Word of God. A few include: indulgences—ways to monetarily pay for forgiveness, the day of worship—they changed the sacred Sabbath to Sunday, they set up a system of priests that replace God's method of forgiveness through His son Jesus Christ.

Parallel language is found in Revelation chapters 13, 17 and 18, and Daniel chapters 7 and 8. The little horn, also called the sea beast, King 7, *"the one that was"*, and the head of Babylon the great, the Mother of Harlots.

"They shall fall by sword and by flame" Refers to the Reformers who became martyrs for God's truth. Protestantism is born in the reformation. The Papacy sets up counter reforms through punishment, inquisitions and deceptions.

"But the people who know their God shall be strong, and carry out great exploits" (Daniel 11:32).

The people with great exploits include Martin Luther, Valdes (founder of the Waldensian group), Jan Hus, John Wycliffe, and many others.

"A god whom his fathers knew not" This god could be the system of worshiping humans, including Mary the mother of Jesus and saints as gods. In the 10th century official recognition of saints was initiated by pope John XV. According to the Roman Catholic Church, saints are venerated—but not worshiped, but they are believed to be the bearers of special powers. Because of this belief in the powers of the saints, their relics are regarded as efficacious.[12]

These saints and relics have been decorated in *"gold, silver, with precious stones and pleasant things,"* and have been idolized, worshiped and made the objects of prayer.

"The most strongholds" This refers to the strongholds of our Lord and Savior— Churches.

"O LORD, my strength and my fortress, My refuge in the day of affliction, The Gentiles shall come to You From the ends of the earth and say, 'Surely our fathers have inherited lies, Worthlessness and unprofitable things'"(Jeremiah 16:19).

"The LORD is good, A stronghold in the day of trouble; And He knows those who trust in Him" (Nahum 1:7).

The Lord is to be our fortress, our stronghold in the day of trouble. The Catholic Church teaches that we should seek the strength and protection from saints (dead humans), inanimate objects or other sacraments.

The End of Time

The next five verses of Daniel 11 are yet future. We do not have history to prove these events 100% accurate, nor do we have a direct revelation from God. But we do have enough confirmation in our past interpretations to make an educated and probably accurate outline of the events shown in these verses.

Verse 40

"At the time of the end the king of the South shall attack him; and the king of the North shall come against him like a whirlwind, with chariots, horsemen, and with many ships; and he shall enter the countries, overwhelm them, and pass through" (Daniel 11:40).

"At the time of the end" Anytime after AD1844. (See the chapter: "Time-lines of Prophecy" for confirmation of this date).

"King of South" This is Islam.

---

12   Roman Catholicism, *Encyclopedia Britannica Deluxe* (India: Magic Software, 2010)

"King of North" The papal system with the pope and his followers.

According to verse 40, Islam (South) will attack the king of the North (papacy) in some form or fashion. The king of the North will retaliate like a *"whirlwind."*

Where does the Papacy get all of the ships?

There is a good possibility that it would be from the false prophet (Revelation 13:11-18).

Verse 41

"He shall also enter the Glorious Land, and many countries shall be overthrown; but these shall escape from his hand: Edom, Moab, and the prominent people of Ammon" (Daniel 11:41).

"He" The papacy. The little horn will enter the glorious land with his allies.

"Glorious land" The land of Canaan that was given to the children of Israel.

"On that day I raised My hand in an oath to them, to bring them out of the land of Egypt into a land that I had searched out for them, 'flowing with milk and honey,' the glory of all lands" (Ezekiel 20:6).

"The glory of all lands" This is a parallel to verse 41.

"Escape" Those who are to be saved, to be delivered.

"Edom" The children of Esau (Genesis 36:1).

"Moab" and "Ammon" The children conceived by Lot from his two daughters (Genesis 19:37).

God has a remnant people in all nations, peoples and religions of the world. In the last days there will only be two groups of people: sheep—followers of Jesus Christ; and goats— those who ignore Jesus Christ and walk their own path apart from Him. Revelation 14 talks about the choice that the entire earth will have to make. If you choose Jesus Christ and worship Him as He asks, you will receive the seal of God. If you worship as you please or choose to follow the papacy and its form of worship then you will receive the *"mark of the beast."*

End of Time Prophecies

Daniel 11:41 I believe is describing this future event when the mark of the beast will be set up and all must choose. I believe parallel passages are found in Revelation 14 and 18.

"Then a third angel followed them, saying with a loud voice, 'If anyone worships the beast and his image, and receives his mark on his forehead or on his hand, 10he himself shall also drink of the wine of the wrath of God'" (Revelation 14:9,10).

"And I heard another voice from heaven saying, 'Come out of her, my people, lest you share in her sins, and lest you receive of her plagues. 5For her sins have reached to heaven, and God has remembered her iniquities'" (Revelation 18:4,5).

Verse 42

"He shall stretch out his hand against the countries, and the land of Egypt shall not escape" (Daniel 11:42).

Here is further evidence that the King of the South is no longer Egypt. It does not use the terms king of the South, but here uses Egypt. This was not the process in the forty-one verses prior to this one. This adds strength that the king of the South is still Islam.

Verse 43

"He shall have power over the treasures of gold and silver, and over all the precious things of Egypt; also the Libyans and Ethiopians shall follow at his heels" (Daniel 11:43).

Daniel 11:43 parallels Revelation 13 and 18.

"And I saw one of his heads as if it had been mortally wounded, and his deadly wound was healed. And all the world marveled and followed the beast" (Revelation 13:3).

"For all the nations have drunk of the wine of the wrath of her fornication, the kings of the earth have committed fornication with her, and the merchants of the earth have become rich through the abundance of her luxury" (Revelation 18:3).

All the world marveled and followed the beast—the king of the North, the papacy, which had power over the treasures of gold, silver and precious things. With these things the merchants of the earth follow her.

Verse 44

"But news from the east and the north shall trouble him; therefore he shall go out with great fury to destroy and annihilate many" (Daniel 11:44).

"News from the east" The book of Revelation describes angel messengers coming from the east.

"Then I saw another angel ascending from the east, having the seal of the living God. And he cried with a loud voice to the four angels to whom it was granted to harm the earth and the sea, ₃saying, 'Do not harm the earth, the sea, or the trees till we have sealed the servants of our God on their foreheads'" (Revelation 7:2,3).

"The east" This is the direction that Jesus Christ will return, and could symbolize any news that proceeds from His presence (Matthew 24:27).

The last two messages sent by God (news from the east), to warn the earth of His coming wrath is found in Revelation 18. These warnings would surely trouble the king of the North and his allies.

"North" The North has been used to symbolize the presence and location of God.

"The joy of the whole earth, Is Mount Zion on the sides of the north, The city of the great King." "God is in her palaces;" (Psalm 48:2, 3).

"'Behold, the days are coming,' says the Lord GOD, 'That I will send a famine on the land, Not a famine of bread, Nor a thirst for water, But of hearing the words of the LORD. ₁₂They shall wander from sea to sea, And from north to east; They shall run to and fro, seeking the word of the LORD, But shall not find it'" (Amos 8:11,12).

From the north to the east, people will seek for the Lord, for His word, but in the last days, after the final warnings are given His word will not be found. It will be too late. God has a probation period. He is now calling all to come to Him. If you choose to ignore His warnings, you will have to suffer the consequences of your choice.

"Then the sixth angel poured out his bowl on the great river Euphrates, and its water was dried up, so that the way of the kings from the east might be prepared" (Revelation 16:12).

e kings from the East are Jesus Christ and His host.

Verse 45

"And he shall plant the tents of his palace between the seas and the glorious holy mountain; yet he shall come to his end, and no one will help him" (Daniel 11:45).

"**And he shall come to his end**" This is parallel to the following texts:

- **Daniel 2:34,35**, the stone that removed every earthly kingdom, including the king of the North.
- **Daniel 7:26**, the little horn's kingdom was taken away by the most High God.
- **Daniel 8:23**, the fierce king—the papacy, shall be broken without human means.
- **Revelation 19:20**, the beast—the papacy, was cast alive into the like of fire.

Daniel's last vision concludes with the setting up of God's kingdom. This is the same conclusion we saw in the metal statue when the stone struck it destroying all the nations before it. This is also the conclusion of Daniel 7 when the thrones are set up and the Son of Man comes to take His kingdom. The book of Revelation will discuss more of the setting up of Jesus' kingdom and the events that proceed it.

Michael Stands Up
Daniel Chapter 12

Daniel 10, 11 & 12 are a complete unit, a single vision given to Daniel.

"At that time Michael shall stand up, The great prince who stands watch over the sons of your people; And there shall be a time of trouble, Such as never was since there was a nation, Even to that time. And at that time your people shall be delivered, Every one who is found written in the book. 2And many of those who sleep in the dust of the earth shall awake, Some to everlasting life, Some to shame and everlasting contempt. 3Those who are wise shall shine Like the brightness of the firmament, And those who turn many to righteousness Like the stars forever and ever" (Daniel 12:1-3).

"At that time" Daniel 12 is a continuation of Daniel 11:45.

What two events occur when Michael stands up?

"And there shall be a time of trouble" (Verse 1).
"And your people shall be delivered" (Verse 1).

What is Michael standing up from? Where was He sitting?

"I watched till thrones were put in place, And the Ancient of Days was seated; His garment was white as snow, And the hair of His head was like pure wool. His throne was a fiery flame, Its wheels a burning fire; 10A fiery stream issued And came forth from before Him. A thousand thousands ministered to Him; Ten thousand times ten thousand stood before Him. The court was seated, And the books were opened" (Daniel 7:9,10).

Thrones were put into place. The court was seated and the books were opened. Jesus Christ and the Ancient of Days are judging those in the book of life. Revelation 14 and the 2300 day prophecy of Daniel 8:14 gives us evidence that the court was seated in AD 1844. Now is the time that all are being judged and weighed in the balances to see if they are found in the book of life. When Jesus Christ stands up, the judgment process will be complete. Jesus Christ is Michael. (Further proof is given in the next chapter: "Michael Our Prince"). When Michael stands up the End of Time will be upon

End of Time Prophecies

the earth, there will be tribulations such as never was since there was a nation, and the people of God will soon be delivered.

These events will be studied in detail when we get into the book of Revelation.

"But you, Daniel, shut up the words, and seal the book until the time of the end; many shall run to and fro, and knowledge shall increase" (Daniel 12:4).

The exact time of the end is only known by the Father in heaven (Matthew 24:36). Daniel was told to shut up his words. His words would be partially opened in the life of John, the author of Revelation, because of the visions he received from Jesus Christ, through the angel. Daniel's words have been shut up until AD 1844 when historical events began to unlock the mysteries of the time-lines.

The book of Daniel has been unlocked.

God is a God of time. He foretold history thousands of years before the events were to transpire, and they occurred exactly as He described.

If this is not evidence that the Word of God is true, I don't know what you are seeking for.

Keep studying to see how the prophecies of Revelation fit perfectly with the prophecies of Daniel.

Michael Our Prince
Who is like God?

Where is the first reference to Jesus Christ in the Bible?

It may surprise you to hear that it is the fourth word in the Bible.

"In the beginning God created the heavens and the earth" (Genesis 1:1).

We know this is Jesus Christ because of John's gospel:

"He [Jesus] was in the world, and the world was made through Him, and the world did not know Him" (John 1:10).

Genesis 1:26 confirms the presence of the Son, the Father, and the Spirit during creation when it says *"Let Us make man in Our image."*

Paul writes in Colossians that:

"He [Jesus Christ] is the image of the invisible God, the firstborn over all creation. 16For by Him all things were created that are in heaven and that are on earth, visible and invisible, whether thrones or dominions or principalities or powers. All things were created through Him and for Him. 17And He is before all things, and in Him all things consist" (Colossians 1:15-17).

Whenever man sees a visible representation of God, they see Jesus Christ, even in the Old Testament.

Jesus walked and talked with His created pair: Adam and Eve (Genesis 3:8). He cautioned Cain to curb his anger (Genesis 4:6,7), and directed Noah how to build an ark (Genesis 6:13,14). The Old Testament stories reveal Jesus as God, Creator, Friend, Judge and Savior.

Can Jesus Christ also be seen as a messenger?

The word *angel* means "messenger." It is a word that describes a function or a job. Today we hear the word *angel* and instantly jump to the image of a created being with wings and a bright light, but this is not always the case. The word *angel* simply means messenger. Some of God's messengers do have wings and are accompanied by bright lights, but what if the messenger is God Himself? Is it possible that Jesus Christ delivered some of His own messages?

"And the Angel of the Lord appeared to [Moses] in a flame of fire from the midst of a bush" "God called to [Moses] from the midst of the bush" (Exodus 3:2,4).

Jesus Christ, the form of the invisible God, called out to Moses from the burning bush. Jesus had a message for Moses. Jesus was the messenger or *angel*. No connotation of a created being is given here.

Further proof that the word *angel* describes the function or act of Jesus as His own messenger is found in Genesis 31:11-13: *"Then the angel of God spoke to me [Jacob]... I am the God of Bethel."* And Genesis 48:16: *"The Angel who has redeemed me from all evil."*

Jesus Christ is the only God, Savior and Redeemer of mankind. The worship of angels is not acceptable to God (Revelation 19:10; Colossians 2:18). Any angel that accepts worship from others must either do so in sin or be God Himself. Here is an important difference between Jesus giving a message and created angels. Angels are not worshiped.

The Old Testament stories take on a new focus when we realize that it was Jesus Christ— the visible form of God, the *"Angel of the Lord"* who directly interacted with fallen man often delivering His own messages. Jacob wrestled with Jesus (Genesis 32; Hosea 12:4). Israel was rescued out of Egypt by Jesus Christ (Isaiah 63:9). Jesus remained visible as a pillar of cloud by day and of fire by night (Exodus 13:21 and 14:19). (Note: the presence of God the Father remained invisible, hidden behind the curtain of the most holy place sitting upon the mercy seat at the center of camp; while Jesus Christ was visible to all in the pillar). Jesus, as the Angel of the Lord, visited Abraham, Sarah, Isaac, Gideon, Samson's mother and Hannah— the mother of Samuel.

Immanuel meaning "God with us" perfectly describes the presence of God through Jesus Christ since the world began.

"For He [Jesus Christ] Himself has said 'I will never leave you nor forsake you'" (Hebrews 13:5 quoting Genesis 28:15).

Who is Michael the archangel?

Michael means "Who is like God?" This name, in the Bible, appears only in apocalyptic passages: Daniel 10:13,21; Daniel 12:1; Jude 9; Revelation 12:7. It is used only in instances where He is in direct conflict with Satan. The name "Who is like God?" is both a question and a challenge. Satan claims *"I will be like the Most High"* (Isaiah 14:14). The name Michael challenges the devils claims, asking who really is like God? Who can create? Who can control time, seasons and planets? The answer is no one except God.

Daniel 10:13 calls Michael one of the chief princes and later in Daniel 12:1 adds that Michael is *"the great prince who stands watch over the sons of your people."* Michael is a prince and a protector. Jude 9 calls Michael the archangel.

Arche can indicate "old", as in *archaeology*— "the study of old things." But it can also indicate "rulership", as in *monarchy*— "the rule of one."

Both terms, *old* and *rulership*, perfectly describe Jesus Christ the Alpha and the Omega. Combined with *"prince"* and *"protector"* of the saints, Michael the archangel is rightly identified as Jesus Christ.

According to 1 Thessalonians 4:16, the *"voice of the archangel"* is associated with the resurrection of the saints at the coming of Jesus Christ. John 5:28 records Christ declaring that the dead in Christ will come forth from their graves when they hear the voice of the Son of man.

Michael is a title given to the Lord Jesus Christ. He is the Arch-Angel in the same way that He is our High Priest, our Comforter, our King, our Savior, our Protector, our Lord and God.

Counterfeit Prophecy
Wheat versus Tares

Sin began with Satan. The details are fuzzy but we do know that ever since sin took root in his heart he has tried to substitute his false theories, fables and gospels in place of the Word and truth of God. Through vague and fanciful interpretations, he works to confuse minds so they will not discern truth. It is a masterpiece of Satan's deceptions to keep the minds of men searching and conjecturing revelations that God has not made known or which God did not intend that men should understand. Important matters concerning our salvation is not clothed in mystery. The Word of God is plain to all who study it with a prayerful heart, and earnest study. Salvation is simple *"Jesus said to him, 'I am the way, the truth, and the life. No one comes to the Father except through Me'"* (John 14:6).

The Devil's Tactics

"Another parable He put forth to them, saying: "The kingdom of heaven is like a man who sowed good seed in his field; 25but while men slept, his enemy came and sowed tares among the wheat and went his way. 26But when the grain had sprouted and produced a crop, then the tares also appeared" (Matthew 13:24-26).

What was sown by the enemy?

Tares among the wheat.

The blades of young grasses or tares can look very similar in nature to the blades of young wheat. It is not until both have matured that the two begin to take on different characteristics identifying each as edible wheat or useless grass.

"So the servants of the owner came and said to him, 'Sir, did you not sow good seed in your field? How then does it have tares?' 28He said to them, 'An enemy has done this.' The servants said to him, 'Do you want us then to go and gather them up?' 29But he said, 'No, lest while you gather up the tares you also uproot the wheat with them. 30Let both grow together until

the harvest, and at the time of harvest I will say to the reapers, First gather together the tares and bind them in bundles to burn them, but gather the wheat into my barn'" (Matthew 13:27-30).

Why couldn't the servants weed out the tares?

They might "also uproot the wheat with them" (Verse 29).

"He answered and said to them: 'He who sows the good seed is the Son of Man. 38The field is the world, the good seeds are the sons of the kingdom, but the tares are the sons of the wicked one. 39The enemy who sowed them is the devil, the harvest is the end of the age, and the reapers are the angels. 40Therefore as the tares are gathered and burned in the fire, so it will be at the end of this age'" (Matthew 13:37-40).

What is the field of wheat and tares?

The world (Verse 38).

Who is the enemy?

The devil (Verse 39).

Jesus Christ warned his church that living among the true members in His church would be false members, sown by Satan. These tares would look, act and behave like true Christians, that is, until the fruits of their labors would be developed.

Satan's Deceptions

The devil wants to be like God (Isaiah 14:14). His tares are designed to turn people away from God's simple truths. Turning away from God makes you, by default, a follower of Satan.

Truth is absolute. There is only one truth that matters and that is Jesus Christ. *"I am the way, the truth, and the life. No one comes to the Father except through Me" (John 14:6).*

Satan's tares are 99.9% correct. They align closely with scriptural truth, but will always differ in some important detail. He has been planting tares for thousands of years; some are just now coming to fruition. Look at the theory of Evolution, there is a lot of *new* science which seems to point to a universe that evolved over time without a creator. Nevertheless there is an equal and greater amount of science that points to a universe planned by a loving God, a Creator. Satan spent generations grooming the right men and cultures to propagate his errors into the scientific world. Three hundred years ago scientists would have been ridiculed if they believed in evolution, today they are mocked if they still believe in creation.

The Testimony of Truth

Living in the End of Time we must be extra cautious with what we believe as truth. Our only safeguard is the Word of God. It is the only document guarded by the Spirit of God to be truthful and accurate (2 Timothy 3:16; 2 Peter 1:21).

Holding on to human traditions, fables, or ideas may be detrimental to your hope of eternal life.

"To the law and to the testimony: if they speak not according to this word, [it is] because [there is] no light in them" (Isaiah 8:20 KJV).

Tares of the Devil

There are two vines.

The vine of Christ, versus the vine of the earth (Revelation 14:18,19).

There are two marks or seals.

The mark of God (Revelation 14:1) versus the mark of the beast (Revelation 13:15,16).

There are many Christs.

Jesus Christ the Messiah versus the many antichrists (1 John 2).

There are two flocks.

Sheep versus goats (Matthew 25:31-33).

End of Time Prophecies

It is by prayerful study and seeking a "Thus Saith the Lord" that truth will be separated from counterfeit. In studying prophecy it is easy to listen to various ideas, concepts and guesses, without checking them against the truth of God's word. If you seek the simple Word of God for all truth, then you will not be led astray.

Israel in Prophecy
A Counterfeit Concept

The church is God's appointed agency for the salvation of men. It was organized for service, and its mission is to carry the gospel to the world. From the beginning it has been God's plan that through His church shall be reflected to the world His fullness and His sufficiency. The members of the church, those whom He has called out of darkness into His marvelous light, are to show forth His glory."[1]

God's church began with Adam and Eve. After they chose to sin God offered them mercy, Grace and hope. Mercy in that He did not instantly give them the penalty of death due their actions, and grace in that He promised to put enmity (hatred) back between them and sin, where now none stood. He gave them the promise of hope that a Son would be born from her seed that would be able to pay the price of sin and would restore mankind back to the perfection they once lived.

The First Church

There are not many details about this early church of Adam, Eve and family, but there are enough details to show that God had imparted to His people His desires, laws, and commandments.

"Also for Adam and his wife the LORD God made tunics of skin, and clothed them" (Genesis 3:21).

Here is the first reference to the sacrifices of a lamb. This sacrifice comforted the sinners. Their physical needs were provided for, by clothing them, and their spiritual needs were met by the sacrificed lamb which symbolically pointed the sin filled couple to the future sacrifice that Jesus Christ would perform for all humanity and forgiveness of sins.

---

[1] White, E.G., *Acts of the Apostles*, (TN: Harvestime Books, 2001), 19.

End of Time Prophecies

"By faith Abel offered to God a more excellent sacrifice than Cain, through which he obtained witness that he was righteous, God testifying of his gifts; and through it he being dead still speaks" (Hebrews 11:4).

Righteous means right doing. God respected Abel because he obeyed God. God did not respect Cain because Cain did not obey God's word. Both Cain and Able were aware of God's law.

Sin is the transgression of the law (Romans 7:7). The law must be present before sin can occur.

"So the LORD said to Cain, 'Why are you angry? And why has your countenance fallen? 7If you do well, will you not be accepted? And if you do not do well, sin lies at the door. And its desire is for you, but you should rule over it'" (Genesis 4:6,7).

We know the results of Cain's choice.

"Then Cain went out from the presence of the LORD and dwelt in the land of Nod on the east of Eden" (Genesis 4:16).

Two Choices for Mankind

After Cain's choice, two groups of humans began to develop. One race chose to follow God and keep His precepts and laws. The other group chose to ignore God and thus by default be counted with Satan.

"Now it came to pass, when men began to multiply on the face of the earth, and daughters were born to them, 2that the sons of God saw the daughters of men, that they were beautiful; and they took wives for themselves of all whom they chose" (Genesis 6:1,2).

The Bible labels the followers of God as the Sons of God (Romans 8:14, Galatians 4:6,7), and those who did not follow God as the sons and daughters of men (Numbers 23:19, Ecclesiastes 9:3).

Shem versus Ham

"Now the sons of Noah who went out of the ark were Shem, Ham, and Japheth. And Ham was the father of Canaan" "And he said: 'Blessed be the LORD, The God of Shem, And may Canaan be his servant. 27May God enlarge Japheth, And may he dwell in the tents of Shem; And may Canaan be his servant'" (Genesis 9:18, & 26, 27).

Name the 3 sons of Noah:

Shem
Ham
Japheth

Which son was blessed?

Shem (Verse 26).

After the flood, Noah's son Shem was given the blessing of carrying on the lineage of the sons of God fulfilling the promise given to Eve that her seed would crush the head of the serpent. Jesus Christ, born of Mary, would have a direct lineage back to Eve of ancestors that believed, trusted and obeyed His commandments.

Ham, through his actions, was cursed, and Japheth would be blessed but would live under the roof of Shem.

Isaac versus Ishmael

"Now the LORD had said to Abram: 'Get out of your country, From your family And from your father's house, To a land that I will show you. 2I will make you a great nation; I will bless you And make your name great; And you shall be a blessing'" (Genesis 12:1,2).

Who was God going to make into a great nation?

Abram.

Abram, a direct descendant of Shem, was visited by God (actually by Jesus Christ Himself) and was given a promise, a covenant, that he would be the father of a large nation. This nation would be one that God could call His own, a nation who respected Him and obeyed Him.

Abram's wife Sarai was barren and both were getting older. In a moment of weak faith, Abram attempted to create this great nation on his own by sleeping with his servant maid Hagar. Ishmael was born, but he was not to be God's ordained nation. God would bless Ishmael and make him into a strong nation, but Ishmael would not carry the name of God's people. It is important to realize that Ishmael is how the Muslim world connects themselves to Abraham and it is through this relationship that they claim to be God's true nation. This is a tare of Satan.

God required Abram's full faith. He waited until Sarah was past the age of childbearing, that is after menopause, then He gave her a son—Isaac. Through this special son God's people would come.

God's Covenant

"And I will establish My covenant between Me and you and your descendants after you in their generations, for an everlasting covenant, to be God to you and your descendants after you. 8Also I give to you and your descendants after you the land in which you are a stranger, all the land of Canaan, as an everlasting possession; and I will be their God." 9And God said to Abraham: 'As for you, you shall keep My covenant, you and your descendants after you throughout their generations'" (Genesis 17:7-9).

Abraham and his descendants had a responsibility, they were to keep God's covenant. As long as Abraham's children honored the covenant, God would be their God and would provide for them—forever.

Isaac had two sons— twins, Esau (the elder) and Jacob. Esau sold his birthright and chose to seek wives from the daughters of Ishmael, and thus, chose not to be called a Son of God. Esau no longer participated in the covenant promise (Genesis 28:9). Jacob, after many struggles, would choose to be called a Son of God and with this choice God would change his name to Israel, meaning Prince with God (Genesis 32:28).

Notice the transformation of God's people. He created mankind as male and female, and intended that they would remain free from sin and forever be called the Sons of God. When sin entered earth, all would have to make the same choice given to Adam and Eve. They could choose to be called a child of God, or they could rebel and choose sin and be known as sons and daughters of men. The sons and daughters of men could always choose to repent, turn from their sins and seek Jesus Christ. Those who did would be called the children of God.

Throughout history, there would always be a group of people who would carry the name of God and would represent those who obey God inviting Him to be the Lord of their life.

Noah carried the name of God's people through the flood. His son Shem chose God and carried the name of God's people. Father Abraham, a direct descendant of Shem, would be the father of Isaac who would bear Jacob whose name was changed to Israel. Here is the first use of the name of Israel to represent the Sons of God. Israel (Jacob) would have many children, more than 12. His children would align themselves with the one true God.

The Nation of Israel

Over time the children of Israel lost sight of their duty to God and became slaves in Egypt.

Moses was sent to deliver his people. After a series of plagues, which will be mirrored at the End of Time, the Pharaoh was almost ready to release the slaves. One more plague would be needed. God warned the Sons of God, those who still believed in Him, that the last plague would be one of death, but He would spare those who believed and showed the correct sign.

"And you shall take a bunch of hyssop, dip it in the blood that is in the basin, and strike the lintel and the two doorposts with the blood that is in the basin. And none of you shall go out of the door of his house until morning. 23For the LORD will pass through to strike the Egyptians; and when He sees the blood on the lintel and on the two doorposts, the LORD will pass over the door and not allow the destroyer to come into your houses to strike you" (Exodus 12:22,23).

What would spare the destroying angel from entering the house?

"Strike the lintel and the two doorposts with the blood" (Verse 22).

Here is the sign of blood, used as a reminder that a Messiah would one day die to save the world. This sign was freely available to all, both Israelite and Egyptian, to choose. All who chose to consecrate themselves before the Lord and partake in His commandments would be spared.

The Israelite throng that escaped Egypt was not all bloodline relatives of Abraham or Israel, yet they were collectively called the Princes of God—Israelites. There were some Egyptians that believed, obeyed and were saved. God's covenant with Abraham was still binding on those who chose, by a profession of faith, to be counted as an Israelite, a child of God.

The nation of Israel was designed to be God's chosen people. But they had a choice to maintain. If they honored God and obeyed His laws and kept His precepts they would remain a blessed nation and would forever be the embodiment of God's people on earth. But if they chose to walk contrary to God then God would let them go. He does not force His love, or His rule upon anyone— Israel included.

The Bible centers most of its message around the nation of Israel. This does not mean that the Word of God was designed only for that nation. This nation was to be God's example to the world. It was His church in the Old Testament. Through this nation God was to be glorified and His people were to be His witnesses to the world.

"'You are My witnesses,' says the LORD, 'And My servant whom I have chosen, That you may know and believe Me, And understand that I am He. Before Me there was no God formed, Nor shall there be after Me'" (Isaiah 43:10).

The Israelites were to reveal to men the principles of God's kingdom. They were to show forth His praise among the heathens, and were to be a light to the Gentiles.

"Indeed He says, 'It is too small a thing that You should be My Servant To raise up the tribes of Jacob, And to restore the preserved ones of Israel; I will also give You as a light to the Gentiles, That You should be My salvation to the ends of the earth'" (Isaiah 49:6).

All mankind would recognize that Israel stood in a special relationship with the God of Heaven. The gentiles would notice the uniqueness of Israel; how they were prosperous and blessed by God, and would see that the God of Israel was the one true God. The material advantages that Israel enjoyed were designed to arrest the attention and catch the interest of the heathens. Heathen ambassadors would come from nations, like the Queen of Sheba to King Solomon, to see if they could determine the great secret of Israel's success as a nation. Returning to their homelands the Gentile ambassadors would counsel their fellow countrymen, *"Let us go to pray before the Lord."*

"The inhabitants of one city shall go to another, saying, 'Let us continue to go and pray before the LORD, And seek the LORD of hosts. I myself will go also.' 22Yes, many peoples and strong nations Shall come to seek the LORD of hosts in Jerusalem, And to pray before the LORD. 23Thus says the LORD of hosts: 'In those days ten men from every language of the nations shall grasp the sleeve of a Jewish man', saying, 'Let us go with you, for we have heard that God is with you'" (Zechariah 8:21-23).

"Moreover, concerning a foreigner, who is not of Your people Israel, but has come from a far country for Your name's sake for they will hear of Your great name and Your strong hand and Your outstretched arm), when he comes and prays toward this temple, 43hear in heaven Your dwelling place, and do according to all for which the foreigner calls to You, that all peoples of the earth may know Your name and fear You, as do Your people Israel, and that they may know that this temple which I have built is called by Your name" (1 Kings 8:41-43).

The House of God in Jerusalem would eventually be called a house of prayer for all people.

"Also the sons of the foreigner Who join themselves to the LORD, to serve Him, And to love the name of the LORD, to be His servants— Everyone who keeps from defiling the Sabbath, And holds fast My covenant— 7Even them I will bring to My holy mountain, And make them joyful in My house of prayer. Their burnt offerings and their sacrifices Will be accepted on My altar; For My house shall be called a house of prayer for all nations" (Isaiah 56:6, 7).

"'Sing and rejoice, O daughter of Zion! For behold, I am coming and I will dwell in your midst,' says the LORD. 11Many nations shall be joined to the LORD in that day, and they shall become My people. And I will dwell in your midst. Then you will know that the LORD of hosts has sent Me to you" (Zechariah 2: 10,11).

Failure to Obey

The Israelite nation was given the same requirements of Cain and Abel. Obey My commandments and you will be a witness to Me in the world.

"But it shall come to pass, if you do not obey the voice of the LORD your God, to observe carefully all His commandments and His statutes which I command you today, that all these curses will come upon you and overtake you:"
"And it shall be, that just as the LORD rejoiced over you to do you good and multiply you, so the LORD will rejoice over you to destroy you and bring you to nothing; and you shall be plucked from off the land which you go to possess" (Deuteronomy 8: 15, 63).

Many today do not like to hear that they must obey God to obtain eternal life. They try to argue that we are saved by grace alone and therefore we are no longer subject to the commandments of God. This contradicts the plain words of Jesus who said *"If you love Me, keep My commandments"* (John 14:15).

Obeying God is, and will always be, the focus of our life— even into eternity. The issue arises when man believes that they can keep the commandments of God on their own.

This is not legalism. God understood that from the first act of sin mankind now loved sin. *"The heart is deceitful above all things, And desperately wicked; Who can know it?" (Jeremiah 17:9).*

God never intended for humans to save themselves. God said He would send His Son, the seed of Eve, to put enmity between the flesh of men and the desires of sin.

This hatred of sin is imparted when we accept God's gift of grace. *"For the grace of God that brings salvation has appeared to all men, [12]teaching us that, denying ungodliness and worldly lusts, we should live soberly, righteously, and godly in the present age,"* (Titus 2: 11, 12). Grace is given to all sinners, teaching us how to live apart from sin. *"For it is God who works in you both to will and to do for His good pleasure" (Philippians 2:13).*

The grace of God came to Cain and warned him of his potential act of sin. God convicted Cain of his choice and made a way possible for Cain to overcome his temptation towards murder. Cain ignored God both in his action of sacrifice and his continual dwelling on the temptation to murder.

God's commandments show us how sinful we are. They reveal how far off the mark we really stand. God's law teaches us that we need a Savior and that our only hope is to fall broken and contrite at His feet asking for Him to save us and lead us away from sin.

Israel chooses to walk away from God

The Israelites were told that their blessings would come only if they fully cooperated with God. If they chose to not follow God, then they would be treated with curses and affliction, in hopes that it would lead them to repent, and return back to God. God clearly warned them that if they continued in ignoring God and His commandments that they would be "*plucked*" off of the land.

The Israelite nation, the sons of Jacob, were divided after the death of Solomon, much like Cain and Abel. This division, though tragic, served to separate Judah, the southern kingdom, from the idolatry that engulfed Israel, the northern ten tribes. In spite of the zealous efforts of Elijah, Elisha, Amos, Hosea and other prophets, the northern kingdom deteriorated.

Israel is Removed

"Yet the LORD testified against Israel and against Judah, by all of His prophets, every seer, saying, "Turn from your evil ways, and keep My commandments and My statutes, according to all the law which I commanded your fathers, and which I sent to you by My servants the prophets." 14Nevertheless they would not hear, but stiffened their necks, like the necks of their fathers, who did not believe in the LORD their God. 15And they rejected His statutes and His covenant that He had made with their fathers, and His testimonies which He had testified against them; they followed idols, became idolaters, and went after the nations who were all around them, concerning whom the LORD had charged them that they should not do like them. 16So they left all the commandments of the LORD their God, made for themselves a molded image and two calves, made a wooden image and worshiped all the host of heaven, and served Baal. 17And they caused their sons and daughters to pass through

End of Time Prophecies

the fire, practiced witchcraft and soothsaying, and sold themselves to do evil in the sight of the LORD, to provoke Him to anger" (2 Kings 17: 13-17).

God worked long with Israel, but they stubbornly chose to ignore the warnings of God. God gave them every opportunity to repent, to acknowledge their sinfulness and to seek Him. Israel refused.

"Therefore the LORD was very angry with Israel, and removed them from His sight; there was none left but the tribe of Judah alone" (2 Kings 17: 13-18).

The Nation of Israel was never promised complete restoration.

"Then it shall be, if you by any means forget the LORD your God, and follow other gods, and serve them and worship them, I testify against you this day that you shall surely perish. 20 As the nations which the LORD destroys before you, so you shall perish, because you would not be obedient to the voice of the LORD your God" (Deuteronomy 8:19,20).

This was not a rash decision by God. Israel, like Cain, chose to walk away from the presence of the Lord. God's church no longer rested upon the Northern Kingdom of Israel. His people were to be found in Judah, composed of the two tribes Judah and Benjamin.

Judah Carries God's Name

Judah would carry the lineage of Eve's seed. As long as they sought the Lord and desired to obey His commandments, they would be a blessed nation. Sadly Judah began to walk contrary to God's laws, as their northern brothers in Israel had done. God attempted to wake up His church sending Judah into captivity under the Chaldeans in Babylon.

God did not forsake His people during their captivity. Like Israel He worked hard to have them return to Him, acknowledge Him as God and obey His commandments. God had promised He would renew His covenant including the blessings if they would love and serve Him. God's blessings would *"come to pass if you [Judah] diligently obey the voice of the LORD your God" (Zechariah 6:15).*

The Jewish Nation

Angel Gabriel revealed to Daniel that the Jews—Judah, the last remnant of the nation of Israel, would be given a second and final chance, as a nation, to return to God and cooperate with His divine plan (Daniel 9:24). This was repeated to Prophet Jeremiah.

"Thus says the LORD: 'Against all My evil neighbors who touch the inheritance which I have caused My people Israel to inherit—behold, I will pluck them out of their land and pluck out the house of Judah from among them.' 15Then it shall be, after I have plucked them out, that I will return and have compassion on them and bring them back, everyone to his heritage and everyone to his land. 16And it shall be, if they will learn carefully the ways of My people, to swear by My name, as the LORD lives, as they taught My people to swear by Baal, then they shall be established in the midst of My people. 17But if they do not obey, I will utterly pluck up and destroy that nation, says the LORD" (Jeremiah 12:14-17).

Judah, the remnant of Israel, had a second chance to follow God. Instead, they held on to a formal worship process that replaced the sincere religion taught by God. They placed human traditions above the Word of God. Instead of becoming a beacon of light unto the world, the Jews shut themselves away from the world hoping to be safeguarded from idolatry. In their meticulous attention to the letter of the law, they lost sight of its spirit.

"I hate, I despise your feast days, And I do not savor your sacred assemblies. 22Though you offer Me burnt offerings and your grain offerings, I will not accept them, Nor will I regard your fattened peace offerings. 23Take away from Me the noise of your songs, For I will not hear the melody of your stringed instruments. 24But let justice run down like water, And righteousness like a mighty stream" (Amos 5:21-24).

"'To what purpose is the multitude of your sacrifices to Me?' Says the LORD. 'I have had enough of burnt offerings of rams And the fat of fed cattle. I do not delight in the blood of bulls, Or of lambs or goats. 12When you come to appear before Me, Who has required this from your hand, To trample My courts? 13Bring no more futile sacrifices; Incense is an abomination to Me. The New Moons, the Sabbaths, and the calling of assemblies— I cannot endure iniquity and the sacred meeting. 14Your New Moons and your appointed feasts My soul hates; They are a trouble to Me, I am weary of bearing them. 15When you spread out your hands, I will hide My eyes from you; Even though you make many prayers, I will not hear. Your hands are full of blood. 16Wash yourselves, make yourselves clean; Put away the evil of your doings from before My eyes. Cease to do evil, 17Learn to do good; Seek justice, Rebuke the oppressor; Defend the fatherless, Plead for the widow'" (Isaiah 1:11-17).

End of Time Prophecies

"These people draw near to Me with their mouth, And honor Me with their lips, But their heart is far from Me. 9And in vain they worship Me, Teaching as doctrines the commandments of men" (Matthew 15:8, 9).

God, in His mercy, still bore with His people until the Messiah came. God would have averted the doom coming upon the Jewish nation, as He had done with Nineveh, if the people would have received Jesus Christ as the Son of God—the Messiah. Sadly, when the Messiah came, His own people, the Jews—Israel, received Him not (John 1:11).

The Jewish Nation Ignores God

"And it shall be, that just as the LORD rejoiced over you to do you good and multiply you, so the LORD will rejoice over you to destroy you and bring you to nothing; and you shall be plucked from off the land which you go to possess. 64Then the LORD will scatter you among all peoples, from one end of the earth to the other, and there you shall serve other gods, which neither you nor your fathers have known—wood and stone" (Deuteronomy 28:63, 64).

The rejection of Jesus by the leaders of Israel meant the permanent, irrevocable cancellation of their special standing before God as a nation. The prophecies of Daniel 9 and Jeremiah had been fulfilled:

"The present day return of the Jews to Palestine and the establishment of the modern state of Israel do not imply reinstatement as God's people, present or future. Whatever the Jews, as a nation, may do, now or in [the future] time to come, is in no way related to the former promises made to them. With the crucifixion of Christ [and the stoning of Stephen] they forever forfeited their special position as God's chosen people. Any idea that the return of the Jews to their ancestral home, that is, to the new state of Israel, may in any way be related to Bible prophecy is without valid scriptural foundation. It ignores the plain statements of the Old Testament that God's promises to Israel were all conditional."[2]

2　　Nichol, Francis D., *Seventh-day Adventist Commentary*, Volume 4, (MD: Review and Herald Pub. Assoc. 1976), 33.

The Church Today

God does not force the human will. Israel's cooperation was essential to the success of God's plan. The nation of Israel ceased to exist because they did not cooperate with God. The Jews, the remnant of Israel, failed to believe and in the Messiah.

"For they [Israel] stumbled at that stumbling stone [Jesus Christ— the Messiah]" (Romans 9:32).

God still sustained His church. In the days of Noah His church was eight souls. God had a church. God's prophet Elijah thought he was alone, but the Lord declared *"I have reserved seven thousand in Israel, all whose knees have not bowed to Baal" (1 Kings 19:18).* God had a church. Daniel's three friends stood up for the God of the universe, despite the flames of the furnace. God had a church. That which God desired to do for the world through Israel He is now accomplishing through His Church on the earth today.

Simply being a child of Abraham never guarantees anyone that they are a child of God. Only those who hold on to the promises of God, obey His commandments, and have faith in the Messiah will be called a child of God.

"But it is not that the Word of God has taken no effect. For they are not all Israel who are of Israel, 7nor are they all children because they are the seed of Abraham; but, 'In Isaac your seed shall be called.' 8That is, those who are the children of the flesh, these are not the children of God; but the children of the promise are counted as the seed" (Romans 9:6-8).

God never intended that a simple birth order—being born into the family of Abraham, would save anyone.

"For the Scripture says, 'Whoever believes on Him will not be put to shame.' 12For there is no distinction between Jew and Greek, for the same Lord over all is rich to all who call upon Him. 13For 'whoever calls on the name of the LORD shall be saved'" (Romans 10:11-13).

"And the Scripture, foreseeing that God would justify the Gentiles by faith, preached the gospel to Abraham beforehand, saying, 'In you all the nations shall be blessed.' 9So then those who are of faith are blessed with believing Abraham" (Galatians 3:8, 9).

End of Time Prophecies

"Brethren, my heart's desire and prayer to God for Israel is that they may be saved. 2For I bear them witness that they have a zeal for God, but not according to knowledge. 3For they being ignorant of God's righteousness, and seeking to establish their own righteousness, have not submitted to the righteousness of God" (Romans 10:1-3).

"Then Peter opened his mouth and said: 'In truth I perceive that God shows no partiality. 35But in every nation whoever fears Him and works righteousness is accepted by Him'" (Acts 10:34, 35).

"And if some of the branches were broken off [Israel], and you, being a wild olive tree [Gentile], were grafted in among them, and with them became a partaker of the root and fatness of the olive tree, 21For if God did not spare the natural branches [Israel], He may not spare you either. 22Therefore consider the goodness and severity of God: on those who fell, severity; but toward you, goodness, if you continue in His goodness. Otherwise you also will be cut off. 23And they also, if they [individuals Jews] do not continue in unbelief, will be grafted in, for God is able to graft them in again" (Romans 11:17, 21-23).

"God did not spare the natural branches" *(Verse 21).* The natural branches are Israel. The nation of Israel walked away from the promises of God. They have been, as a nation, cut off forever— *"plucked from off the land" (Deuteronomy 8:63).*

"For by grace you have been saved through faith, and that not of yourselves; it is the gift of God, 9not of works, lest anyone should boast. 10For we are His workmanship, created in Christ Jesus for good works, which God prepared beforehand that we should walk in them. 11Therefore remember that you, once Gentiles in the flesh— who are called Uncircumcision by what is called the Circumcision made in the flesh by hands— 12that at that time you were without Christ, being aliens from the commonwealth of Israel and strangers from the covenants of promise, having no hope and without God in the world. 13But now in Christ Jesus you who once were far off have been brought near by the blood of Christ" (Ephesians 2:8-13).

All who will enter the Kingdom of Heaven will enter through faith in Jesus Christ. Hebrews 11 proves that it was the faith in a future Messiah that saved and not some birth into a nation or people.

Looking to the nation of Israel or to the Jews to fulfill any End of Time prophecy is an error and will lead to erroneous ideas and interpretations that are not supported in Scripture.

Introduction to Revelation
The Apocalypse of Christ

The book of Revelation opens with this statement "*The Revelation of Jesus Christ.*" The word *revelation* comes from the Greek word *apokalypsis* or *apocalypse,* which means "to uncover, to unveil, or to reveal." The last book of the Bible reveals the central purpose, theme and focus of the entire Bible, that is, Jesus Christ.

The book of Revelation was not designed to be confusing or hard to understand. Confusion and deception is the work of the devil, not the God of love. God through His messenger came to reveal not hide the work of Jesus Christ. God even added a blessing to the simple reading of His Word.

"Blessed is he who reads and those who hear the words of this prophecy," (Rev. 1:3).

The book of Revelation was designed to be understood. It uses symbols from Hebrew history—recorded in the Old Testament, to reveal truths about Jesus Christ. Most of these symbols come from the Old Testament tabernacle and its services. The Old Testament system of sacrifices was instituted by God when Adam and Eve sinned (Genesis 3:21). Each sacrifice pointed the sinner forward to the eventual sacrifice of Jesus Christ on the cross, paying the penalty of sin for all who believe, trust and declare Him Lord of their lives. Moses created the first tabernacle on earth as God directed him. This tabernacle held items such as the golden lampstand, the altar of incense, the table of shewbread and more. Each of these items along with the services surrounding them were familiar to the Jews, and anyone who has studied the Old Testament. Revelation takes these familiar and common symbols and reveals the work of Christ.

End of Time Prophecies

Three Ways to Study Revelation

"The Revelation of Jesus Christ, which God gave Him to show His servants— things which must shortly take place. And He sent and signified it by His angel to His servant John, ₂who bore witness to the Word of God, and to the testimony of Jesus Christ, to all things that he saw. ₃Blessed is he who reads and those who hear the words of this prophecy, and keep those things which are written in it; for the time is near." "₁₉Write the things which you have seen, and the things which are, and the things which will take place after this" (Revelation 1:1-3, 19).

God reveals three ways to study the book of Revelation.

1. Reading the book to uncover or reveal Jesus Christ (Verse 1).

2. Prophecy is the record of things past, present, and future (Verse 2, 19).

3. Simply reading, hearing, and keeping the words in Revelation will add a blessing to life.

The focus of our study will be on reading Revelation for its prophetic message. This subject alone encompasses more than we have space to write. In fact 1 Peter 1:12 tells us that the study of Revelation, and the many mysteries of God and His Word, are *"things which angels desire to look into."* This tells me that we will spend eternity learning more about Jesus Christ— the focus of Revelation.

Before we dive into prophecy let's look briefly at the other two ways to read and study revelation.

The Revealing of Jesus Christ

What does Revelation reveal or uncover about Jesus Christ?

Revelation affirms that Jesus was at work in the **past**, is working **now**, and will have a **future** work (Revelation 1:19).

Where was Jesus in the past? What was His work?

Searching Scriptures, we find the first mention of Jesus Christ: *"In the beginning God created the heavens and the earth"* (Genesis 1:1).

Introduction to Revelation

The story of creation is the first mention of Jesus Christ! The book of Colossians confirms that this is Christ.

"He is the image of the invisible God, the firstborn over all creation. 16For by Him all things were created that are in heaven and that are on earth, visible and invisible, whether thrones or dominions or principalities or powers. All things were created through Him and for Him. 17And He is before all things, and in Him all things consist" (Colossians 1:15-17).

Jesus Christ, the focus of Colossians, is the image of the invisible God. Anytime anyone in the scriptures, Old or New Testaments saw God, or the form of God, they were seeing the person called Jesus Christ. Jesus Christ is God; there is no separation between the Son and the Father. Jesus Christ is the creator, He is the beginning God.

Noah saw Jesus Christ and received the instructions to build an ark. Abraham and Sarah saw Jesus Christ and laughed when He said a child would be born. Jacob wrestled with Jesus Christ. Moses saw Jesus Christ in the burning bush and then saw His presence pass before the mountain top cave. The three in the furnace stood next to Jesus Christ.

The New Testament gospels revealed a Jesus Christ in the flesh as the perfect sacrifice for mankind. Jesus is God incarnate, living among and living as His people (in human form).

What is Jesus' current work?

To answer this question, allow me to ask another question…

If Jesus Christ died on the cross to conquer sin (and He did!) why does sin still exist?

The book of Revelation answers this question. Using symbols from Hebrew history and the Old Testament, Revelation reveals truths about Jesus' current work.

The Old Testament tabernacle system was a copy or a shadow of the heavenly tabernacle system (Hebrews 8:1,2,5).

The book of Revelation takes the framework of the Old Testament tabernacle, and compares it to the work of Christ in the heavenly sanctuary.

Jesus Christ Revealed in the Tabernacle System

Insights into the duties of Christ are revealed when we compare the outline of the entire book of Revelation to the items used in the Old Testament tabernacle system.

Where was the tabernacle located, within the Israelite camp?

Old Testament: The tabernacle, the house of God, sat in the middle of His people. God the Father resided in the Most Holy Place, sitting on the mercy seat, invisible to the camp, while the visible form of God, Jesus Christ, hovered over the camp in the form of a cloud by day and pillar of fire by night (Numbers 2:17).

Revelation 1:12, 13: *"Then I turned to see the voice that spoke with me. And having turned I saw seven golden lampstands, 13and in the midst of the seven lampstands One like the Son of Man, clothed with a garment down to the feet and girded about the chest with a golden band."*

Christ, the Son of Man, is in the middle of His people—here designated by the seven lampstands.

In the Old Testament, what was the purpose of the sacrificial lambs?

Old Testament: The sacrifices pointed to a future Messiah whose blood would atone for the sins of those who believe in Christ by faith (John 1:29; Isaiah 53:7; Leviticus 4:20; Exodus 12:13).

Revelation 5:6, 9: *"And I looked, and behold, in the midst of the throne and of the four living creatures, and in the midst of the elders, stood a Lamb as though it had been slain, having seven horns and seven eyes, which are the seven Spirits of God sent out into all the earth."*

"And they sang a new song, saying: 'You are worthy to take the scroll, And to open its seals; For You were slain, And have redeemed us to God by Your blood Out of every tribe and tongue and people and nation,'"

Jesus Christ is the lamb slain for the sins of the earth.

Introduction to Revelation

In the Old Testament why did the priests offer morning and evening sacrifices?

Old Testament: The morning and evening sacrifices were for the Israelites who may have been away from the camp and thus unable to perform their own sacrifices for the forgiveness of sins. Through these sacrifices a person could turn back towards the camp and remember that sacrifices were being offered for his sins (Exodus 29:38-46).

Revelation 8:4: *"And the smoke of the incense, with the prayers of the saints, ascended before God from the angel's hand."*

Jesus Christ, as our high priest, now stands in the Heavenly sanctuary receiving the prayers of His saints, represented by the smoke of the incense. He offered His life as a sacrifice for you, covering your sins, if you turn to Him. All who by faith look to heaven and believe that Jesus Christ is their savior and that He died for them will be afforded the benefits of the perfect sacrifice of Jesus' death on the cross.

What yearly event cleaned the Old Testament camp from sin?

Old Testament: The Day of Atonement. This solemn ceremony ended the yearly tabernacle cycle. The high priest would prepare himself and the camp, and then he would enter into the Most Holy place to stand before God offering the sacrifices of the people as an atoning offering. If it was accepted, the sins of the camp and all who had participated throughout the year would be removed forever (Leviticus 16:16,19).

Revelation 11:19: *"Then the temple of God was opened in heaven, and the ark of His covenant was seen in His temple. And there were lightnings, noises, thunderings, an earthquake, and great hail."*

According to Daniel 8:14 the Heavenly Day of Atonement– the cleansing of the sanctuary, began in AD1844. At this time, Jesus Christ, as our high priest, entered the Most Holy Place.

This is where we stand in time. This is why sin still exists on earth, because the work of Jesus Christ is not yet complete. Soon, when the judgment is done and Jesus Christ (Michael) stands up, the final events in earth's history will unfold. Jesus will return to take His people home and sin will be destroyed forever.

This is Jesus Christ's present work. The books are now opened and all are being judged to see if they have asked for His blood to cover them or to see if they squandered away Jesus' gift of grace.

In the Old Testament system, what evidence was given that God accepted the atonement offering?

Old Testament: God's spirit filled the entire tabernacle pushing the priest out. All services were suspended during this time (1 Kings 8:11; 2 Chronicles 5:14).

Revelation 15:8: *"The temple was filled with smoke from the glory of God and from His power, and no one was able to enter the temple till the seven plagues of the seven angels were completed."*

Evidence is given that at the end of the judgment in heaven God's glory will fill the temple. Man will then have to stand before God without a mediator. This is future and begins when the time of trouble begins.

What symbol, in the Old Testament, was used to represent the removal of sins?

Old Testament: The sacrifices did not remove sins; they simply transferred them to the sanctuary. The Day of Atonement was the removal of sins, for those who honored God's precepts and continued to walk in a life of faith in God. It was the act of banishing a scapegoat that symbolized the removal of sins from the camp—forever (Leviticus 16:21,22).

Revelation 20:1-3: *"Then I saw an angel coming down from heaven, having the key to the bottomless pit and a great chain in his hand. 2He laid hold of the dragon, that serpent of old, who is the Devil and Satan, and bound him for a thousand years; 3and he cast him* *into the bottomless pit, and shut him up, and set a seal on him, so that he should deceive the nations no more till the thousand years were finished. But after these things he must be released for a little while."*

Satan, the father of sin, will be banished completely from the universe of God. He will be utterly destroyed, and with it all sin and sinners.

At the conclusion of the Old Testament sanctuary cycle no sin remained in the camp. This will be the state of God's universe. Not a trace of sin will be found, not even in hell (which is a moment in time, and not an everlasting place with beings living a life of torture. See the chapter "Hell and Death").

The Old Testament is no accident. Every story, every word, every symbol points us to a Creator, a Savior, and a God who desires that none *"should perish but that all should come to repentance" (2 Peter 3:9).*

The revealing of Jesus Christ's current work, as outlined against the Old Testament sanctuary, shows us that sin still exists because the work of Christ is not yet complete.

Studying Revelation, it will be seen that we are now living in the days of last atonement process in heaven (Leviticus 16 & 21; Daniel 8:14; Revelation 11:19; 15:8).

Sin is not yet eradicated because Christ—our high priest, is still within the Most Holy place completing His priestly work.

Soon Jesus Christ, will stand up and the End of Time will be seen.

The apocalypse or revealing of Jesus Christ is John's most important work. It reveals that Jesus, the meek, lowly, and humble man, who walked the earth and allowed Himself to suffer wrong even to the point of death, is more than a man—He is God of the universe. Jesus Christ is no simple prophet or philosopher, He is God. He is bigger than time— even existing before time ever was. He is the first and the last. He is the lion, the king, and the rightful heir to Judah, Israel, and all creation.

The Reading of Revelation

"Blessed is he who reads and those who hear the words of this prophecy, and keep those things which are written in it; for the time is near" (Revelation 1:3).

Revelation was a letter from John. It was meant to be read aloud in church. The Word of God simply states that he who reads, hears and keeps the words of this prophecy will be blessed.

Reading Revelation builds faith, gives strength to endure, adds hope, edifies its readers and gives guidance and correction so that we can stay on the straight and narrow path.

Reading Revelation describes God's people: *"Here is the patience of the saints; here are those who keep the commandments of God and the faith of Jesus"* (Revelation 14:12).

Reading Revelation edifies our Christian walk. Read the first three chapters, talking about the seven churches, and notice how each church could represent a particular type of Christian. Which personality are you? What edification is given? What reproof is shared? Can you see something that will help you in your walk with the Savior?

If you study Revelation only for the symbols and prophecy, you will miss the big picture—Jesus Christ. If you ignore Revelation because it is too confusing you will miss a special blessing that is given by just reading and hearing it. Glance at the end of the book, notice that those who hold on to Christ win!

Chiasm: A Hebrew way of thought

Before we get deeper into our study of prophecy it is important that we understand the writing style of John.

Chiasm is a fancy name for the Hebrew way of organizing thoughts. A Chiasm is like a journey to a mountaintop. We start at the base A, climb up the side B, and reach the top C, then we descend down side B' and reach the base A' but from the other side. As we descend, we pass the same objects but with a new, fuller meaning. The crux of the argument is at the center C, and not the end.

Introduction to Revelation

The first chapter of Revelation includes a basic Chiasm.

"His head and hair were white like wool, as white as snow, and His eyes like a flame of fire; 15His feet were like fine brass, as if refined in a furnace, and His voice as the sound of many waters; 16He had in His right hand seven stars, out of His mouth went a sharp twoedged sword, and His countenance was like the sun shining in its strength" (Revelation 1: 14-16).

                        Voice

              Feet   Right Hand

                Eyes   Mouth

     Head, Hair   Face, Countenance

The crux of these verses is the center, the voice of God.

The next two verses expand upon the center of the Chiasm: the voice of God.

"And when I saw Him, I fell at His feet as dead. But He laid His right hand on me, saying to me, "Do not be afraid; I am the First and the Last. 18I am He who lives, and was dead, and behold, I am alive forevermore. Amen. And I have the keys of Hades and of Death" (Revelation 1:17, 18).

The Center of Revelation

There are several chiastic patterns found in Revelation, depending on the focus. Looking at the entire book for Old Testament Sanctuary references we can see a Chiasm of topics. The center of this view, the main idea, is found in Chapter 11.

"Saying: 'We give You thanks, O Lord God Almighty, The One who is and who was and who is to come, Because You have taken Your great power and reigned. 18The nations were angry, and Your wrath has come, And the time of the dead, that they should be judged, And that You should reward Your servants the prophets and the saints, And those who fear Your name, small and great, And should destroy those who destroy the earth.' 19Then the temple of God was opened in heaven, and the ark of His covenant was seen in His temple. And there were lightnings, noises, thunderings, an earthquake, and great hail" (Revelation 11:17-19).

Here is the ultimate Good News! The Lord God Almighty has come, and is ready to reward His servants and saints.

End of Time Prophecies

Prophecy

There are many layers to a prophetic interpretation of Revelation. Some layers are literal, some figurative and symbolic (most will be symbolic), and some are a combination of them all. Many passages are allusions, parallels or references to Old Testament language and themes; therefore a study of Old Testament is required.

Revelation is a jumble of visions written one after another. It is not designed to be read chronologically, that is from start to finish as a straight line. The visions of Daniel proved this. Daniel had multiple visions that described the same set of events, furthermore whole chapters in Daniel were out of place, showing us that Daniel did not happen in the order we read it. Just like Daniel, the book of Revelation is a series of visions, each one unique. Each vision speaks to the same set of events in the history of earth, but adds more information and details.

One way of viewing the scope of Revelation is to view it like a TV Guide. Imagine all of the major TV news channels are reporting on a single major news event. Each news network would present the same story but from their political slant or angle. Revelation is a series of TV channels that report on the End of Time, each one reporting on prophetic events from its own point of view.

Introduction to Revelation

The Outline of Revelation— a T.V. Guide

News Channel	Station	Point of View
The 7 Churches	Rev. 2,3	The body of believers in Jesus Christ— the true church.
The 7 Seals	Rev. 4-6,8:1	The Apostate church— believers of a false religion and a false savior.
The 7 Trumpets	Rev. 8,9,11	The secular and political world surrounding the church.
The 2 Witnesses	Rev. 10,11	God's Word, the Bible is under attack.
The Dragon's War	Rev. 12-14	The Great Controversy between Satan and the Son of God.
3 Angels Message	Rev. 14	The last warnings issued to the world before God's wrath is poured out.
Judgment of Babylon	Rev. 17,18	The discovery of what Babylon represents.
Last Day Events	Rev. 15,16	Descriptions of the plagues from God's wrath.
The Second Coming	Rev. 19,20	Jesus Christ Returns to the Earth to gather His saints.
The New Earth	Rev. 21,22	Events sealing up the end of sin and the beginning of Eternity in paradise.

The Seven Churches
Revelation 1-3

The seven churches represent seven time periods in the life and growth of the true Christian church. Each period follows the one before it. The Old Testament marked the history of the church, God's people, prior to the life of the Messiah. The New Testament, including Revelation, discusses the history of God's church from the earthly ministry of Jesus Christ until the End of Time.

"The mystery of the seven stars which you saw in My right hand, and the seven golden lampstands: The seven stars are the angels of the seven churches, and the seven lampstands which you saw are the seven churches" (Revelation 1:20).

"To the angel of the church of Ephesus write, 'These things says He who holds the seven stars in His right hand, who walks in the midst of the seven golden lampstands:'" (Revelation 2:1).

Seven is often used to denote completeness, as in the seven days of creation. The first three chapters of Revelation speak about seven churches. There were more than seven churches during the time of John. The number seven alerts us that Christ is here referencing information that will be applicable to all of His churches, throughout all ages.

What are the seven stars?

Angels of the seven churches (Verse 20).

The Greek word *angelos* translated here as *angel* means "messenger." God has in his right hand messengers prepared for every church in every age.

"And to the angel of the church in Sardis write, 'These things says He who has the seven Spirits of God and the seven stars: "I know your works, that you have a name that you are alive, but you are dead"'" (Revelation 3:1).

End of Time Prophecies

What are the seven spirits of God?

The seven spirits of God and the seven stars are related. This can help us identify what they are.

"And from the throne proceeded lightnings, thunderings, and voices. Seven lamps of fire were burning before the throne, which are the seven Spirits of God" (Revelation 4:5).

The seven spirits are called seven lamps of fire.

Proverbs 20:27 calls the spirit of man *"the lamp of the Lord."*

"And I looked, and behold, in the midst of the throne and of the four living creatures, and in the midst of the elders, stood a Lamb as though it had been slain, having seven horns and seven eyes, which are the seven Spirits of God sent out into all the earth" (Revelation 5:6).

Revelation 5:6 describes the seven eyes of the Lamb as the seven spirits of God. Zechariah 4:10 identifies men as the eyes of the Lord. Men are filled with the Spirit of God and shine forth as lamps to a dark world.

Isaiah 11:2 mentions seven Spirits or characteristics that would rest upon, or within Jesus Christ as He ministered in human flesh: *1) Spirit of the Lord, 2)Wisdom, 3)Understanding, 4)Counsel, 5)Might, 6)Knowledge, 7)Fear of the Lord.*

The seven spirits of God refer to those, in all generations, who posses the characteristics of Christ.

Seven Messengers for Seven Ages

The seven lampstands represent each church age from the Apostolic church through Laodicea. Each of the seven churches mentioned by name represented a real church body during the time of John. The characteristics of each church applied to the era in which each would represent. Each praise and admonition revealed would fit both the local church and the church age.

There are seven stars in Christ's hand (Revelation 1:1); these represent the seven angels or seven messengers of each church age which will spread the light of God's message to each church in every age. God's plan has always been to use mankind to spread His Word, His love, and His gospel to a darkened world.

John is writing to each angel or messenger, plural. His writings are for us, not the angels. We are sent out into all the earth (Revelation 5:6).

It is possible that the lampstands could represent the church body, and the burning lamp or flames would represent the people who are filled with the oil of the Holy Spirit (Zechariah 4:1-6; 1 John 2:20,27; Isaiah 61:1). These are the people who are letting their light shine out into the world (Matthew 5:14-16).

The seven characteristics of the seven spirits (Isaiah 11:2), shows us the character that God's messengers, His saints, must possess.

The seven Spirits of God represent His messengers to the world. A named church is used to introduce each age, or span of time that God's people— His church would have to endure before Christ's return. I believe it may be possible to select a specific messenger that epitomes the spirit of each church age.

With this thought in mind, the messenger to the first church age comes down to a selection between Peter and Paul.

Peter was present at Pentecost and witnessed the outpouring of the Holy Spirit upon the young Christian church. But at this time the probation of the Jews had not yet closed. According to Daniel 9 this would come about 3 ½ years after the crucifixion of Christ.

Paul's Damascus road conversion, years after the crucifixion, helped mark the message of Christ's Gospel being spread to the gentile world.

"Paul, an apostle (not from men nor through man, but through Jesus Christ and God the Father who raised Him from the dead)" (Galatians 1:1).

Apostle, *apostolos* in Greek, refers to "a messenger" or to "one who is sent." Though Peter was an apostle, sent to preach the Word of God to the world, Paul more broadly shined the light of Jesus to the world outside of the Jews.

Paul, I believe, is the messenger to the new church, and by him we must compare all future spokespersons for God.

"For I neither received it from man, nor was I taught it, but it came through the revelation of Jesus Christ. 13For you have heard of my former conduct in Judaism, how I persecuted the church of God beyond measure and tried to destroy it. 14And I advanced in Judaism beyond many of my contemporaries in my own nation, being more exceedingly zealous for the traditions of my fathers. 15But when it pleased God, who separated me from my mother's womb and called me through His grace, 16to reveal His Son in me, that I might preach Him among the Gentiles, I did not immediately confer with flesh and blood, 17nor did I go up to Jerusalem to those who were apostles before me; but I went to Arabia, and returned again to Damascus. 18Then after three years I went up to Jerusalem to see Peter, and remained with him fifteen days. 19But I saw none of the other apostles except James, the Lord's brother" (Galatians 1:12-19).

Ephesus

"Unto the angel of the church of Ephesus write; These things saith he that holdeth the seven stars in his right hand, who walketh in the midst of the seven golden candlesticks; 2I know thy works, and thy labour, and thy patience, and how thou canst not bear them which are evil: and thou hast tried them which say they are apostles, and are not, and hast found them liars: 3And hast borne, and hast patience, and for my name's sake hast laboured, and hast not fainted. 4Nevertheless I have [somewhat] against thee, because thou hast left thy first love. 5Remember therefore from whence thou art fallen, and repent, and do the first works; or else I will come unto thee quickly, and will remove thy candlestick out of his place, except thou repent. 6But this thou hast, that thou hatest the deeds of the Nicolaitanes, which I also hate. 7He that hath an ear, let him hear what the Spirit saith unto the churches; To him that overcometh will I give to eat of the tree of life, which is in the midst of the paradise of God" (Revelation 2:1-7 KJV).

Church: Ephesus
The Apostolic Church
AD31 – 100

AD31   The disciples are filled with the Holy Ghost at Pentecost (Acts 2).

AD100   Death of the last apostle, John.

The messenger is apostle Paul (died in AD67 or 68).

Ephesus means "relaxes." The church during this age becomes relaxed and begins to drift away from its first love and from the Word of God (Acts 20:29-31).

Who are the Nicolaitans?

Nikao = to conquer.

Laos or Laity = the common people.

Nicolaitans are some group of people that have been conquered or controlled.

"But this you have, that you hate the deeds of the Nicolaitans, which I also hate" (Revelation 2:6).

During first church age there are deeds of the Nicolaitans.

Deeds are actions, usually random, unorganized and unforced.

"Thus you also have those who hold the doctrine of the Nicolaitans, which thing I hate" (Revelation 2: 15).

Two ages later, during the Pergamos church, the deeds have now turned into doctrines.

Doctrines are something that is established, set in place and often enforced.

Nicolaitans is a symbol showing that a set of errors would begin in the church as random deeds and subtle actions. Later, in the third church age of Pergamos, these actions would be codified into doctrines of faith based on error and human tradition instead of the Word of God.

The Bible warns the church members of every age to be careful of false beliefs and doctrines.

"Therefore take heed to yourselves and to all the flock, among which the Holy Spirit has made you overseers, to shepherd the church of God which He purchased with His own blood. 29For I know this, that after my departure savage wolves will come in among you, not sparing the flock. 30Also from among yourselves men will rise up, speaking perverse things, to draw away the disciples after themselves" (Acts 20:28-30).

End of Time Prophecies

The apostle Paul is warning the church that *"savage wolves will come in among you."* Wolves use a tactic of dividing the flock to conquer the weak. The errors of the Nicolaitans would begin as small subtle deeds during the Ephesus age, able to deceive the weak. Each error advanced within the church and left uncorrected would develop into doctrines of error.

Smyrna

"And unto the angel of the church in Smyrna write; These things saith the first and the last, which was dead, and is alive; 9I know thy works, and tribulation, and poverty, (but thou art rich) and [I know] the blasphemy of them which say they are Jews, and are not, but [are] the synagogue of Satan. 10Fear none of those things which thou shalt suffer: behold, the devil shall cast [some] of you into prison, that ye may be tried; and ye shall have tribulation ten days: be thou faithful unto death, and I will give thee a crown of life. 11He that hath an ear, let him hear what the Spirit saith unto the churches; He that overcometh shall not be hurt of the second death" (Revelation 2:8-11 KJV).

Church: Smyrna
The Persecuted Church
AD 100 – 313

AD 313 Roman Emperor Constantine issues the Edict of Nantes giving religious tolerance to Christians.

The messenger may be Iranaeus who was a disciple of Polycarp who was a disciple of John.

Smyrna means "bitter." This word is from the root *myrrh* which was used in embalming the dead. This age is a bitter age with lots of death.

"You will have tribulation ten days" Rome began persecuting the Christians under the rule of Nero. This continued strongly until Emperor Constantine at the end of this age. The last great period of tribulation was under Diocletian, which lasted exactly 10 years (10 prophetic days) from AD 303 – 313.

The Seven Churches

Pergamos

"And to the angel of the church in Pergamos write; These things saith he which hath the sharp sword with two edges; 13I know thy works, and where thou dwellest, [even] where Satan's seat [is:] and thou holdest fast my name, and hast not denied my faith, even in those days wherein Antipas [was] my faithful martyr, who was slain among you, where Satan dwelleth. 14But I have a few things against thee, because thou hast there them that hold the doctrine of Balaam, who taught Balac to cast a stumblingblock before the children of Israel, to eat things sacrificed unto idols, and to commit fornication. 15So hast thou also them that hold the doctrine of the Nicolaitanes, which thing I hate. 16Repent; or else I will come unto thee quickly, and will fight against them with the sword of my mouth. 17He that hath an ear, let him hear what the Spirit saith unto the churches; To him that overcometh will I give to eat of the hidden manna, and will give him a white stone, and in the stone a new name written, which no man knoweth saving he that receiveth [it.]" (Revelation 2:12-17 KJV).

Church: Pergamos
The Exalted Church
AD313- 538

AD538 marks the beginning of a central state run church—Roman Catholicism.

The messenger is probably Martin of Tours (AD316-397). Tradition teaches that Martin raised the dead to life on three different occasions. Other humans who were given the Holy Spirit to raise the dead include: Peter (Acts 9), Paul (Acts 20), and Elijah, twice (1 Kings 17, 2 Kings 4).

Pergamos means "polygamy." During this age Emperor Constantine created the Council of Nicene to try and unify the different religious factions that existed. One group believed that Jesus was not the Son of God, while the other held to the Word of God. Constantine attempted to gain political favor. He compromised some of the truths in Christianity with non-Christian or pagan beliefs, blending truth and error, some which stand to this day. This was the beginning of a mixing of church (religious) and state (political) entities, or polygamy.

End of Time Prophecies

During this age, Emperor Justinian, in AD533, made the bishop of Rome the supreme bishop over the entire empire. Three of Rome's ten divisions did not agree with this decision. Through conquest these three powers, the Heruli, Ostrogoths, and Vandals, were *'plucked up'* and ceased to exist.

AD538 marks the beginning of the 1260 year prophecy (Daniel 7:25; 12:7; and Revelation 11:2,3).

"Doctrine of Nicolaitans" The Roman Catholic doctrine of making the priests, bishops and the pope (papa bishop) into overlords instead of servants is one of the Nicolaitans errors that became doctrine during this age.

"Doctrine of Balaam" Balaam was hired by Balac (Balak) to curse God's people—the Israelites (Numbers chapters 23-31). Balaam could not utter a single curse. God changed the curses into blessings. Balaam devised a new plan. He requested that the beautiful women of Balac's kingdom display themselves openly before the eyes of God's people. God's people became enamored with the beauty of the women and joined in fornication and idolatry. Many Christians today are being led astray by pomp, circumstance, and rituals that hide the truth behind these false doctrines.

"Hidden Manna" Manna is God's Word—the Bible. During this age the Bible was hidden away from the common people, the laity.

"White Stone" This represents the acquittal of sins. Black and white stones were used by juries for casting votes. Black stones were cast for guilty, white meant acquittal.

Thyatira

"And unto the angel of the church in Thyatira write; These things saith the Son of God, who hath his eyes like unto a flame of fire, and his feet [are] like fine brass; 19I know thy works, and charity, and service, and faith, and thy patience, and thy works; and the last [to be] more than the first. 20Notwithstanding I have a few things against thee, because thou sufferest that woman Jezebel, which calleth herself a prophetess, to teach and to seduce my servants to commit fornication, and to eat things sacrificed unto idols.

The Seven Churches

21And I gave her space to repent of her fornication; and she repented not. 22Behold, I will cast her into a bed, and them that commit adultery with her into great tribulation, except they repent of their deeds. 23And I will kill her children with death; and all the churches shall know that I am he which searcheth the reins and hearts: and I will give unto every one of you according to your works. 24But unto you I say, and unto the rest in Thyatira, as many as have not this doctrine, and which have not known the depths of Satan, as they speak; I will put upon you none other burden. 25But that which ye have [already] hold fast till I come. 26And he that overcometh, and keepeth my works unto the end, to him will I give power over the nations: 27And he shall rule them with a rod of iron; as the vessels of a potter shall they be broken to shivers: even as I received of my Father. 28And I will give him the morning star. 29He that hath an ear, let him hear what the Spirit saith unto the churches" (Revelation 2:18-29 KJV).

Church: Thyatira
The Church in the Wilderness
AD538-1517

October 31, 1517 Martin Luther nailed his 95 theses to the church door in Wittenberg.

The Messenger could be Saint Columba (521 – 597). His vast ministry was accompanied by supernatural signs, evidence of the strength of God. He was an observer of the Biblical Sabbath—worship on the seventh-day Sabbath.

Thyatira means "continual sacrifice." Many tortures were inflicted upon the church at this time.

"That woman Jezebel" Ahab, king of Israel, married Jezebel as a political maneuver to strengthen his kingdom and secure it. This is exactly what the church did when it united or married with the state under Constantine. Their actions were for political reasons, despite the attempt to cloak it in an air of spirituality. The church compromised its core beliefs to satisfy politics. When Jezebel got the power of the state behind her, she forced her religion upon her subjects, killing the prophets and priests of the Most High God (1 Kings 18; 2 Kings 9).

The Roman Church, united with the political state and played the role of Jezebel forcing God's people—His church to go into hiding.

End of Time Prophecies

Small bands of true Christians conducted their services secretly in open fields, meadows, barns, or where ever safety could be found. The Waldenses and Albigenses were Christian groups who suffered persecution at this time. In AD1208 pope Innocent III declared a holy war on these groups. This extermination occurred on so vast and terrible a scale that it may well constitute the first case of genocide in modern European history. In the French town of Be'ziers alone, at least fifteen thousand men, women and children were slaughtered, many in the sanctuary of the church. When an officer inquired of the pope's representative how he might distinguish heretics from true believers, the reply was "Kill them all. God will recognize His own."

Sardis

"And unto the angel of the church in Sardis write; These things saith he that hath the seven Spirits of God, and the seven stars; I know thy works, that thou hast a name that thou livest, and art dead. ₂Be watchful, and strengthen the things which remain, that are ready to die: for I have not found thy works perfect before God. ₃Remember therefore how thou hast received and heard, and hold fast, and repent. If therefore thou shalt not watch, I will come on thee as a thief, and thou shalt not know what hour I will come upon thee. ₄Thou hast a few names even in Sardis which have not defiled their garments; and they shall walk with me in white: for they are worthy. ₅He that overcometh, the same shall be clothed in white raiment; and I will not blot out his name out of the book of life, but I will confess his name before my Father, and before his angels. ₆He that hath an ear, let him hear what the Spirit saith unto the churches" (Revelation 3:1-6 KJV).

Church: Sardis
The Church of the Reformation
AD1517 – 1798

AD1798 marks the deadly wound that was inflicted upon the little horn (Revelation 13:3). This marks the end of the 1260 year prophecy and the rampant rule of the pope over the nations of Europe.

AD1798 Rome falls to the hands of Berthier a French general. The pope—Pius VI, is taken prisoner and dies in captivity on August 29, 1799. The rule of the pope's is ended for a while, but the office of pope would continue, though without its former power or prestige, with pope Pius VII.

The messenger is Martin Luther (b. 1483 – 1546). He nailed 95 thesis' or questions on the door of the local Roman Catholic Church. He was questioning the direction that the church had drifted and outlined how it now differed from the true Word of God.

Sardis means "That which remains." It is fitting for this church which had to remain until the little horn would receive its wound at the end of this age.

Philadelphia

"And to the angel of the church in Philadelphia write; These things saith he that is holy, he that is true, he that hath the key of David, he that openeth, and no man shutteth; and shutteth, and no man openeth; 8 I know thy works: behold, I have set before thee an open door, and no man can shut it: for thou hast a little strength, and hast kept my word, and hast not denied my name. 9Behold, I will make them of the synagogue of Satan, which say they are Jews, and are not, but do lie; behold, I will make them to come and worship before thy feet, and to know that I have loved thee. 10Because thou hast kept the word of my patience, I also will keep thee from the hour of temptation, which shall come upon all the world, to try them that dwell upon the earth. 11Behold, I come quickly: hold that fast which thou hast, that no man take thy crown. 12Him that overcometh will I make a pillar in the temple of my God, and he shall go no more out: and I will write upon him the name of my God, and the name of the city of my God, [which is] new Jerusalem, which cometh down out of heaven from my God: and [I will write upon him] my new name. 13He that hath an ear, let him hear what the Spirit saith unto the churches" (Revelation 3:7-13 KJV).

Church: Philadelphia
The missionary Church
AD 1798 – 1844

AD 1844 This marks the end of the 2300 year prophecy, first recorded in Daniel 8:14.

The messenger could be John Wesley (1703 – 1791). His early ministry focused on works or methods of salvation and led to his followers being called Methodist. Later in his ministry he understood the method of salvation was grace and not works, and began to preach the Gospel of Jesus Christ.

Philadelphia means "Brotherly Love" and is an appropriate title for this church age describing the opening of the world's mission fields. Missionaries traveled and explored the far reaches of the planet spreading the Gospel of Jesus Christ.

"I have set before you an open door" Paul's missionary ministry to the world was through an open door (2 Corinthians 2:12). During this age, the missionary door was opened again, paving the way for missionaries to reach the furthest parts of the earth, spreading the Gospel of Jesus Christ to every nation, tongue and people.

Another reference to the open door is that of the door to the Most Holy Place in heaven being opened at the end of this age. Christ moved into the Most Holy Place, completing the work of atonement, ushering in the cleansing of the sanctuary.

Laodicean

"And unto the angel of the church of the Laodiceans write; These things saith the Amen, the faithful and true witness, the beginning of the creation of God; 15I know thy works, that thou art neither cold nor hot: I would thou wert cold or hot. 16So then because thou art lukewarm, and neither cold nor hot, I will spue thee out of my mouth. 17Because thou sayest, I am rich, and increased with goods, and have need of nothing; and knowest not that thou art wretched, and miserable, and poor, and blind, and naked: 18I counsel thee to buy of me gold tried in the fire, that thou mayest be rich; and white raiment, that thou mayest be clothed, and [that] the shame of thy nakedness do not appear; and anoint thine eyes with eyesalve, that thou mayest see. 19As many as I love, I rebuke and chasten: be zealous therefore, and repent. 20Behold, I stand at the door, and knock: if any man hear my voice, and open the door, I will come in to him, and will sup with him, and he with me. 21To him that overcometh will I grant to sit with me in my throne, even as I also overcame, and am set down with my Father in his throne. 22He that hath an ear, let him hear what the Spirit saith unto the churches" (Revelation 3:14-22 KJV).

Church: Laodicea
The End of Time Church
1844 - End of Time

The Messenger is Ellen G. White (1827 - 1915). She is the author of more than 130 books and is the world's most translated woman author. Her works appear in more than 150 languages. She exalted Jesus Christ and continually pointed to the Scriptures as the basis of faith. She has several recorded and witnessed prophetic visions that shed light on the gospel of Jesus and the messages found in the Word of God.

Laodicea mean "people's rights" or "a just people." This period is the last of the church ages and will culminate in the just of all ages finally being vindicated for their steadfast faith in God.

"You are neither cold nor hot" This is a perfect description of our present age. Today many are complacent in their Christian walk. Many claim to be a Christian, but it is in name only— their actions are missing. This is the lukewarm condition that is cautioned against. Many are fooling themselves that they are "*rich*" in the graces of God, but in truth are "*wretched, and miserable, and poor, and blind, and naked.*" Matthew 7:22,23 records the fate of those who are lukewarm and do not "*buy of me [Jesus Christ] gold tried in the fire.*"

The Seven Churches

Name	Age	Title
Ephesus	31-100	The Apostolic Church
Smyrna	100-313	The Persecuted Church
Pergamos	313-538	The Exalted Church
Thyatira	538-1517	The Church in the Wilderness
Sardis	1517-1798	The Church of the Reformation
Philadelphia	1798-1844	The Missionary Church
Laodicea	1844-End of Time	The Last Day Church

The Seven Seals
Revelation 4, 5, 6

Revelation 3 concludes the vision of the Church Age. Chapter 4 is a new vision, a new channel of news. This new vision covers the same span of earth's history as the seven churches— from Christ on earth until the End of Time. The focus of this vision is the seven seals. Each seal reveals more about an apostate church, one that looks a lot like Christ's true church, but is full of deceptions, fables and traditions of men.

The Throne Room

"After this I looked, and, behold, a door [was] opened in heaven: and the first voice which I heard [was] as it were of a trumpet talking with me; which said, Come up hither, and I will shew thee things which must be hereafter. 2 And immediately I was in the spirit: and, behold, a throne was set in heaven, and [one] sat on the throne. 3And he that sat was to look upon like a jasper and a sardine stone: and [there was] a rainbow round about the throne, in sight like unto an emerald. 4And round about the throne [were] four and twenty seats: and upon the seats I saw four and twenty elders sitting, clothed in white raiment; and they had on their heads crowns of gold. 5And out of the throne proceeded lightnings and thunderings and voices: and [there were] seven lamps of fire burning before the throne, which are the seven Spirits of God. 6And before the throne [there was] a sea of glass like unto crystal: and in the midst of the throne, and round about the throne, [were] four beasts full of eyes before and behind" (Revelation 4:1-6 KJV).

What was John describing?

God's throne set in heaven (Verse 2).

How many seats sat around the throne?

Twenty-four (Verse 4).

How many beasts were around the throne?

Four living creatures (Verse 6).

End of Time Prophecies

This new vision begins as John returns to the state of being "*in the spirit.*" He begins by describing what he sees as he stands in the throne room of heaven.

Who are the 24 Elders?

"And the graves were opened; and many bodies of the saints who had fallen asleep were raised; 53and coming out of the graves after His resurrection, they went into the holy city and appeared to many" (Matthew 27:52, 53).

"Therefore He says: 'When He ascended on high, He led captivity captive, And gave gifts to men'" (Ephesians 4:8).

"Having disarmed principalities and powers, He made a public spectacle of them, triumphing over them in it" (Colossians 2:15).

These texts might explain the 24 elders. Matthew records a special group of saints that were raised to life at the crucifixion of Christ. Paul in Ephesians and Colossians describes their ascent into heaven, as proof that Jesus overcame both sin and death. John is now viewing 24 elders sitting in heaven around the throne. The number 24 may be symbolic of the 12 tribes of Israel (Old Testament), who are inscribed on the 12 gates of the New Jerusalem, and the 12 apostles (New Testament), who are written on the 12 foundations of the New Jerusalem. 24 would cover both Old and New Testaments—God's complete Word.

These twenty-four elders may be the jury, made up of the inhabitants of this sinful world, seated to witness the justice of God.

Lamps of Fire

"Who makes His angels spirits, His ministers a flame of fire" (Psalm 104:4).

"Are they not all ministering spirits sent forth to minister for those who will inherit salvation?" (Hebrews 1:14).

"And I looked, and behold, in the midst of the throne and of the four living creatures, and in the midst of the elders, stood a Lamb as though it had been slain, having seven horns and seven eyes, which are the seven Spirits of God sent out into all the earth" (Revelation 5:6).

What do the Lamps of Fire represent?

Angels are ministers; a flame of fire (Psalms).
Seven eyes are seven Spirits of God (Revelation).

The seven lamps of fire, which are before the throne of God, represent the Spirit of God, which fills His ministering angels and messengers. The first vision of Revelation introduced seven messengers sent to each of the church ages. Each of these messengers, also called angels, or spirits were filled with the singular Holy Spirit of God.

Four Living Creatures

"And the first beast [was] like a lion, and the second beast like a calf, and the third beast had a face as a man, and the fourth beast [was] like a flying eagle. 8And the four beasts had each of them six wings about [him;] and [they were] full of eyes within: and they rest not day and night, saying, Holy, holy, holy, Lord God Almighty, which was, and is, and is to come. 9And when those beasts give glory and honour and thanks to him that sat on the throne, who liveth for ever and ever, 10The four and twenty elders fall down before him that sat on the throne, and worship him that liveth for ever and ever, and cast their crowns before the throne, saying, 11Thou art worthy, O Lord, to receive glory and honour and power: for thou hast created all things, and for thy pleasure they are and were created" (Revelation 4:7-11 KJV).

The Beasts

The first beast was like a lion.
The second beast is like a calf.
The third beast had a face like a man.
The fourth beast was like a flying eagle.

Two words from Greek can be translated into the English word for beast; *zoon*, meaning "living creature;" and *therion*, meaning "fiendish or wild beast." Daniel's reference to the word beast was *therion*, a wild beast. It was used to represent a power or a kingdom. Revelation here uses the Greek word *zoon*, meaning a living creature such as an angel or human. The four beasts are not to represent kingdoms as they did with Daniel. Later Revelation 13 uses the Greek word *therion* for beast and therefore is discussing a nation, power or kingdom.

End of Time Prophecies

How many wings did the living creatures have?

Six wings (Verse 8).

"Above it stood seraphim; each one had six wings: with two he covered his face, with two he covered his feet, and with two he flew" (Isaiah 6:2).

What is another name for these living creatures?

Seraphim.

These living creatures will serve a purpose later in this chapter.

A Little Book

"And I saw in the right hand of Him who sat on the throne a scroll written inside and on the back, sealed with seven seals. 2Then I saw a strong angel proclaiming with a loud voice, "Who is worthy to open the scroll and to loose its seals?" 3And no one in heaven or on the earth or under the earth was able to open the scroll, or to look at it. 4So I wept much, because no one was found worthy to open and read the scroll, or to look at it" (Revelation 5:1-4).

"But you, Daniel, shut up the words, and seal the book until the time of the end; many shall run to and fro, and knowledge shall increase" (Daniel 12:4).

"Now when I looked, there was a hand stretched out to me; and behold, a scroll of a book was in it. 10Then He spread it before me; and there was writing on the inside and on the outside, and written on it were lamentations and mourning and woe" (Ezekiel 2:9, 10).

What does the little book hold?

"And written on it were lamentations and mourning and woe" (Ezekiel).

"And one of the elders saith unto me, Weep not: behold, the Lion of the tribe of Juda, the Root of David, hath prevailed to open the book, and to loose the seven seals thereof. 6And I beheld, and, lo, in the midst of the throne and of the four beasts, and in the midst of the elders, stood a Lamb as it had been slain, having seven horns and seven eyes, which are the seven Spirits of God sent forth into all the earth. 7And he came and took the book out of the right hand of him that sat upon the throne. 8And when he had taken the book, the four beasts and four [and] twenty elders fell down before the Lamb, having every one of them harps, and golden vials full of odours, which are the prayers of saints. 9And they sung a new song, saying, Thou art worthy to

take the book, and to open the seals thereof: for thou wast slain, and hast redeemed us to God by thy blood out of every kindred, and tongue, and people, and nation; 10And hast made us unto our God kings and priests: and we shall reign on the earth. 11And I beheld, and I heard the voice of many angels round about the throne and the beasts and the elders: and the number of them was ten thousand times ten thousand, and thousands of thousands; 12Saying with a loud voice, Worthy is the Lamb that was slain to receive power, and riches, and wisdom, and strength, and honour, and glory, and blessing. 13And every creature which is in heaven, and on the earth, and under the earth, and such as are in the sea, and all that are in them, heard I saying, Blessing, and honour, and glory, and power, [be] unto him that sitteth upon the throne, and unto the Lamb for ever and ever. 14And the four beasts said, Amen. And the four [and] twenty elders fell down and worshipped him that liveth for ever and ever" (Revelation 5:5-14 KJV).

Who is the lamb?
Jesus Christ (John 1:29).

This vision continues into chapter six. Remember chapter divisions and verses were added years later by scholars in an effort to help study and locate texts.

The First Four Seals
The Four Horses
"Now I saw when the Lamb opened one of the seals; and I heard one of the four living creatures saying with a voice like thunder, "Come and see." 2And I looked, and behold, a white horse. He who sat on it had a bow; and a crown was given to him, and he went out conquering and to conquer. 3When He opened the second seal, I heard the second living creature saying, "Come and see." 4Another horse, fiery red, went out. And it was granted to the one who sat on it to take peace from the earth, and that people should kill one another; and there was given to him a great sword. 5When He opened the third seal, I heard the third living creature say, "Come and see." So I looked, and behold, a black horse, and he who sat on it had a pair of scales in his hand. 6And I heard a voice in the midst of the four living creatures saying, "A quart of wheat for a denarius, and three quarts of barley for a denarius; and do not harm the oil and the wine." 7When He opened the fourth seal, I heard the voice of the fourth living creature saying, "Come and see." 8So I looked, and behold, a pale horse. And the name of him who sat on it was Death, and Hades followed with him. And power was given to them over a

fourth of the earth, to kill with sword, with hunger, with death, and by the beasts of the earth" (Revelation 6:1-8).

The first four seals are introduced by one of the four beasts. Each seal unleashes a different colored horse. What is the significance of the colored horses? Are they good or evil?

At a first glance, the horses appear to be good. White is often a symbol of purity (Revelation 3:4,5), but the next three horses bring about killing, harm and death. Perhaps the white horse, along with the other colored horses, does not represent goodness.

Colored horses are mentioned in Zechariah 1:8,9 and 6:2,3. The prophet Zechariah asks what do these horses represent and he is told: *"These are the ones whom the Lord has sent to walk to and fro throughout the earth"* (Zechariah 1:9). This statement has a parallel in Job 1:7 when the devil confronts God *"And the LORD said to Satan, 'From where do you come?' So Satan answered the LORD and said, 'From going to and fro on the earth, and from walking back and forth on it'"* (Job 1:7).

Here is evidence that perhaps these horses are a representation of Satan. The devil's greatest tool is deception. Deception is appearing to be one thing, while the truth is something different. Eve was deceived, she thought she was talking to a snake, she thought she was doing something grand by eating of the special fruit. Lucifer deceived Eve.

Recall that the book of Revelation is like a whole bunch of TV channels. Each vision (TV channel) describes events in earth's history, but shows it from a different perspective. The first three chapters of Revelation described the Church of God.

What is the perspective of the seven seals?

Looking closely at the seals it appears that each seal that follows moves away from being pure towards destruction. The destruction gets so bad that at some point in time a group of people (the wicked) are calling out for the rocks to fall on them and hide them from the face of the Lord (Verse 16).

I believe the perspective of the seven seals is the apostate church. The seals follow the growth of a church that looks and acts like the true church, but within this church deceit is practiced and it prospers.

It is not strange that the devil would have a church that emulates the church of Christ. Christ warned us that there would be tares that look like the wheat. Later in our study of Revelation we will see that John is amazed because there is an apostate church, called *"the mother of harlots and of the abominations of the earth"* (Revelation 17:5).

The seven seal shows how this apostate church developed.

The Rider of the Four Horses

I believe the rider of the four horses is the same. It is the devil. It is not the devil that changes in each era but the horse or his method of deception that changes as he establishes his apostate church.

Jesus Christ promised that he would not leave anyone comfortless (John 14:18). Christ prepared four special creatures symbolizing the outpourings of His Spirit to help combat the four horses or methods the devil would use to introduce deception into God's true church. Each colored horse is introduced by a living creature—a beast who is able to help combat the error and apostasy that is being set up.

The Four Living Creatures

The *lion* is a symbol of Jesus Christ, who was born into the line of Judah and is the head of the Church (Genesis 49:9).

The *cow* is one of the creatures of sacrifice. This would be the spirit needed by the true church to endure the persecutions and martyrdom of this age.

Man represents wisdom and knowledge. The spirit of truth would be needed by the true church to counter the lies, heresies and false religion that would exist in this third age.

The *eagle* represents speed and swiftness. This would be strength to a church in hiding.

The Four Living Beasts

	Beast	Horse	Rider's Item
Seal 1	Lion	White	Given a crown

"he went forth conquering and to conquer."

Seal 2	Calf	Red	Given a sword

"to take peace from the earth."

Seal 3	Man	Black	A Pair of Balances

"hurt not the oil and the wine."

Seal 4	Eagle	Pale	His name was death

"to kill with sword, and with hunger and with death."

Seal 1: A White Horse
AD 31 – 100
Introduced by the Lion Creature

The white horse of the devil mimics Christ's pure white horse and his Church (Revelation 19:11). The devil has a bow in his hands but no arrows. The devil will sow false teachings into the true church but these can do no damage (no arrows), unless they are believed. A crown is given to the rider meaning that his power is given to him by some authority who is larger than himself. Satan is currently the god of this world (Matthew 4:8; 2 Corinthians 4:4). God is allowing Satan to work, for a time, until the universe can see the true character of sin and the father of lies.

"Conquering and to conquer" Both words are the Greek word *Nikao*. We saw this word introduced during the letters to the seven churches in the word *Nicolaitans* (Revelation 2:6,15). This connection strengthens the concept that the seven seals are describing an apostate church. This church is under the direction and deception of Satan.

Seal 2: A Red Horse
AD100 – 313
Introduced by the Cow Creature

The red horse denotes blood and bloodshed. Power is given to the rider by some authority to persecute the true church. The sword he is given is one sided, not as powerful as Christ's two-edged sword. It is able to kill the body, but the soul (the life) it is unable to touch (Revelation 1:16; Hebrews 4:12; Matthew 10:28).

Seal 3: A Black Horse
AD313 – 538
Introduced by the man creature

The black horse brings ignorance and darkness to the church. The pair of balances is the combining of two powers, balancing a political power (pagan Rome) with a religious power (papal Rome).

Jesus Christ, His Words, His gospel, and His life, is the bread of life (John 6:35). Oil and wine are symbols of the Holy Spirit and the Word of God (Zechariah 4; Matthew 25; Leviticus 8:12). Wine represents the rejuvenation of the Spirit or the Spirit energized (Acts 2).

During this age the Word of God would be restricted from the people. This apostate church would actually charge their parishioners to receive the free gift of grace. The Roman Catholic Church, which gained world power during this age, would introduce the concept of buying and selling indulgences or buying and selling the forgiveness of sins bypassing true repentance and a return to Christ. (This was instituted by Tetzel). The bread of life, offered free, was now being sold.

Seal 4: A Pale Horse
AD538 – 1517[1]
Introduced by the eagle creature

This pale or sickly horse is one reeking of putrid and death. The joint political and religious power created in the previous age is now given power to harm the true church. The political aspect of this power is able to kill with the sword. The religious aspect is able to kill the spirit by removing the Word of God and by adulterating the truth that is plainly taught in the Scriptures.

The apostate church is fully functioning during this seal. It began with deeds and a few errant ideas. Over time it developed into a power that is unlike any which has ever existed.

Daniel describes this joint power in Daniel 7:19: *"Then I wished to know the truth about the fourth beast, which was different from all the others, exceedingly dreadful, with its teeth of iron and its nails of bronze, which devoured, broke in pieces, and trampled the residue with its feet;"*

This dreadful power is the papacy. This apostate Christian religion was foretold to Daniel, John and the disciples of Christ. Jesus personally described the events that would occur under the seven seals to His disciples. This is recorded in Matthew chapter 24.

Seals	Revelation	Matthew
Seal 1	Rev. 6:2	Mt. 24:4,5
Seal 2	Rev. 6:3,4	Mt. 24:6
Seal 3	Rev. 6:5,6	Mt. 24:7,8
Seal 4	Rev. 6:7,8	Mt. 24:9-12
Seal 5	Rev. 6:9-11	Mt. 24:13
Seal 6	Rev. 6:12-17	Mt. 24:14-29
Seal 7	Rev. 8:1	Mt. 24:30,31

---

1 This date could be AD1449, the beginning of the second woe (Revelation 9:13-21), But since the focus of this vision is the Church, AD1517 is used, referencing the Reformation.

The Last Three Seals

The last three seals do not have a horse and rider. There is no need for a living beast to introduce them. The focus of the seals was to introduce the apostate church. God's Spirit, symbolized by the four beasts, sustained the true church during the rise of the apostate one. God's Spirit is not withdrawn in the last seals, but the need to counteract a new deception or a new horse is not required. The apostate church (papacy) is still, today, fully functioning and deceiving all who are unaware. The last three seals introduce closing events in the history of the earth.

Fifth Seal

"When He opened the fifth seal, I saw under the altar the souls of those who had been slain for the Word of God and for the testimony which they held. 10And they cried with a loud voice, saying, "How long, O Lord, holy and true, until You judge and avenge our blood on those who dwell on the earth?" 11Then a white robe was given to each of them; and it was said to them that they should rest a little while longer, until both the number of their fellow servants and their brethren, who would be killed as they were, was completed" (Revelation 6:9-11).

Seal 5: An Altar with Slain Souls.
AD1517 – End of Time

This seal encourages the true church to stay the course until the end. This seal warns that the antichrist (the papal system) is fully developed in the world and will continue to persecute and sow lies and untruths until its end in the lake of fire.

"Under the altar" This altar is the altar of burnt offering. In the sanctuary service this altar is where the sacrifice was consumed by fire, symbolizing the destruction of sin and the wrath of God due to sin. Prior to the burning of this sacrifice the blood was collected by the priest. *"For the life of the flesh is in the blood, and I have given it to you upon the altar to make atonement for your souls; for it is the blood that makes atonement for the soul"* (Leviticus 17:11).

Blood, the symbol of life, was transferred to the sanctuary and used in the atonement process, of which Jesus Christ is the focus. Any excess blood was poured out at the base of the altar of burnt offerings.

It is this blood that John saw in his vision. The life *"is in the blood."* This seal is not describing ethereal or spirits of humans. Blood cannot speak. It is symbolically crying out—personifying the victims of those slain. Souls in Greek is *Psyche* meaning "life or breath." The people, symbolized by the blood poured at the base of the altar, are told to *"rest a little while longer."* Death is a sleep, not a transition to some other form (Ecclesiastes 9:5; 1 Corinthians 15:51; Psalm 6:5; John 11:9-14). (See the chapter: "Hell and Death" for a deeper discussion of this topic).

Sixth Seal

"I looked when He opened the sixth seal, and behold, there was a great earthquake; and the sun became black as sackcloth of hair, and the moon became like blood. 13And the stars of heaven fell to the earth, as a fig tree drops its late figs when it is shaken by a mighty wind. 14Then the sky receded as a scroll when it is rolled up, and every mountain and island was moved out of its place. 15And the kings of the earth, the great men, the rich men, the commanders, the mighty men, every slave and every free man, hid themselves in the caves and in the rocks of the mountains, 16and said to the mountains and rocks, 'Fall on us and hide us from the face of Him who sits on the throne and from the wrath of the Lamb! 17For the great day of His wrath has come, and who is able to stand?'" (Revelation 6:12-16).

Seal 6: Natural Disasters
AD1517 – End of Time

This seal includes many of the natural disasters that will occur throughout the earth. Individual disasters have been associated with the events outlined in this seal such as the Lisbon earthquake, the dark day of AD1780, and the falling stars in AD1833. While these natural disasters are unique, it is believed that these natural disasters will be repeated throughout the earth just before Christ returns (Matthew 24:29; Joel 2:31).

"A great earthquake" The deadliest earthquake on record to date occurred in AD1556 in Shensi, China. The most destructive earthquake to civilization occurred on November 1, 1755 in Lisbon, Portugal. It was felt throughout all of Europe and beyond by both direct vibrations and huge tidal waves. Lisbon was hit with a third destructive force—fire, started by candles overturned in the initial quake. Lisbon was home to many libraries, rare books, and paintings. Ninety percent of Lisbon was destroyed. Scripture points to even larger earthquakes prior to Christ's return (Psalm 18:7; Revelation 16:18; Joel 2:10; Nahum 1:5).

"The sun became black and the moon as blood" There was a dark day recorded on May 19, 1780. It began at 10a.m. and continued until the middle of the next night. The planets were not aligned to produce an eclipse. The moon was full the night before but shone with the appearance of blood on this evening. It was so dark during the day that the animals returned to their roosts thinking it was night. Candles were required to see. There will come a time when the sun will not shine (Jeremiah 4:20-31; Ezekiel 32:7,8; Isaiah 13:10; Isaiah 34:4; Matthew 24:29).

"Stars of heaven fell" A meteor shower of unparalleled proportions occurred on November 13, 1833. The shower began at 9pm and lasted until daybreak. It was seen all over North America from east to west. The spectacle was more grand and explosive than any single recorded fireworks display in the world.

Seventh Seal

"When He opened the seventh seal, there was silence in heaven for about half an hour" (Revelation 8:1).

Seal 7: Silence of half an hour
Some Future Date

This silence ushers in the final events of Jesus Christ appearing in the clouds above. This silence of a half an hour will be discussed in the chapter: "The Last Plagues."

We skipped chapter 7. It will be discussed in its own chapter, "The 144,000". Several of Johns visions are divided, that is they are interrupted by another idea or theme. I believe this style of writing reveals how John received the visions. I believe that these interludes were meant to calm John, to give him comfort and peace.

Receiving foreknowledge of events can be traumatizing. Isaiah writes: "*A distressing vision is declared to me; The treacherous dealer deals treacherously, And the plunderer plunders. Go up, O Elam! Besiege, O Media! All its sighing I have made to cease. 3Therefore my loins are filled with pain; Pangs have taken hold of me, like the pangs of a woman in labor. I was distressed when I heard it; I was dismayed when I saw it. 4My heart wavered, fearfulness frightened me; The night for which I longed He turned into fear for me*" (Isaiah 21:2-4). Daniel records: "*And I, Daniel, fainted and was sick for days; afterward I arose and went about the king's business. I was astonished by the vision, but no one understood it*" (Daniel 8:27).

John was in and out of visions. Having just seen four colored horses introduced by weird living creatures, John may need a breather. He may need to sit down and put his head between his knees.

I believe the interludes were for John's comfort and state of mind. The sealing of the 144,000 (Revelation 7) is comfort. It shows that God will take care of His own. It shows that despite the apostate Christian church and the destruction it would cause, God will reward His faithful saints with eternal life.

The Antichrist
"Is now already in the world." 1 John 4:3

Many today are seeking after the antichrist. They focus their watch on when, who or what he will be; but he is already at work in the world. Our focus should be on truth— on Jesus Christ. Scripture warns us to guard our focus. Christ warned that His return to deliver His saints would take many by surprise. Many are not focused on the right thing, that is, a saving and real relationship with Jesus Christ (Matthew 24:44, 2 Peter 3:10).

Who is the antichrist?

"Little children, it is the last hour; and as you have heard that the Antichrist is coming, even now many antichrists have come, by which we know that it is the last hour" (1 John 2:18).

What is an antichrist?

Scripture reveals scripture.

"And every spirit that does not confess that Jesus Christ has come in the flesh is not of God. And this is the spirit of the Antichrist, which you have heard was coming, and is now already in the world" (1 John 4:3).

"For many deceivers have gone out into the world who do not confess Jesus Christ as coming in the flesh. This is a deceiver and an antichrist" (2 John 1:7).

The prefix *anti*, used in antichrist, has the meaning of: "in place of" as in contrast, "in exchange for", or "one after another."

John reveals that even in his day many antichrists had come trying to stand in the place of Jesus Christ, exchanging His method of salvation for some other means.

Studying all of Revelation, it is evident that there will appear three extreme antichrists. All three will find their end when they are cast alive into a lake of fire. All three play key roles in deceiving the world and implementing the mark of the beast.

Revelation 19:20 describes the beast and the false prophet being *"cast alive into the lake of fire burning with brimstone."* Revelation 20:10 confirms this and adds that the devil will be *"cast into the lake of fire and brimstone where the beast and the false prophet are."*

"The beast" This is a system of false Christianity. The little horn is this beast.

"The false prophet" This entity will force the world to set up an image to the beast, and will force the world to worship that image.

"The dragon" This is the first and greatest adversary of God. He is also called the devil, or Satan.

Here are the three major antichrist's or antichrist powers that will exist and become more prominent as the End of Time develops. These are the ones who will be performing signs, speaking blasphemies, and deceiving the whole world to follow the father of lies (Revelation 16:13,14).

The Beast

The beast is described in Revelation 13:1-10. It looks like a leopard, a bear, and a lion— all direct references to Daniel 7. The descriptions for this beast is not limited to Revelation 13— Daniel 7:8,20,21,25; 8:9-12; 12:7; Revelation 11:2; 12:6; 17:3-8.

The beast is a system that is worshiped. A system that is able to persecute, make war, and torment those who do not believe as it desires. Daniel called this system the little horn. There is abundant evidence supplied within the scriptures to implicate the Roman system of the papacy as this beast. History allows us to look back and apply the beast's events to the prophecies found in the Word of God. No other system fits the portrayal of this beast than that of the papacy.

"Let no one deceive you by any means; for that Day will not come unless the falling away comes first, and the man of sin is revealed, the son of perdition, ₄who opposes and exalts himself above all that is called God or that is worshiped, so that he sits as God in the temple of God, showing himself that he is God. ₅Do you not remember that when I was still with you I told you these things? ₆And

now you know what is restraining, that he may be revealed in his own time. ₇For the mystery of lawlessness is already at work; only He who now restrains will do so until He is taken out of the way. ₈And then the lawless one will be revealed, whom the Lord will consume with the breath of His mouth and destroy with the brightness of His coming. ₉The coming of the lawless one is according to the working of Satan, with all power, signs, and lying wonders, ₁₀and with all unrighteous deception among those who perish, because they did not receive the love of the truth, that they might be saved" (2 Thessalonians 2:3-10).

Verse 9 tells us that Satan is not the *"man of sin"* or the antichrist mentioned in these texts. This antichrist would do his work *"according to the working of Satan."*

The antichrist described in this verse is speaking of the beast. He receives his power from Satan, and is the focal point of deception among those who perish in the last days. This beast power was already at work during the writing of John, but it was restrained for a time. This beast would not receive its full power until AD538.

The False Prophet

The false prophet is described in Revelation 13:11-18. This power prophesies to *"those who dwell on the earth to make an image to the beast who was wounded by the sword and lived"* (Revelation 13:14).

The false prophet is not worshiped like the beast, but is a political power that is able to force the world to worship the beast. Studying history, the biblical time lines, and descriptions of the false prophet, many scholars label the United States as this false prophet, a power that looks like a lamb but speaks as a dragon (Revelation 13:11). The U.S. is a nation that was built on "In God We Trust" and freedom of religion but today is beginning to speak out and turn its back on these core beliefs.

The Devil

The devil goes by many names: The great dragon, that serpent of old, Satan, author of sin, the enemy, angel of light, adversary of God, and Lucifer (Revelation 12:7-12; Matthew 13:39; 1 Peter 5:8;

1 John 3:8; 2 Corinthians 11:14; Isaiah 14:12). He is the one who gives power to the beast and the false prophet (Revelation 13:2).

Satan's Greatest Deception

The greatest deception of Satan is yet to come. Satan will attempt to impersonate Christ Himself. We are warned of this coming deception:

"For false christs and false prophets will rise and show great signs and wonders to deceive, if possible, even the elect. 25See, I have told you beforehand. 26Therefore if they say to you, 'Look, He is in the desert!' do not go out; or 'Look, He is in the inner rooms!' do not believe it. 27For as the lightning comes from the east and flashes to the west, so also will the coming of the Son of Man be" (Matthew 24:24-27).

This coming deception will be unlike anything the world today has seen. Satan will transform himself *"into an angel of light"* (2 Corinthians 11:14). Miracles of healing will accompany his transformation. It will appear as if Christ has returned. Satan has been sowing his tares in the world for millenniums. Many today blindly follow the mainstream voices in religion. They have not shown themselves to be faithful stewards of God's Word. They do not rightly divine truth from error. Many who hold on to the traditions of men will be deceived by the glory, brightness, and miracles that accompany this angel of light.

Satan will announce that he is Christ. Satan will proclaim that God has changed His mind and now desires the world to worship on Sunday— to honor His Son. Furthermore, the devil will claim that it is because the whole world is not worshiping on Sunday that the turmoil, ruin and degradation of the planet exists. This will put a target on the backs of all faithful Christians who desire to hold on to the plain Word of God— the Bible.

"To the law and to the testimony! If they do not speak according to this word, it is because there is no light in them" (Isaiah 8:20).

The 144,000
Revelation 7

The seven seals were opened before John and he was able to witness the sequence of events that would lead up to and surround Jesus' second coming. Daniel fainted when he saw these events. John fell at the feet of his angel presence, fearful of what he saw. John's pulse rate probably skyrocketed throughout his many visions. I believe each time John began to be overwhelmed God would present him with a vision of comfort and calm. The vision of the 144,000 is one of comfort and peace. This vision reveals the sealing of God's children and a promise of redemption from sin.

"And after these things I saw four angels standing on the four corners of the earth, holding the four winds of the earth, that the wind should not blow on the earth, nor on the sea, nor on any tree. 2And I saw another angel ascending from the east, having the seal of the living God: and he cried with a loud voice to the four angels, to whom it was given to hurt the earth and the sea, 3Saying, Hurt not the earth, neither the sea, nor the trees, till we have sealed the servants of our God in their foreheads" (Revelation 7:1-3 KJV).

"Thus says the LORD of hosts: 'Behold, disaster shall go forth From nation to nation, And a great whirlwind shall be raised up From the farthest parts of the earth'" (Jeremiah 25:32).

Wind and whirlwind are prophetic terms for strife, war, or evil. The four angels hold back the strife that will come upon the earth until *"we have sealed the servants of our God on their foreheads"* (Verse 3).

"And these words which I command you today shall be in your heart. 7You shall teach them diligently to your children, and shall talk of them when you sit in your house, when you walk by the way, when you lie down, and when you rise up. 8You shall bind them as a sign on your hand, and they shall be as frontlets between your eyes" (Deuteronomy 6:6-8).

"Keep my commands and live, and my law as the apple of your eye. 3Bind them on your fingers; write them on the tablet of your heart" (Proverbs 7:2, 3).

What is bound to the fingers, hand and heart?

These words, which I command you today (Verse 6).

End of Time Prophecies

The heart does not store memory. It is the frontlet between your eyes, your brain, that is able to remember and store up the commandments of God.

The seal of God will be given to those who remember God's laws. More than knowledge of God's law, it will require action. Action is symbolized by binding the law to the fingers and hand.

Seeing and Hearing

"And I heard the number of them which were sealed: [and there were] sealed an hundred [and] forty [and] four thousand of all the tribes of the children of Israel. ₅Of the tribe of Juda [were] sealed twelve thousand. Of the tribe of Reuben [were] sealed twelve thousand. Of the tribe of Gad [were] sealed twelve thousand. ₆Of the tribe of Aser [were] sealed twelve thousand. Of the tribe of Nepthalim [were] sealed twelve thousand. Of the tribe of Manasses [were] sealed twelve thousand. ₇Of the tribe of Simeon [were] sealed twelve thousand. Of the tribe of Levi [were] sealed twelve thousand. Of the tribe of Issachar [were] sealed twelve thousand. ₈Of the tribe of Zabulon [were] sealed twelve thousand. Of the tribe of Joseph [were] sealed twelve thousand. Of the tribe of Benjamin [were] sealed twelve thousand" (Revelation 7:4-8 KJV).

How many are sealed?

144,000

12,000 from each tribe is too perfect of a number to be an exact figure. We are in the book of Revelation and most of the descriptions so far have been symbolic, it is easy to see that this number is most likely symbolic as well. Perhaps it is some reference to the 12 tribes of Israel (Old Testament) and the 12 apostles (New Testament), or 12x12=144.

Did John see or hear this number?

John heard the number of 144,000 (Verse 4).

"After this I beheld, and, lo, a great multitude, which no man could number, of all nations, and kindreds, and people, and tongues, stood before the throne, and before the Lamb, clothed with white robes, and palms in their hands; ₁₀And cried with a loud voice, saying, Salvation to our God which sitteth upon the throne, and unto the Lamb" (Revelation 7:9,10 KJV).

Did John see or hear the great multitude?

John now sees the great multitude (Verse 9).

The concept of sight versus hearing is important when reading Revelation. Many times throughout the recording of Revelation John first *hears* about something. He writes what he heard; then John *sees* what he heard about and records his own explanation of what he saw.

John was told the sealed servants of God would number 144,000; but when he looked, he saw a vast multitude that was difficult if not impossible to count.

Who is this multitude?

There are two possible answers, it is either the entire throng of saints from Adam up to the last person saved, or it is a subgroup of the entire saints, sharing a common theme. We can answer this.

"And one of the elders answered, saying unto me, What are these which are arrayed in white robes? and whence came they? 14And I said unto him, Sir, thou knowest. And he said to me, These are they which came out of great tribulation, and have washed their robes, and made them white in the blood of the Lamb" (Revelation 7:13,14).

How are the 144,000 defined?

"These are they which came out of great tribulation" (Verse 14).

Here is a reference to something more than a tribulation, this is a great tribulation. This wording sounds similar to Daniel 12:1 *"a time of trouble,"* and Matthew 24:21 *"For there will be great tribulation such has not been since the beginning of the world until this time, no, nor ever shall be."*

Ellen G. White writes, "These are they which came out of great tribulation; they have passed through the time of trouble such as never was since there was a nation; they have endured the anguish

End of Time Prophecies

of the time of Jacob's trouble; they have stood without an intercessor through the final outpouring of God's judgments."[1]

This information lends credibility to the concept that the 144,000, while symbolic in number, is a subset—a special group of the saints that will total God's kingdom.

Not Defiled by Women

"And I looked, and, lo, a Lamb stood on the mount Sion, and with him an hundred forty [and] four thousand, having his Father's name written in their foreheads. ₂And I heard a voice from heaven, as the voice of many waters, and as the voice of a great thunder: and I heard the voice of harpers harping with their harps: ₃And they sung as it were a new song before the throne, and before the four beasts, and the elders: and no man could learn that song but the hundred [and] forty [and] four thousand, which were redeemed from the earth. ₄These are they which were not defiled with women; for they are virgins. These are they which follow the Lamb whithersoever he goeth. These were redeemed from among men, [being] the firstfruits unto God and to the Lamb. ₅And in their mouth was found no guile: for they are without fault before the throne of God" (Revelation 14:1-5 KJV).

Here again the 144,000 are mentioned.

Who are the 144,000?

"*These are they which were not defiled with women; for they are virgins.*"

"*These were redeemed from among men, [being] the firstfruits unto God and to the Lamb.*"

Symbols of adulterous women are used throughout Revelation referring to powers, false churches and people who walked contrary to God's Word. Virgins are here symbolic of people who remained true to God's Word and did not follow after seducing lies or fancy fables.

---

1 White, E.G., *The Great Controversy*, (CA: Pacific Press, 1888, 1971), 649.

"Firstfruits" This implies that there is more fruit to follow. The 144,000 appears is a special group within God's complete number of saved people.

> *"And I saw as it were a sea of glass mingled with fire: and them that had gotten the victory over the beast, and over his image, and over his mark, [and] over the number of his name, stand on the sea of glass, having the harps of God. ₃And they sing the song of Moses the servant of God, and the song of the Lamb, saying, Great and marvellous [are] thy works, Lord God Almighty; just and true [are] thy ways, thou King of saints. ₄Who shall not fear thee, O Lord, and glorify thy name? for [thou] only [art] holy: for all nations shall come and worship before thee; for thy judgments are made manifest" (Revelation 15:2-4 KJV).*

> *"Before the throne there was a sea of glass, like crystal. And in the midst of the throne, and around the throne, were four living creatures full of eyes in front and in back" (Revelation 4:6).*

Where do the four living creatures stand?

Around the throne.

Look back at Revelation 14:3. The 144,000 sang a new song while standing before the four living creatures. The living creatures stood on the glass sea. The 144,000 sing a song no one can learn except them.

In Chapter 15 John sees this same group—the 144,000, standing on the sea of glass, singing a song. These are *"them that had gotten the victory over the beast, and over his image, and over his mark, [and] over the number of his name"* (Revelation 15:2).

The 144,000 cannot include Adam and Eve, because the image to the beast (Revelation 13:14) was not set up. In fact, at the writing of this book in 2016 the mark of the beast and its image is not yet set upon the world. The beast—the little horn is present, but the mark is not yet here.

Ellen White supports this description of the 144,000. She describes them as the living saints during the last plague. Later she describes the scene as the trumpet of God awakens the sleeping [dead] saints:

"The graves opened, and the dead [saints] came up clothed with immortality. The 144,000 [living saints] shouted, 'Alleluia!' as they recognized their friends who had been torn from them by death, and in the same moment we [the 144,000] were changed and caught up together with them to meet the Lord in the air."[2]

The 144,000 will be composed of all believers who come out of Babylon; who wash their robes in the blood of Jesus Christ making Him Lord, ruler and God of their lives. The 144,000 will be the saints of God who endure the trials that will be poured out at the End of Time. They will be those who follow all of the commandments of God, including the 4th—keeping the seventh-day Sabbath, and who have the faith of Jesus Christ (Revelation 14:12).

The 144,000 represents an untold number of living saints from around the world who will endure the last plagues. The idea that the saints must endure a period of tribulation or a time of trouble is not foreign. Noah and his family endured a worldwide destruction—saved in an ark. Daniel faced lions, but God shut their mouths. Elijah endured three years of famine, but God provided.

Do not believe the devil's tare that the church will be raptured away from this time of trouble. Begin now to practice your faith and trust in God so that you will be prepared to meet the troubles coming.

2　　White, E.G., *Early Writings*, (MD: Review and Herald Publishing Association, 2000), 16.

The Seven Trumpets
Revelation 8:2-13; Rev. 9; Rev. 11:14-19

Trumpets are used to announce war and political strife. The seven angels with trumpets are sent to proclaim the changes that would take place in the political world. The political world in focus is the one that surrounds the Glorious Land— Jerusalem and surrounding area.

"And I saw the seven angels which stood before God; and to them were given seven trumpets. ₃And another angel came and stood at the altar, having a golden censer; and there was given unto him much incense, that he should offer [it] with the prayers of all saints upon the golden altar which was before the throne. ₄And the smoke of the incense, [which came] with the prayers of the saints, ascended up before God out of the angel's hand. ₅And the angel took the censer, and filled it with fire of the altar, and cast [it] into the earth: and there were voices, and thunderings, and lightnings, and an earthquake. ₆And the seven angels which had the seven trumpets prepared themselves to sound" (Revelation 8:2-6 KJV).

What was carried on the smoke of the incense?

The prayers of the saints (Verse 4).

The altar of incense is found within the tabernacle in the first room, the Holy Place. This altar was lit twenty-four seven and represented the prayers of the saints ascending to God. A sinner would offer a sacrifice to be killed and place it on the altar of burnt offering in the courtyard. The priest would take some of the blood from this offering and sprinkle it on the altar of incense. The sweet smell of fragrance—our prayers, mixed with the blood of the sacrificial lamb would ascend to heaven. Through symbols, it was represented that only through the blood of Christ would our prayers be heard before God.

Unifying Revelation

John is trying to relate events he saw in words, a difficult task especially if multiple events are occurring simultaneously. The seven trumpets occur during the seven seals, which occur during the seven church ages, which corresponds to events outlined in Daniel. This is why the Old Testament tabernacle and its services are being used to explain the actions seen in the visions. Understanding the tabernacle services will help the reader understand these visions.

"The angel casting the censor to the earth" Here is a direct reference to a specific act in the Sanctuary service. A typical morning in Herod's Tabernacle looked like this[1]: Prior to sunrise a priest would awake and cast lots to determine who would do the various duties of the day.

At daybreak, a lamb would be brought to the outer court where a single priest would prepare to slaughter the lamb. Another priest would enter the temple cleaning out the dead coals from the altar of incense and would maintain the lit lamps and its oil. Here is a reference to the seven lamps found in Revelation chapters 1-3.

When these duties were complete, the door into the temple was opened signaling the priest to slay the lamb. (This imagery was seen in Revelation 4 and 5). The blood of the lamb would be collected and used for dipping and sprinkling of the blood appropriately. The remainder of the blood was poured out at the base of the altar of burnt offerings; represented in Revelation 6:9 with the opening of the fifth seal.

Coals from the altar of burnt offerings would be carried into the tabernacle to be added to the altar of incense. Incense would be added to the fire. The shovel that carried in the hot coals would be thrown down to the ground outside of the tabernacle.

---

1 Edersheim, Alfred, *The Temple: Its Ministry and Services*, (MA: Hendrickson Publishers Inc., 2009)

During this transfer of coals, the slaughter of the lamb, and the casting down of the shovel there would be a break in the singing of the temple choir. A moment of silence would exist. During this silence seven priests would blow seven trumpets. (The number of trumpets in the tabernacle service could change. It would never be less than two or more than one hundred twenty. Seven is used here referencing completeness).

The tabernacle theme is the backbone of Revelation. The action surrounding the priest casting down the coals, integrates the sanctuary rituals with the visions or television news channels of Revelation. These events are simultaneous events, and not a single set of events that follow one after another.

The Seven Trumpets

The seven trumpets tell of the political changes to the world. The first four trumpets mark the decline of the Roman Empire. The last three trumpets, called woes, describe a new power that is thrust upon the earth. This new power is not strictly a political kingdom but it is also a combination of political powers and religious ideology. This power will fight against the Papal Roman power. This power is Islam. We saw these same events played out in Daniel chapter 11.

The First Trumpet

"The first angel sounded, and there followed hail and fire mingled with blood, and they were cast upon the earth: and the third part of trees was burnt up, and all green grass was burnt up" (Revelation 8:7 KJV).

Trumpet 1: Alaric the Visigoth
AD 395 – 410

The first trumpet marks the beginning decline of the Empire of Rome, particularly western Rome. The Visigoths (Goths) under Alaric invaded the empire slaughtering thousands, razing fields and destroying cities.

"**Hail**" This is a reference to the origin of the invaders—from above, the North.

"**Hail and fire**" Both hail and fire destroy mercilessly, as did the Visigoths.

"**Mingled with blood**" Blood was shed on purpose by Alaric, just because.

"**Third part**" The Roman Empire was divided into 3 parts by the sons of Constantine (AD337). Frequent remarks in Revelation of a "*third part*" is an allusion to a third part of the empire which was under scourge. Alaric invaded the territory once held by Constans (a son of Constantine), that of Italy and Illyricum.

The Second Trumpet

"And the second angel sounded, and as it were a great mountain burning with fire was cast into the sea: and the third part of the sea became blood; 9And the third part of the creatures which were in the sea, and had life, died; and the third part of the ships were destroyed" (Revelation 8:8,9 KJV).

Trumpet 2: Gaiseric the Vandal
AD428 – 468

AD439 The Vandals capture Carthage in a huge naval victory.

AD455 The Vandals invade Rome.

This second trumpet relates to the next invasion of Rome. Gaiseric (Genseric) resolved to create a naval power, and in doing so became sovereign of the Mediterranean sea.

"**Into the sea**" The conquests were mostly naval. From the port of Carthage, Gaiseric preyed on Roman commerce and waged war against the empire.

The Third Trumpet

"And the third angel sounded, and there fell a great star from heaven, burning as it were a lamp, and it fell upon the third part of the rivers, and upon the fountains of waters; 11And the name of the star is called Wormwood: and the third part of the waters became wormwood; and many men died of the waters, because they were made bitter" (Revelation 8:10,11 KJV).

Trumpet 3: Attila the Hun
AD445 – 453

"**There fell a great star**" Like a meteor that flashes briefly across the sky, Attila would enter the political scene quickly and disappear as fast.

"**It fell upon rivers and waters**" The principle operations of Attila were in the region of the Alps—the headwaters of the Roman Empire, where the rivers flowed into Italy.

"**Wormwood**" This means "bitter." The areas, which suffered under Attila, were indeed made bitter. It was the boast of Attila that the grass never grew on the spot, which his horse had trod. *The Scourge of God*, was a name he appropriated to himself.

The Fourth Trumpet

"And the fourth angel sounded, and the third part of the sun was smitten, and the third part of the moon, and the third part of the stars; so as the third part of them was darkened, and the day shone not for a third part of it, and the night likewise. ₁₃And I beheld, and heard an angel flying through the midst of heaven, saying with a loud voice, Woe, woe, woe, to the inhabiters of the earth by reason of the other voices of the trumpet of the three angels, which are yet to sound!" (Revelation 8:12,13 KJV).

Trumpet 4: Odoacer the Heruli
AD453 – 493

AD476 The end of the Western Roman Empire.

Romulus Augustulus—Emperor of Western Rome seeks to make allies with Odoacer to help fight off the Huns. After successful military campaigns Augustulus refuses to hand over land settlements for Odoacer and his army. Odoacer revolts in AD476 ending the reign of the Western Roman Empire. Odoacer becomes king of Italy. The Eastern Empire of Rome continues to thrive under the banner of the Byzantine Empire; its capital is located in Byzantium or Constantinople (Istanbul).

"**The third part of them was darkened**" Western Rome ceased to exist—it was darkened.

End of Time Prophecies

The Three Woes

Three trumpets remain to be sounded; three woes are to appear. These three woes were introduced in Daniel 11:29. There was a *"former"* and a *"latter"* set of events. These would be the first and the third woe. These woes centered on a period of conflict between the king of the North (the little horn), and the king of the South (Islam).

The Roman Empire is all but dissolved at this point in history. The woes will announce a new power (Islam) on the world scene, one that is carried over through the last trumpet.

The First Woe
The Fifth Trumpet

"And the fifth angel sounded, and I saw a star fall from heaven unto the earth: and to him was given the key of the bottomless pit. 2And he opened the bottomless pit; and there arose a smoke out of the pit, as the smoke of a great furnace; and the sun and the air were darkened by reason of the smoke of the pit. 3And there came out of the smoke locusts upon the earth: and unto them was given power, as the scorpions of the earth have power. 4And it was commanded them that they should not hurt the grass of the earth, neither any green thing, neither any tree; but only those men which have not the seal of God in their foreheads. 5And to them it was given that they should not kill them, but that they should be tormented five months: and their torment [was] as the torment of a scorpion, when he striketh a man. 6And in those days shall men seek death, and shall not find it; and shall desire to die, and death shall flee from them. 7And the shapes of the locusts [were] like unto horses prepared unto battle; and on their heads [were] as it were crowns like gold, and their faces [were] as the faces of men. 8And they had hair as the hair of women, and their teeth were as [the teeth] of lions. 9And they had breastplates, as it were breastplates of iron; and the sound of their wings [was] as the sound of chariots of many horses running to battle. 10And they had tails like unto scorpions, and there were stings in their tails: and their power [was] to hurt men five months. 11And they had a king over them, [which is] the angel of the bottomless pit, whose name in the Hebrew tongue [is] Abaddon, but in the Greek tongue hath [his] name Apollyon. 12One woe is past; [and,] behold, there come two woes more hereafter" (Revelation 9:1-12 KJV).

Woe 1: The Fall of Eastern Rome
AD610 – 1449

AD610 Islam is spread by Muhammad.

AD1449 The Byzantine Empire—Eastern Roman Empire, ends.

"**A star falls to the earth**" This meteor is widespread over the entire earth, unlike the specific star called wormwood of the third trumpet, which fell to a specific location. This reference can either be a reference to Islam, or a reference to Satan when he fell from heaven like a falling star.

"**Bottomless pit**" The Greek word used is *abyssos* which means "bottomless, or the place of the dead." This same word was used in the Septuagint to describe the condition of earth prior to Creation (Genesis 1:2). *Abyssos* is used to describe the state of the earth during the millennium, when Satan is bound to it for a thousand year period (Revelation 20:2,3). The word here is used to describe the "*king over them*" and is an appropriate symbol for the devil—the de facto king of everyone who does not submit to Jesus Christ as the King of their lives. Islam does not teach that Jesus Christ is God.

"**Smoke arose out of the pit**" This is a reference to Islam, which spread its anti-Christian beliefs throughout the entire world. Compared to the Bible, Islam is a false religion. Islam fills the earth with darkness and delusion—smoke.

Muhammad (b. AD570), the claimed founder of Islam, was born in the city of Mecca, to a family of the Quarish tribe— a tribe of traders. Orphaned early in life, he entered the service of a rich widow whom he later married, along with others. Around AD610, he believed he heard a voice from heaven, that of Gabriel, telling him that there was no God but Allah alone. This and other messages served as a basis for a new religion—Islam.

AD622 Muhammad and his followers are pushed out of Mecca and they move north to Yathrib—renaming it Medina, the city of the prophet. From this location, Muhammad led his followers on military raids of Quraish caravans to survive. In AD630 he reenters

Mecca in triumph, obtaining rule over the city. Islam begins to prosper. By AD 1071 the Seljuk Turks—an Islamic people, begin to invade the lands of the Byzantine Empire.

"Tormented five months" Five months in prophetic time is exactly 150 years. July 27, 1299 Osman I (Othman), an Islamic Turk, invades Nicomaedia, a major city of the Byzantine Empire. Exactly 150 years later to the day, on July 27, 1449 the successor to the Byzantine throne—Constantine XI Palaeologus, would not venture to ascend the throne without consent from the Turkish (Islamic) sultan. Power now rested with the Ottoman Turks.

July 27, 1449 marked the beginning of the second woe.

The Second Woe
The Sixth Trumpet

"And the sixth angel sounded, and I heard a voice from the four horns of the golden altar which is before God, 14Saying to the sixth angel which had the trumpet, Loose the four angels which are bound in the great river Euphrates. 15And the four angels were loosed, which were prepared for an hour, and a day, and a month, and a year, for to slay the third part of men. 16And the number of the army of the horsemen [were] two hundred thousand thousand: and I heard the number of them. 17And thus I saw the horses in the vision, and them that sat on them, having breastplates of fire, and of jacinth, and brimstone: and the heads of the horses [were] as the heads of lions; and out of their mouths issued fire and smoke and brimstone. 18By these three was the third part of men killed, by the fire, and by the smoke, and by the brimstone, which issued out of their mouths. 19For their power is in their mouth, and in their tails: for their tails [were] like unto serpents, and had heads, and with them they do hurt. 20And the rest of the men which were not killed by these plagues yet repented not of the works of their hands, that they should not worship devils, and idols of gold, and silver, and brass, and stone, and of wood: which neither can see, nor hear, nor walk: 21 Neither repented they of their murders, nor of their sorceries, nor of their fornication, nor of their thefts" (Revelation 9:13-21 KJV).

Woe 2: The Ottoman Empire
AD 1449 – 1840

"**Loose the four angels**" These are the four Principal Sultanas' (dynasties) of which the Ottoman Empire was composed; located in Aleppo, Baghdad, Damascus and Iconium.

"**Fire, smoke, and brimstone**" The Ottoman Turks used firearms, gunpowder and canons in their battles; unique to the world at this time.

AD 1453 Mahomet II laid siege to Constantinople. Using gunpowder and canons he overtook the city and completely ended the Byzantine rule—Eastern Roman Empire was done.

"**Prepared for 1 hour, 1 day, 1 month, 1 year**" This empire would reign for this exact amount of prophetic time: 391 years and 15 days. A year = 360, month= 30, day=1. A prophetic day = year; one hour = 15 days.

Josiah Litch, a minister during the 1800's, is first credited with seeing the connection between the "*five months*" in the first woe and the 391 years, 15 days of the second woe. Furthermore Josiah Litch made a prediction, based on the time-lines in Revelation 9, that the second woe would end on exactly August 11, 1840. Litch reasoned that since the Ottoman supremacy was done by a voluntary acknowledgment on the part of the Christian Emperor, that the end of the Ottoman supremacy would be in a similar fashion.

Josiah reasoned that the start of the "*five months*" from the first woe began on July 27, 1299 with the invasion of Nicomaedia by the Turk Osman I. Counting exactly 150 years brought the end of the first woe on July 27, 1449.

Events surrounding AD 1449 are recorded in history. Late in AD 1448, nearing the close of the 150 years, John Palaeologus, Emperor of Eastern Rome (Byzantine) died without leaving a son to follow him. His brother Constantine XI Palaeologus, the lawful successor, would not venture to ascend the throne without the consent of the Turkish sultan. Ambassadors were sent to receive permission. Early in 1449

Constantine was crowned. Eastern Rome's independence (Byzantine Empire) was in the hands of the Turks.

Prior to AD1840 the Ottoman Empire was at war with Egypt. In 1839, at the Battle of Nizip (June 24), the Turks were defeated by Ibrāhīm, A son, or adopted son, of Muhammad Alī— pasha of Egypt. The Turks had most of their fleet captured. Fearing the disintegration of the Ottoman Empire, the European powers negotiated the Treaty of London in July 1840. This Treaty was created with the assistance of England, Russia, Austria and Prussia. The Turks agree to allow these European powers to work out a settlement. This treaty was really an ultimatum. The Ottoman Empire would agree to give up Egypt and parts of Syria— for life; Mehemet Ali would evacuate the other parts of the Ottoman empire and would return the Ottoman fleet taken at the Battle of Nizip. If Mehemet Ali (Egypt) did not agree to these terms, then the combined European powers were allowed to take matters into their own hands using any means necessary.

This ultimatum was drafted on July 15, 1840 in London. It would take a few weeks for the treaty to reach the desk of Mehemet Ali in Alexandria, Egypt. It arrived by steamer ship on August 11, 1840, exactly 391 years and 15 days after the Ottoman Empire began to exercise its supremacy. On this date the Ottomans, by voluntary acknowledgment, agreed to let go of the supremacy it once felt.

The Second Woe is finished.

The Third Woe
The Seventh Trumpet

Before John is given the last woe, there are two visions of comfort and hope. These are discussed in the next two chapters.

"The second woe is past; [and,] behold, the third woe cometh quickly. 15And the seventh angel sounded; and there were great voices in heaven, saying, The kingdoms of this world are become [the kingdoms] of our Lord, and of his Christ; and he shall reign for ever and ever. 16And the

four and twenty elders, which sat before God on their seats, fell upon their faces, and worshipped God, 17Saying, We give thee thanks, O Lord God Almighty, which art, and wast, and art to come; because thou hast taken to thee thy great power, and hast reigned. 18And the nations were angry, and thy wrath is come, and the time of the dead, that they should be judged, and that thou shouldest give reward unto thy servants the prophets, and to the saints, and them that fear thy name, small and great; and shouldest destroy them which destroy the earth. 19And the temple of God was opened in heaven, and there was seen in his temple the ark of his testament: and there were lightnings, and voices, and thunderings, and an earthquake, and great hail" (Revelation 11:14-19 KJV).

Woe 3: The End of Time
AD1844 – The End of Time

The seventh trumpet is not a single event, but like the preceding trumpets, this one covers a span of time. This last trumpet introduces events in our future. We are interpreting events that have not yet occurred. We do not have a direct revelation from God, and therefore must wait on history to prove our interpretations. However, from our study and the growth in prophecy that God has given us, we can make an accurate interpretation of the remaining prophecies, at least outlining the general events left to occur. This woe is the final confrontation between Islam and the little horn; the kings of the South and North respectfully (Outlined in Daniel 11:40-45).

"**The Nations were angry**" This could be the anger felt by the powers under the influence of the papacy—the little horn, when Islam, the king of the South attacks the king of the North. This could also be the time when the nations are angry at the Son of God for His judgment and wrath that He has poured out upon the kingdoms of this earth.

"**Your wrath has come**" The wrath of God is poured out during the last plagues.

"**You should reward Your servants**" The Lord God Almighty rewards His servants, the saints, who have been waiting for the promise of salvation and eternal life.

"**The ark of His covenant was seen in His temple**" God's commandments, located within the ark of the Covenant, will be the judging factor. The nations, peoples and tongues of the earth will have to realize that God's word is truth.

"**And should destroy**" Here is God destroying the wicked that remain (Revelation 19:21). Here is the stone of Daniel 2 which removes the kingdoms of this earth. It is at this time that Jesus Christ comes in the clouds with His angels and collect His saints, both living and dead, to be resurrected and live with Him forever. This is the first resurrection.

The Rise of the Empires
A View of History

BC - Before Christ
King 1 Babylonians (Chaldeans)
(Revelation 17:10)

612BC Babylonians capture Nineveh.
580BC Nebuchadnezzar captures Jerusalem.

King 2 Medes and Persians
(Revelation 17:10)

539BC Cyrus captures Babylon.
509BC Rome exists as a republic, but is not yet a world power.
457BC Artaxerxes gives the command to restore and build Jerusalem (Daniel 9:25; Ezra 7.)
408BC Tabernacle rededicated (Nehemiah 13)

Kings 3,4,5 & 6 Grecians
(Revelation 17:10)

331BC Alexander the Great, *the notable horn*, defeats Persia, the taller horn.
June 13, 323BC Alexander the Great dies in the prime of his life.
  Four kings appear, each a general under Alexander who divides his kingdom four ways.
280BC Rome becomes leader of a loose confederation of Latin cities in central Italy.
264- 146BC Rome expands its empire.
49-44BC Julius Caesar is dictator of Rome.
27BC Gaius Octavius is the sole ruler of the Roman Empire, becoming its first emperor and calls himself Augustus (Daniel 11:20; Luke 2:1).
4BC Jesus Christ is Born (Luke 2).

AD - anno Domini

27 Jesus Christ begins His earthly ministry (Daniel 9:25; Luke 3).
31 Jesus Christ is crucified (Daniel 9:26,27; John 19).
31 **Ephesus Church Age & White Horse Seal** (Rev. 2:1-7; 6:1,2).
34 Stoning of Stephen at the hands of the Jews (Daniel 9:24; Acts 6, 7).
  This marks the end of the 70 week (490 year) prophecy of Daniel 9.
  This is the complete rejection by the Jews of the gospel of Jesus Christ.
67 Death of apostle Paul.
70 Rome destroys Jerusalem (Matthew 24:2; Daniel 11:28).
100 Death of John the Revelator.
100 **Smyrna Church Age & Red Horse Seal** (Revelation 2:8-11; 6:3,4).

End of Time Prophecies

284-313 Diocletian is Emperor of Rome (Revelation 2:10). He divides the empire into two provinces and appoints Maximian – a soldier, to be co-emperor who will rule the Western province. He persecutes the Christians. This may be the beginning of the division of the two legs as seen in the metal statue of Daniel 2.
303 Diocletian forbids Christian worship.
306 Constantine is named co-emperor of Western Rome.
313 **Pergamos Church Age & Black Horse Seal** (Revelation 2:12-17; 6:5,6).
313 Edict of Milan. Constantine with Licinius (who then ruled in Eastern Rome), jointly grant Christians freedom of worship.
324 Constantine defeats Licinius and rules the entire Empire.
330 Constantine moves the capital from Rome to Byzantium, renames it Constantinople—the Eastern Empire of Rome.
330-476 Western Rome exists until Odoacer overruns Rome.
337 Death of Constantine. His heirs fight for control of the Empire. His sons include: Constantine II, Constans, Constantius.
337-340 Constantine II rules Britain, Gaul, and Spain.
337-350 Constans rules Africa, Italy, Illyricum (Macedonia & Greece).
337-361 Constantius rules Eastern Rome.
379-395 Theodosius I rules Eastern Rome.
380 Theodosius I establishes Christianity as the official Roman religion.
388 Theodosius I rules Western and Eastern Empire after the death of Maximus.
395 Death of Theodosius I. The Roman Empire is formally split into two prefectures or divisions: East and West.
East: Illyricum (Macedonia, Greece), Syria, Judea, Egypt, Thrace.
West: Gaul, Spain, Britain, Franks, Italy, N. Africa.

Trumpet 1 Revelation 8:7
395-410 Alaric of the Goths or Visigoths invades Gaul (Western Rome).
410 Alaric sacks Rome.

Trumpet 2 Daniel 11:30; Revelation 8:8,9
428-468 Gaiseric (Genseric) of the vandals invades Africa (Western Rome). His conquests were mostly naval and he dominates the Mediterranean Sea.
439 Gaiseric captures Carthage.
455 Gaiseric invades Rome.

Trumpet 3 Revelation 8:10,11
445- 453 Attila the Hun devastates much of Rome's Eastern Empire.
451 Attila invades Gaul and loses.
452 Attila raids Northern Italy.

The Rise of the Empires

Trumpet 4 Revelation 8:12

453-493 Odoacer the Ostrogoth, a German chief, allies himself with Romulus Augustulus, who is Emperor of Western Rome.

476 Odoacer revolts against Augustulus when the latter refused to reward the German allies with lands for settlements. This ends the Western Roman Empire.

493 The Heruli are destroyed (Daniel 7:20). They are one of the three horns plucked up.

496 The pagan French king Clovis converts to Catholicism.

508 **Beginning of the 1335 and 1290 prophecies.**

508 Clovis consolidates his rule into a powerful Christian state rule. This marks the setting up of the *abomination of desolation*—the papal rule (Daniel 11:31, Daniel 12:11-13).

533 Emperor Justinian begins wars against the Vandals and the Goths. Wishing to obtain influence with the bishop in Rome and the Catholic supporters he issues a decree which constitutes the bishop of Rome as the pope, the head of all churches. This decree can't fully be implemented until all rival are removed.

534 The Vandals are destroyed. This is one of the three horns that are plucked up.

King 7 The papacy is in power and will remain in power until 1798.

Beginning of the 1260 year prophecy.

538 All rivals to Justinian's decree are crushed. The pope becomes the head of all churches orchestrated by the state (Daniel 7:24-26; 8:9-12).

Thyatira Church Age & Sickly Horse Seal (Revelation 2:18-29; 6:7,8).

Trumpet 5 - Woe 1 - Revelation 9:1-12

610-1449 The fall of Eastern Rome—the Byzantine Empire.

610 Muhammad begins to write the Koran.

622 Muhammad and his followers are pushed out of Mecca, they move to Yathrib, renaming it Medina.

630 Muhammad and his followers conquer Mecca. Islam as a religion begins to prosper.

July 27, 1299 – July 27, 1449 *"They should be tormented five months."* The Byzantine Empire is invaded and ultimately gives up control in 1449 (Revelation 9:5).

Trumpet 6 - Woe 2 - Revelation 9:13-21

1449 The Ottoman Empire is in power until August 11, 1840.

1453 Mahomet II sieges Constantinople using gunpowder and cannons representing fire and brimstone (Revelation 9:17).

October 31, 1517 Martin Luther nails 95 theses, critical of Catholic Church

End of Time Prophecies

practices, to the Wittenberg church door starting the Reformation.

1517 **Sardis Church Age & Seal Five** (Revelation 3:1-6; 6:9-11).

1789 George Washington becomes the first president of the United States.

November 1793 France, by legislation, declares there is no God and forbids the Bible to be read by its citizens (Revelation 11:7,8).

June 1797 France, again by legislation, allows freedom of all religions. This is exactly 3 ½ years after it abolished it (Revelation 11:9-11).

1798 General Berthier, with a French army, enters Rome, takes the pope captive and inflicts a "*deadly wound*" upon the papacy.

1798 **Philadelphia Church Age & Seal Six** (Revelation 3:7-13; 6:12-17; 17:11).

The 1290 and 1260 year time-lines end in 1798

August 11, 1840 The Ottoman Empire surrenders its power back into the hands of Christian powers. This is exactly 391 years and 15 days or prophetically 1 hour, 1 day, 1 month, 1 year (Revelation 9:15).

1844 Beginning of God's Judgment hour.

1844 **Laodicean Church Age & Seal Seven** (Daniel 12:13; Revelation 3:14-22).

The 2300 and 1335 day prophecies end in 1844

1800's The gospel is opened to the world through missionary work, publishing Bibles and revivals in many Christian denominations.

1860-1877 U.S. Civil War.

1900's U.S.A. emerges as a world economic power.

1914 – 1918 World War I

1922 The Ottoman Empire come to its end when it is replaced by the Turkish Republic and various successor states in southeastern Europe and the Middle East.

1922 Egypt became formally independent.

1929 Benito Mussolini gives the pope full authority over the nation of the Vatican City. The deadly wound is beginning to be healed.

1939 – 1945 World War II

July 16, 1945 The first atomic bomb is detonated in Alamogordo, New Mexico at 5:30a.m. This may be the fire from heaven (Revelation 13:13).

August 6, 1945 Hiroshima is attacked by an atomic bomb at the hands of the U.S.

August 9, 1945 Nagasaki is attacked by an atomic bomb at the hands of the U.S.

1989 The false prophet (U.S.A.) joins hands with the beast (papacy) to remove the power of Communism.

2014 The false prophet (U.S.A.) again joins hands with the beast (papacy) to reestablish trade and communication with Cuba.

Future - King 8

The papacy will return to former glory and power (Revelation 17:11-14).

Future **Woe 3 Trumpet 7 - Woe 2 - Revelation 1:14-19**

The Little Book And The Seven Thunders
Revelation 10

Chapter 10, along with chapter 11, is inserted within the vision of the Seven Trumpets. The purpose for this arrangement may be to give John a break, a breather so he would have time to restore his strength before God reveals more to him. Think about the information that John has been revealed, wars, rumors of wars, angels, trumpets, churches and so much more; this is heavy information. John is essentially told to sit down, put his head between his knees and relax. God's got this.

"I saw still another mighty angel coming down from heaven, clothed with a cloud. And a rainbow was on his head, his face was like the sun, and his feet like pillars of fire. 2He had a little book open in his hand. And he set his right foot on the sea and his left foot on the land, 3and cried with a loud voice, as when a lion roars. When he cried out, seven thunders uttered their voices" (Revelation 10:1-3).

"I saw" This is the language John uses to begin a new vision or some new section of prophecy. This helps us differentiate between this information and the seven trumpets, which have their conclusion in the last half of chapter 11.

What is the condition of the little book?

It is sitting opened in his hand.

Who is holding this book?

The one who cried with a loud voice, as when a lion roars.

Jesus Christ is the lion of the tribe of Judah (Revelation 5:5).

"The sea is His, for He made it; And His hands formed the dry land" (Psalm 95:5). Jesus, the Creator, made the sea and his hands formed the dry land. He is the one who stands on the sea and the earth.

"A little book open in his hand" This is the same book we read about in Revelation 5 that was sealed with seven seals. This sealed book was the book of Daniel that God "*Sealed up until the time of the end*" (Daniel 12:4). The prophecies of Daniel were revealed to John. History would help John understand some of the visions. Today we can use history to help us understand the rest of the sealed book and mysteries of Daniel.

Seven Thunders

"Now when the seven thunders uttered their voices, I was about to write; but I heard a voice from heaven saying to me, "Seal up the things which the seven thunders uttered, and do not write them." ₅The angel whom I saw standing on the sea and on the land raised up his hand to heaven ₆and swore by Him who lives forever and ever, who created heaven and the things that are in it, the earth and the things that are in it, and the sea and the things that are in it, that there should be delay no longer, ₇but in the days of the sounding of the seventh angel, when he is about to sound, the mystery of God would be finished, as He declared to His servants the prophets" (Revelation 10:4-7).

"There should be delay no longer" This is comfort to John. More than describing that the End of Time is near, God is declaring that there will be no more time-lines. John has just witnessed the sixth seal; this seal introduced the last events that occur just prior to the conclusion of Daniel's 2300 year prophecy (ending in AD1844). Daniel became faint and was sick for days when he was given information that extended beyond the 70 year time-line given by Jeremiah. God is here comforting John that there are no more time-lines.

Today, after AD1844, all set time-lines have concluded. However, there are events yet prophesied which must come to pass. This concept, of prophetic events occurring after a strict time-line was given, is seen in Daniel 9. After the 70 weeks (490 year), the time-line was fulfilled; but the prophecy warned of another event— the destruction of Jerusalem, that would occur after the 490 years concluded. These warnings are given to provide comfort to the wise saints who will hear, understand, and obey, just like the Christians who escaped the destruction of Jerusalem in AD70, when they heeded the warnings and signs given by Jesus to His disciples in Matthew 24.

The Little Book And The Seven Thunders

"The seven thunders" The seven thunders hint at something tumultuous or troublesome. Sometimes it is best not to know a head of time the exact details of the trials that we must face. There is strong evidence to support the idea that the seven thunders described the disappointment felt around the world by Christians of all denominations who believed that the second coming of Christ was the event foretold as *"the cleansing of the sanctuary"* in AD 1844. This great disappointment turned out to be a key event in unlocking the mysteries of Daniel's sealed book and Revelation.

A Bitter Book

"Then the voice which I heard from heaven spoke to me again and said, 'Go, take the little book which is open in the hand of the angel who stands on the sea and on the earth.' 9So I went to the angel and said to him, 'Give me the little book.' And he said to me, 'Take and eat it; and it will make your stomach bitter, but it will be as sweet as honey in your mouth.' 10Then I took the little book out of the angel's hand and ate it, and it was as sweet as honey in my mouth. But when I had eaten it, my stomach became bitter. 11And he said to me, 'You must prophesy again about many peoples, nations, tongues, and kings'" (Revelation 10:8-11).

What is John asked to do?

Take the book and eat it.

John does as he is instructed. He takes the book and eats it.

"Moreover He said to me, 'Son of man, eat what you find; eat this scroll, and go, speak to the house of Israel.' 2So I opened my mouth, and He caused me to eat that scroll. 3And He said to me, 'Son of man, feed your belly, and fill your stomach with this scroll that I give you.' So I ate, and it was in my mouth like honey in sweetness. 4Then He said to me: 'Son of man, go to the house of Israel and speak with My words to them'" (Ezekiel 3:1-4).

Why is this book sweet?

The Word of God gives hope. It is good news; it is sweet.

End of Time Prophecies

Why does it become bitter?

The news that John would receive showed of the trials, tribulations, and struggles that the church would have to endure before the End of Time.

The book is sweet because it is the Word of God. The message that is being revealed to John is proof that the End of Time is approaching, and that one day, soon, the children of God will be collected to join Jesus Christ in eternity. But the word becomes bitter in John's stomach. The message is difficult to digest. There are many events left to happen. There will be struggles, tortures and many other trials that the children of God must face.

John gains strength from this interlude. He re-accepts the mission given to him of sharing the revelation of Jesus Christ with the world. The message may be taxing, confusing and even stressful, and it might not all make sense to John but the message is important enough that Jesus Christ is asking him to share it.

The Two Witnesses
Revelation 11:1-13

Before the last woe is announced to John, he is given a brief peek at the end of the story. John is reminded that Christ's side wins and all who have suffered for the side of truth will soon have their reward and vindication.

"Then I was given a reed like a measuring rod. And the angel stood, saying, 'Rise and measure the temple of God, the altar, and those who worship there. 2But leave out the court which is outside the temple, and do not measure it, for it has been given to the Gentiles. And they will tread the holy city underfoot for forty-two months'" (Revelation 11:1,2).

John is told to measure the temple of God, but he never records these measurements. This is quite different from his records on the New Jerusalem (Revelation 21). There he records detailed measurements.

John measures *"the altar, and those who worship there"* (Verse 1). How do you measure a person? Is John to record the height and weight of each saint? The answer lies in the Greek word *metreo,* which is translated "measure or measuring." This word is used in 2 Corinthians 10:12: *"For we dare not class ourselves or compare ourselves with those who commend themselves. But they, measuring themselves by themselves, and comparing themselves among themselves, are not wise."* Paul is using the word *metreo* to measure people. This measure is figuratively speaking about character. It is not wise to compare ourselves to other sinners, because all of us have fallen short of the Glory of God (Romans 3:23). The only comparison that matters is Jesus Christ. Are we new creatures? Has all of our old passed away? Have we become new? (2 Corinthians 5:17).

The focus of John's measuring is *"the temple of God and the altar",* the courtyard is not to be measured. This is significant because Christ's work in the courtyard was completed at Calvary. The altar is not the altar of burnt offering; this sat in the courtyard and was not to be measured. This altar is the altar of incense— the altar that represents our prayers before the presence of God. This is the role

End of Time Prophecies

of Christ. Jesus is the person we will be measured against. This is sobering but comforting. We are sinners— we will never measure up to the standards of Christ, but He died for us. He is our sacrifice. By His acts, we can all be saved.

John's measuring is parallel to the courts being set in heaven (Daniel 7). Judging is required. Those who accept the grace of Jesus and apply it to their lives will develop characters that begin to emulate Christ. Those whose characters are "cowardly, unbelieving, abominable, murderers, sexually immoral, sorcerers, idolaters, and all liars shall have their part in the lake which burns with fire and brimstone, which is the second death" (Revelation 21:8).

The Two Witnesses

"And I will give power to my two witnesses, and they will prophesy one thousand two hundred and sixty days, clothed in sackcloth. ₄These are the two olive trees and the two lampstands standing before the God of the earth. ₅And if anyone wants to harm them, fire proceeds from their mouth and devours their enemies. And if anyone wants to harm them, he must be killed in this manner. ₆These have power to shut heaven, so that no rain falls in the days of their prophecy; and they have power over waters to turn them to blood, and to strike the earth with all plagues, as often as they desire" (Revelation 11:3-6).

How long will the two witnesses prophecy?

1260 prophetic days, or 1260 literal years.

How long are the gentiles to tread the holy city underfoot?

42 months is 3 ½ years which are 1260 days.

Here is the same time period as verse 2. This exact time period is found in Revelation 12:6, 14; 13:5; Daniel 7:25; 12:7. All of these texts are describing the exact same period of history, each reference adds a new dynamic or a new characteristic to the 1260 year time period. This helps us in our interpretation and understanding of this time period and the events connected with it.

The Two Witnesses

The 1260 years began in AD538 with the official setting up of the papacy, the little horn, the abomination of desolation, the antichrist, the sea beast.

The two witnesses operate during this time period. Note that it is 1260 years and not 3 ½ years as many false interpretations attempt to say.

The Olive Trees and Lampstands

"Then I answered and said to him, 'What are these two olive trees— at the right of the lampstand and at its left?' 12And I further answered and said to him, 'What are these two olive branches that drip into the receptacles of the two gold pipes from which the golden oil drains?' 13Then he answered me and said, 'Do you not know what these are?' And I said, 'No, my lord.' 14So he said, 'These are the two anointed ones, who stand beside the Lord of the whole earth'" (Zechariah 4:11-14).

"Olive trees" Olive trees produce oil. Oil is a symbol that represents God's Holy Spirit (Matthew 25). The lampstand uses the oil to shine its light. In the first chapter of Revelation we saw that each lamp represented the churches of God. God's people— the church, are filled with the Holy Spirit (oil) and are used to proclaim the Word of God to the world.

"The two anointed ones" This describes the system of light fueled by the oil of the Holy Spirit. While this could be understood to be two people, there is stronger evidence to deny this belief. If these represent humans, they would be as limited as Christ was when He was on the Earth. Christ (as a human) was only able to be at one place at a time. Zechariah and John declare that these two stand next to God of the whole earth.

"Your word is a lamp to my feet And a light to my path" (Psalm 119:105).

The two olive trees— the two lampstands— the two anointed ones— are the Word of God! God's Word is filled with the oil of the Holy Spirit, and it is through God's Word that we are able to preach, believe and have faith in Jesus as our Savior. The two lampstands represent both the Old and New Testaments of God's Word. Elijah used the Word of God to shut up the heavens from raining, and later produce the fire from heaven. Moses used the Word of God to turn water into blood and ushered in the other horrible plagues upon Egypt.

The two witnesses or two anointed ones were to prophecy for 1260 years— a feat that is impossible by sinful man who now lives less than 120 years.

The Witnesses are Killed

"When they finish their testimony, the beast that ascends out of the bottomless pit will make war against them, overcome them, and kill them. ₈And their dead bodies will lie in the street of the great city which spiritually is called Sodom and Egypt, where also our Lord was crucified. ₉Then those from the peoples, tribes, tongues, and nations will see their dead bodies three-and-a-half days, and not allow their dead bodies to be put into graves. ₁₀And those who dwell on the earth will rejoice over them, make merry, and send gifts to one another, because these two prophets tormented those who dwell on the earth. ₁₁Now after the three-and-a-half days the breath of life from God entered them, and they stood on their feet, and great fear fell on those who saw them. ₁₂And they heard a loud voice from heaven saying to them, "Come up here." And they ascended to heaven in a cloud, and their enemies saw them. ₁₃In the same hour there was a great earthquake, and a tenth of the city fell. In the earthquake seven thousand people were killed, and the rest were afraid and gave glory to the God of heaven" (Revelation 11:7-13).

How long were the two witnesses to be dead in the streets?

3 ½ days is prophetically 3 ½ years.

How can anyone kill the scriptures?

How would they be seen dead in the streets of Sodom and Egypt?

The key lies in verse 13 "*a tenth of the city fell.*" The Roman Empire would be divided into ten divisions. One tenth of the city would equate to one of the ten kingdoms. The Franks—or France, fulfills this reference. During the French Revolution of the late 1700's France discarded the Bible and formally denied the existence of

God; similar to the inhabitants of Sodom, the pharaoh of Egypt and those who crucified Jesus—all denied Jesus was the Son of God.

November 1793, by an act of the legislature, the people of France abolished the Bible. They uplifted a Goddess of Reason in place of the Word of God. Divorce was legalized, and the family structure was dissolved. Atheism ruled. The seven-day week, established at creation and celebrated by the worship of God on the seventh-day Sabbath, was changed to a ten day cycle. Bibles were burned and those holding on to its truths were tortured and martyred. It was during this time that the use of the guillotine was first put in use.

June 1797, exactly three years and six months after the Scriptures were abolished in legislation, new legislation was constructed which gave freedom of religion back to the people. The Spirit of God had returned to the Scriptures and they "*stood up*" and were revived.

Since this time, the two witnesses—the Old and New Testaments have ascended to heights not reached by any other book in the history of mankind. The Bible has more prints, more copies and more translations than any other book in the world.

The Dragon's War
Revelation 12, 13, 14:1-5

Chapter 12 is the History Channel of Revelation. The other news channels or lines of prophecy like the seven churches, seven seals, and the seven trumpets begin after Christ and extends to the End of Time. Revelation 12 begins prior to Christ's life on earth.

"Now a great sign appeared in heaven: a woman clothed with the sun, with the moon under her feet, and on her head a garland of twelve stars. 2Then being with child, she cried out in labor and in pain to give birth" (Revelation 12:1,2).

"Woman" This is a symbol that represents believers (both in God or in any false god) (Isaiah 54:5,6; 2 Corinthians 11:2; Ephesians 5:25). There are chaste— virgin women; these represent the believers of God— the true church (Revelation 14:3,4). There are adulterous— harlots, which represent the believers in something other than Jesus Christ and His truth (Revelation 17:5, 15). This concept should not be strange to us; we saw the seven churches represent God's believing people and the seven seals represent an apostate church that tries to look like God's believing people but in truth is full of deceptions and lies.

Sun, Moon and Stars. Here is a connection to the Creator. The twelve stars is a direct reference to Joseph's dream and the twelve tribes of Israel (Genesis 37:9; Genesis 42:32).

The woman mentioned in these texts represents the believer's in Christ— the Creator.

"And another sign appeared in heaven: behold, a great, fiery red dragon having seven heads and ten horns, and seven diadems on his heads. 4His tail drew a third of the stars of heaven and threw them to the earth. And the dragon stood before the woman who was ready to give birth, to devour her Child as soon as it was born" (Revelation 12:3,4).

Who is the Dragon?

No guessing is required, verse 9 reveals the answer:

End of Time Prophecies

"So the great dragon was cast out, that serpent of old, called the Devil and Satan, who deceives the whole world; he was cast to the earth, and his angels were cast out with him" (Revelation 12:9).

Who are the stars?

Angels or messengers (Revelation 1:20).

John is taken back in history to a time before there was sin. Sin developed within Lucifer (Ezekiel 28:15). Instead of repenting and turning away from his sin of pride, Lucifer deceived a third of the angels in heaven. There came a point in time in which Lucifer and his angels were "*cast to the earth*" (Revelation 12:9).

"She bore a male Child who was to rule all nations with a rod of iron. And her Child was caught up to God and His throne. 6Then the woman fled into the wilderness, where she has a place prepared by God, that they should feed her there one thousand two hundred and sixty days. 7And war broke out in heaven: Michael and his angels fought with the dragon; and the dragon and his angels fought, 8but they did not prevail, nor was a place found for them in heaven any longer. 9So the great dragon was cast out, that serpent of old, called the Devil and Satan, who deceives the whole world; he was cast to the earth, and his angels were cast out with him. 10Then I heard a loud voice saying in heaven, "Now salvation, and strength, and the kingdom of our God, and the power of His Christ have come, for the accuser of our brethren, who accused them before our God day and night, has been cast down. 11And they overcame him by the blood of the Lamb and by the word of their testimony, and they did not love their lives to the death. 12Therefore rejoice, O heavens, and you who dwell in them! Woe to the inhabitants of the earth and the sea! For the devil has come down to you, having great wrath, because he knows that he has a short time." 13Now when the dragon saw that he had been cast to the earth, he persecuted the woman who gave birth to the male Child. 14But the woman was given two wings of a great eagle, that she might fly into the wilderness to her place, where she is nourished for a time and times and half a time, from the presence of the serpent. 15So the serpent spewed water out of his mouth like a flood after the woman, that he might cause her to be carried away by the flood. 16But the earth helped the woman, and the earth opened its mouth and swallowed up the flood which the dragon had spewed out of his mouth. 17And the dragon was enraged with the woman, and he went to make war with the rest of her offspring, who keep the commandments of God and have the testimony of Jesus Christ" (Revelation 12:5-17).

The story line flip-flops between heaven and earth, past and present.

"She" This is the woman— the church of true believers. She bore Jesus Christ was born, died as our perfect sacrifice, rose again the third day, and then was *"caught up to God."*

The church of believers would flee into the wilderness because of tortures and persecutions at the hands of the apostate church (Roman Catholicism). This would last for 1260 days. This is the same number that we have encountered before. This was a period of years starting in AD538 and ending in AD1798.

The story then flips back to heaven, prior to the devil being cast to the earth. There John saw war in heaven. *"Michael [Jesus Christ] and His angels fought with the dragon."*

What living creature introduced the fourth seal?

A Flying eagle (Revelation 4:7).

The fourth seal began in AD538 at the beginning of the 1260 years that the little horn would rule. The apostate church was fully developed at this time. John witnesses God's church being helped by the living eagle creature— the Spirit of God.

"Time, times and half a time" This period of time is once again 42 months, 3 ½ years, or 1260 days. If you haven't made the connection yet, please start your study afresh. This time period is specific to the little horn. It is repeated in multiple ways so that no one can miss who is described. The little horn will be the beast that one day will have a mark associated with it (not a physical mark, but an action or belief). If you were the church in AD538, it would be important to know who the little horn was. If you are the church today, it will be important to know who the little horn is.

Satan, the great dragon, is enraged with God's church of believers. He is still making war with the church. This will continue until the End of Time, when sin is destroyed forever and the devil finds his end in the lake of fire.

End of Time Prophecies

The Sea Beast

"Then I stood on the sand of the sea. And I saw a beast rising up out of the sea, having seven heads and ten horns, and on his horns ten crowns, and on his heads a blasphemous name" (Revelation 13:1).

Where did this beast rise from?

The sea.

"Then he said to me, 'The waters which you saw, where the harlot sits, are peoples, multitudes, nations, and tongues'" (Revelation 17:15).

What does water represent?

Water represents peoples, nations, and multitudes.

The beast (*therion*) rises to power among civilizations and many people. Later in Revelation 13:11 there is another beast which rises from the earth, or a location that is not full of established people, civilizations and ruling kingdoms (at least not those mentioned expressly in the scriptures).

"Now the beast which I saw was like a leopard, his feet were like the feet of a bear, and his mouth like the mouth of a lion. The dragon gave him his power, his throne, and great authority. ₃And I saw one of his heads as if it had been mortally wounded, and his deadly wound was healed. And all the world marveled and followed the beast. ₄So they worshiped the dragon who gave authority to the beast; and they worshiped the beast, saying, "Who is like the beast? Who is able to make war with him?" ₅And he was given a mouth speaking great things and blasphemies, and he was given authority to continue for fortytwo months. ₆Then he opened his mouth in blasphemy against God, to blaspheme His name, His tabernacle, and those who dwell in heaven. ₇It was granted to him to make war with the saints and to overcome them. And authority was given him over every tribe, tongue, and nation" (Revelation 13:2-8).

"Forty two months" Here is the period of time that we have seen throughout Daniel and Revelation. It is associated with the little horn (Daniel 7:25), the persecution of the saints (Revelation 12:6, 14), and now the beast that rises from the sea. All are the same. The beast is the Roman Catholic Church! It can be no other entity on earth.

Notice what this sea beast is composed of: lion, bear and leopard parts. This is the fourth beast of Daniel 7.

"**One of his heads**" The dreadful and terrible fourth beast had ten horns; three were plucked up when another horn, a little horn appeared. This horn had eyes and a mouth like a man.

"**Mortally wounded**" The little horn, the one with the features of a head, would rule extensively for forty-two months, and then would receive a drastic wound. This occurred in AD 1798 when the French general Berthier disagreed with the pope, took him prisoner, and put a huge wound upon the influence and control that the Catholic Church once had over the nations of the earth.

"**Wound was healed**" Benito Mussolini, AD 1929, signed a document giving the pope full authority over Vatican City, an independent nation. Once again the pope was a civil ruler as well as a religious leader.

The traits of this sea beast match identically to the traits of the little horn described in Daniel 7 and 8.

Worship of the Beast

"All who dwell on the earth will worship him, whose names have not been written in the Book of Life of the Lamb slain from the foundation of the world. 9If anyone has an ear, let him hear. 10He who leads into captivity shall go into captivity; he who kills with the sword must be killed with the sword. Here is the patience and the faith of the saints" (Revelation 13:8-10).

These events have not yet occurred. The statement is plain "*All who dwell on the earth will worship him [the sea beast]*." There will only be two choices— obey God and suffer the persecution at the hands of the beast, or worship the beast and have your name blotted from the book of life.

The Beast from the Earth

"Then I saw another beast coming up out of the earth, and he had two horns like a lamb and spoke like a dragon. ₁₂And he exercises all the authority of the first beast in his presence, and causes the earth and those who dwell in it to worship the first beast, whose deadly wound was healed. ₁₃He performs great signs, so that he even makes fire come down from heaven on the earth in the sight of men" (Revelation 13:11-13).

Here is a new beast. This second beast is called the false prophet (Revelation 16:13, 14; 19:20) and will be easy to identify by four key descriptions.

"**Then I saw another beast**" This beast would come to power at the end of the 1260 year rule of the first beast. It would be coming to power around AD1798 and would remain in power until Jesus' second coming (Revelation 19:20).

"**Coming up out of the earth**" This best would arise from the earth, instead of the sea. If water as a prophetic symbol represents people, dry land—the earth, must represent an area lacking a large number of people.

"**Makes fire come down from heaven**" This has two possible interpretations in prophecy; both may apply. The first possible interpretation is that this is a firsthand description of the power involved in an atomic bomb. "The lightning effects beggared descriptions" wrote General Thomas Farrell of the explosion created from an atomic bomb. "The whole country was lighted by a searchlight with the intensity many times that of the midday sun. It was golden, purple, violet, gray and blue. It lighted every peak, crevasse and ridge of the nearby mountain range with a clarity and beauty that cannot be described but must be seen to be imagined."[1] The only nation who has ever made fire from heaven come down in the sight of men is the United States of America when it dropped two bombs on

---

1   Guillen, Ph.D., Miachael, *Five Equations that Changed the World,* (NY: Hyperion, 1995), 263.

Japan. The second possible interpretation is that this is a future reference to Armageddon and a repeat of the Mt. Carmel experience.

"**Two horns like a lamb**" This indicates youth, innocence and gentleness. The two horns or forms of power could easily be compared to the Declaration of Independence that declares all men equal; and the Constitution that guarantees the people the right to self-government and freedom of religion. The two horns represent two sovereignties ruling together. Here is a description of the State and federal sovereignties that make up the United States of America."

Regardless of the views shared these descriptions fit only one nation: The United States of America. It is prophesied that America will change from its lamb-like beginnings to a power that "*speaks as a dragon*."

The Image to the Sea Beast

"And he deceives those who dwell on the earth by those signs which he was granted to do in the sight of the beast, telling those who dwell on the earth to make an image to the beast who was wounded by the sword and lived. 15He was granted power to give breath to the image of the beast, that the image of the beast should both speak and cause as many as would not worship the image of the beast to be killed" (Revelation 13:14, 15).

What does the lamb-like beast ask of the earth?

"To make an image to the beast who was wounded by the sword and lived" (Verse 14).

An image is a likeness or representation of the real thing. This image will be some act, object, devotion, process, or facsimile that represents the first beast. The first beast was a persecuting union of church and state, a religious system that was allied with governments in order to enforce *orthodoxy* and combat those it considered heretics.

The papacy is the first beast, the beast of the sea. When it was in power for 1260 years it tortured, killed and murdered thousands upon thousands of Christians who would not bow down to its image, its power and its authority. Tyndale, Zwingli, the Waldenses, Jerome, John Huss, Luther and others are part of an endless list of men who were murdered for their trust in the Word of God over that of men and their traditions.

"**The image of the beast should speak**" A country "*speaks*" or expresses itself through its legislative processes and the treaties it makes. This prophecy predicts that the land beast—America, will enact some law which will enforce a spirit of intolerance and persecution. The enforcement of this act will be an act of homage to the papacy.

The Mark of the Beast

*"He causes all, both small and great, rich and poor, free and slave, to receive a mark on their right hand or on their foreheads, 17and that no one may buy or sell except one who has the mark or the name of the beast, or the number of his name. 18Here is wisdom. Let him who has understanding calculate the number of the beast, for it is the number of a man: His number is **666**" (Revelation 13:16-18).*

"**A mark**" Here is referenced the mark of the beast.

"Then a third angel followed them, saying with a loud voice, 'If anyone worships the beast and his image, and receives his mark on his forehead or on his hand, 10he himself shall also drink of the wine of the wrath of God, which is poured out full strength into the cup of His indignation. He shall be tormented with fire and brimstone in the presence of the holy angels and in the presence of the Lamb. 11And the smoke of their torment ascends forever and ever; and they have no rest day or night, who worship the beast and his image, and whoever receives the mark of his name.' 12Here is the patience of the saints; here are those who keep the commandments of God and the faith of Jesus" (Revelation 14:9-12).

"And I saw thrones, and they sat on them, and judgment was committed to them. Then I saw the souls of those who had been beheaded for their witness to Jesus and for the Word of God, who had not worshiped the beast or his image, and had not received his mark on their foreheads or on their hands. And they lived and reigned with Christ for a thousand years" (Revelation 20:4).

How does one receive the mark of the beast?

Those who worship the image of the beast.

What happens to those who do not worship the beast?

They will live and reign with Christ.

Nebuchadnezzar created an image of gold that represented his power and sovereignty. He forced the nations to bow down to his image. The image that will be set up is something that will point to the sea beast, it will point to the little horn, it will be something that clearly represents the papal system. This image will center on worship, for it will be worshiped.

The mark of the beast is received when one worships the image of the beast. Those who worship this image will receive the mark of the beast. This mark is not a physical mark.

Where is the mark received on the person?

In their right hand or in their forehead.

"Therefore you shall lay up these words of mine in your heart and in your soul, and bind them as a sign on your hand, and they shall be as frontlets between your eyes" (Deuteronomy 11:18).

The right hand is a reference to actions. Your brain— *"frontlets between your eyes"*, symbolizes knowledge or mentally assenting to accept the mark. Receiving the mark of the beast will be the result of a choice you will make. Eve's simple choice came down to appetite and desire. To eat or not to eat. The simple choice that will define the mark of the beast at the End of Time will be worship. Will you worship God as He desires? Or will you worship Him how you desire, believe or are told to do?

The mark of the beast will be Sunday worship. The Roman Catholic Church takes ownership of changing the day of worship from the seventh-day Sabbath to the first day Sunday. They are proud to acknowledge that the change in worship was their doing. They claim that God gave them power to change His times and laws (Daniel 7:25).

End of Time Prophecies

Anyone who worships on this day— contrary to the Bible, is paying homage to the image of the Catholic Church (little horn).

God does not change. Christ declared that not *"one jot or one tittle will by no means pass from the law till all is fulfilled"* (Matthew 5:18). (Jots and tittles are little accent marks used when writing Hebrew. They are the smallest marks that can be made when writing in Hebrew).

Revelation 11 shows John measuring the temple. The dimensions being measured were not the length and width, but the character of those who were worthy to enter into the temple and be called saints of God. Character is measured against the Scriptures and not what man sets up or changes. God's Word does not change. His word has not changed. All of the Ten Commandments apply today just as they did when they were first given to Adam, Eve, Cain, Able, Abraham and written in stone when given to Moses.

Society has moved away from the truths found in God's word. Abortion—the murder of children, is legal today. Lying, stealing, and coveting are commonplace in the world today and propagated through media, advertising and more.

The mark of the beast specifically involves worship. Many Christians have trampled upon the Sabbath, the fourth commandment (Exodus 20:8-11). They believe that this commandment was changed from the seventh-day to the first day. Yet there is not one single Bible text, which clearly says the Sabbath was changed from Saturday to Sunday. Man changed it. The papacy changed it. God did not change it—He is perfect. God's commandments are needed today to be a mirror for us showing how in need we are of God's grace, and His free gift of salvation.

If the U.S. is truly the false prophet, then it will ask the world to honor Sunday as the day of worship effectively making the image to the beast.

Those who trample on God's laws will receive the mark of the beast. They will be counted as goats and not as sheep (Matthew 25:31-46).

The Dragon's War

"Then I looked, and behold, a Lamb standing on Mount Zion, and with Him one hundred and forty-four thousand, having His Father's name written on their foreheads. ₂And I heard a voice from heaven, like the voice of many waters, and like the voice of loud thunder. And I heard the sound of harpists playing their harps. ₃They sang as it were a new song before the throne, before the four living creatures, and the elders; and no one could learn that song except the hundred and forty-four thousand who were redeemed from the earth. ₄These are the ones who were not defiled with women, for they are virgins. These are the ones who follow the Lamb wherever He goes. These were redeemed from among men, being firstfruits to God and to the Lamb. ₅And in their mouth was found no deceit, for they are without fault before the throne of God" (Revelation 14:1-5).

Here is the end of the dragon's war. The redeemed, including the 144,000 are in heaven.

"The Father's name written on their foreheads" This is the seal of God from Revelation 7. The fourth commandment is the only one that contains a descriptive title, which distinguishes the true God from all false gods. The true God is the Creator, the same who created the seventh-day Sabbath. He could have left creation at day 6, but He created the seventh-day, to be a holy day. In fact this is the only day that He added a blessing to it.

"Thus the heavens and the earth, and all the host of them, were finished. ₂And on the seventh day God ended His work which He had done, and He rested on the seventh day from all His work which He had done. ₃Then God blessed the seventh day and sanctified it, because in it He rested from all His work which God had created and made" (Genesis 2:1-3).

"Virgins" Once again we see a reference to a virtuous woman. This is a symbol for the redeemed, for believers who *"keep the commandments of God and the faith of Jesus"* (Revelation 14:12).

The dragon's war is complete. God's side wins. The war began in heaven when the devil allowed pride to overtake him. The devil was cast out. The war is to be completed in the near future when Jesus Christ returns in the clouds to redeem His saints, and then, after the millennium, He will finish the war once and forever.

The Seal of God
The Sabbath

What role, if any, does the worship of the seventh-day Sabbath have on our salvation and the End of Time events?

The seventh-day Sabbath is the fourth commandment, therefore we can ask, "What role, if any, does the keeping of God's Ten Commandments have on our salvation and the End of Time events?" The short answer is both nothing, and everything.

Nothing, in the sense that sinful man, alone, is unable to keep the commandments of God. For we are *"Carnal, sold under sin. 15For what I am doing, I do not understand. For what I will to do, that I do not practice; but what I hate, that I do"* (Romans 7:14, 15). *"For all have sinned and fall short of the glory of God,"* (Romans 3:23).

As sinners, the law cannot save us. The Jewish nation fell into this trap, believing that they could earn salvation through works, and keeping the law.

However, keeping the commandments of God means everything too. Revelation 14:12 defines the saints as those who keep the commandments of God and have the faith of Jesus Christ. Christ said, *"If you love Me, keep My commandments"* (John 14:15).

A loving relationship is what God desires to develop with us. Sin broke our original relationship with Him, putting enmity into our hearts against God. When Jesus Christ died and rose again, a way was eternally made whereby a permanent relationship with God could be reestablished. Our very existence depends upon the love and grace of our Creator. Developing a relationship with God requires that we humbly realize this position. Here is the freedom of choice: we can choose to deny ourselves and follow Jesus Christ fully, or we can deny Christ and follow our plans for life. One leads to eternal life, the other will have an end.

Faith restores a relationship with God. Faith is our belief and trust in God's plan of redemption. As our relationship with God matures we discover that everything He does centers on loving and caring for us. This included His Ten Commandments.

The law of God is a revelation of His will, a transcript of His character. God is love. His law is love. *"Love is the fulfillment of the law"* (Romans 13:10). A character formed by obedience to the law will be holy.

God's law— the Ten Commandments, are meant for our enjoyment and delight. God knows that these laws will only improve the quality of life and our relationship with Him.

Keeping the Ten Commandments as a means to obtain salvation is impossible, but desiring to keep all of the Ten Commandments, for the purpose of growing in Christ, is our delight. If we discover some item in our lives that is contrary to His plan for us or is in opposition to one of His commandments, it is our desire to have this changed. We trust that anything God asks is for our good.

God Never Changes

God's commandments have never been changed, altered, or removed. If any one of them has been changed then God is not a perfect God. God's ten moral laws were given to humankind to show us how sinful we really are. *"I would not have known sin except through the law"* (Romans 7:7).

Jesus Christ is the only remedy for sin. *"For the wages of sin is death, but the gift of God is eternal life in Christ Jesus our Lord"* (Romans 6:23). There is no other solution to sin.

God, being a perfect God, cannot randomly forgive one who trespasses His law. If He could, then He would be a liar for declaring that death was the penalty for sin. But through Jesus Christ, God is not a liar; death was paid, and now through His atoning sacrifice, Jesus Christ is able to impute His forgiveness to all who trust, believe, and have faith in Him and His act on the cross.

The Seal of God

If one of His commandments could have been altered then Jesus Christ would not have had to die on the cross.

God's law is perfect, just, and immutable; it is unchangeable.

The Fourth Commandment

God's commandments will play a crucial role during the End of Time. Worship will become a deciding factor for determining who receives the Seal of God or the mark of the beast.

They *worshiped* the dragon (Revelation 13:4).
They *worshiped* the beast (Revelation 13:4).
Those *worship* the first beast (Revelation 13:12).
Worship the image of the beast (Revelation 13:15).
If anyone *worships* the beast (Revelation 14:9).

Clearly, there is some form of worship that is contrary to God's worship because He warns us not to *worship* the sea beast and the image that represents this beast. God's perfect law has only one commandment that speaks of worship, the fourth commandment: *"Remember the Sabbath day, to keep it holy. 9Six days you shall labor and do all your work, 10but the seventh-day is the Sabbath of the LORD your God" (Exodus 20:8-10).*

Some will try to argue that one in seven days is all that is required by this commandment, but this would be a lie and would deny God's own words.

"Thus the heavens and the earth, and all the host of them, were finished. 2And on the seventh day God ended His work which He had done, and He rested on the seventh day from all His work which He had done. 3Then God blessed the seventh day and sanctified it, because in it He rested from all His work which God had created and made" (Genesis 2:1-3).

God created the seventh-day, Saturday, to be His day of worship, His Sabbath day of rest. Any other day set aside for worship is blasphemy against God and His commandments.

Others try to argue that the Sabbath day of worship was moved to Sunday in celebration of Christ's resurrection. This is a fable of man; a tradition orchestrated by the Catholic Church. The disciples of Christ continued to worship on the seventh-day Sabbath. They never taught converts that Sunday was the new day of worship (Acts 13:14; 18:4; 17:2; 19:8).

Judgment

Judgment is not a one-part process. There is a trial or a determination that a person is either innocent or guilty. After the trial there is the sentencing: freedom if acquitted, punishment if found guilty. Other parts of judgment include an appeal process and the execution of the sentence or the carrying out of the judgment determined. We are now living during the trial phase of God's judgment. The courts are seated and every name is being judged as guilty or innocent (Daniel 7:10). The only way to be counted innocent is to be covered in Christ's righteousness and perfection.

The purpose of judgment is not to teach God anything that He doesn't already know. God knows who is just and who is unjust. He knows who believes, trusts, and through faith, accepts the merits of Jesus' gift of salvation—He is God and knows all. The courts are seated so that the mind of God can be shown to be just. Satan, once the covering Cherub (Ezekiel 28:16; Isaiah 14:12), accuses God of being unfair, unjust and unloving. Satan claims that God's character is not love. Satan claims that God's universe is one of restrictions and not freedoms. Satan claims that God's character is not love, but is judgmental and dictatorial in nature. God is opening His motives, and actions for the whole universe to see.

The court has been set. Before the entire universe, beginning with Abel (the first death), God is reviewing each life. It will be shown whether or not they are believers in Jesus Christ and His atoning blood. This process is easy for those who have died, their life is complete and their choices are made sure. However, what about those who are now living? How can the universe, of created beings, see the future? Only God knows the future. There must come a period when probation closes. There must be some test of loyalty given to those alive that would clearly define whether that person is a follower of Christ or not.

The Final Test

The final test given to the world will be one of worship. It will come down to a choice between worshiping the God of creation and heaven, or worshiping the beast, the dragon, and the image set up. This test of worship will not be lightly given. It will become evident that to worship the beast is in contrast to God. None will err in choosing sides.

God declared that the seventh-day, Saturday, is His Sabbath day—His day of worship. He has not changed.

The sea beast, also called the little horn, is the papal church and this church has declared that its day of worship is on Sunday, the first day of the week.

Soon the world will have to decide whom they will worship.

"Choose for yourselves this day whom you will serve" (Joshua 24:15).

Will you choose to worship God, on the seventh-day that He created, or will you choose to worship on the false day, Sunday, and follow along with the beast and the dragon?

The Last Angel Messengers
Revelation 14, 18

My daughter read the story of Achan, an Israelite who was stoned to death because he disobeyed God. She asked me "Isn't this murder?" adding, "I thought God said 'Thou shalt not murder'" (Joshua 7).

How can God condone the stoning of Achan and yet command against the act of murder? It would appear that a contradiction exists in the Bible. It does not! The answer lies within the story of Achan and the simple fact that *"the wages of [all] sin is death"* (Romans 6:23).

God Desires Repentance

Prior to their conquest of Jericho, God warned the Israelite camp: *"By all means abstain from the accursed things [treasures], lest you become accursed when you take of the accursed things, and make the camp of Israel a curse, and trouble it"* (Joshua 6:18). God would send at least six more warning to the Israelites and Achan, warning them about choosing sin over the Word of God.

Achan sinned. He stole precious treasures from the city of Jericho and disobeyed God's commandment. Israel would suffer defeat in their next battle, against the tiny city of Ai. Here was the next message of warning from God. The camp of Israel had been cursed. Achan needed to repent. He did not.

Joshua confronts God and is told, *"Israel has sinned."*

"Get up, sanctify the people, and say, 'Sanctify yourselves for tomorrow, because thus says the LORD God of Israel: "There is an accursed thing in your midst, O Israel; you cannot stand before your enemies until you take away the accursed thing from among you." 14*In the morning therefore you shall be brought according to your tribes. And it shall be that the tribe which the LORD takes shall come according to families; and the family which the LORD takes shall come by households; and the household which the LORD takes shall come man by man"* (Joshua 7:13,14).

The multi-step process of determining who sinned gave Achan, and his family, multiple opportunities to step forward, confess, repent, and seek for forgiveness. God did not immediately seek to punish or kill Achan. God must erase sin, but He *"is long-suffering toward us [and Achan], not willing that any should perish but that all should come to repentance"* (2 Peter 3:9). This text does not state that God will excuse any sin, but it is a text of grace revealing that God wishes everyone would repent and accept His free gift of salvation. Some will accept it; many will not.

Achan ignored the warning signs. His tribe was chosen. He did not confess. His family was chosen, then his household, and at last he was chosen. Only when he was confronted with facing the consequences of his sin did he finally confess. By this step, it was too late.

God was a merciful God to Achan, but God hates sin. Sin cannot exist in His universe. The only reason He has allowed it to exist for this long is to show the earth and the inhabitants of His universe how terrible sin really is (Job 2:1).

Achan was destroyed because he continued to disobey God despite the clear warnings given. God did not murder as much as He eradicated sin.

God has promised two things to the inhabitants of this sinful world:

1) He will destroy sin and everything attached to it (1 Peter 4:17,18; Revelation 21:6-8).
2) He will save everyone who believes, trusts and follows Jesus Christ—no matter their past (John 3:15-18).

Before God destroys the earth and those living in sin He will send messages—like those sent to Achan, to warn the world of His coming wrath and eradication of sin. During these last messages, there is opportunity for confession and repentance. When the last message is finished—probation will close and all will have sealed their fate.

"He who is unjust, let him be unjust still; he who is filthy, let him be filthy still; he who is righteous, let him be righteous still; he who is holy, let him be holy still" (Revelation 22:11).

The Last Angel Messengers

The last messages given to the earth are commonly called the three angel's messages. These three angel messengers are found within a group of seven angels all performing the last items required at the End of Time.

1ˢᵗ Angel's Message

"Then I saw another angel flying in the midst of heaven, having the everlasting gospel to preach to those who dwell on the earth—to every nation, tribe, tongue, and people— ₇saying with a loud voice, 'Fear God and give glory to Him, for the hour of His judgment has come; and worship Him who made heaven and earth, the sea and springs of water'" (Revelation 14:6,7).

The hour of God's judgment began in AD1844. This was the conclusion of the 2300 day prophecy in Daniel 8 that promised the atonement process would begin in the heavenly sanctuary. This process is the trial phase of God's judgment on sin. The courtroom seats are set up (Daniel 7) and the judges—Jesus Christ and God, visit every case—every life that ever lived beginning with Abel (the first to die). Each case is decided for life or death. Those who held on to Jesus Christ by faith will be saved (Hebrews 11). Those who ignored God's free gift will be set aside for eternal destruction.

This phase of the judgment must take place before Christ returns in the clouds. His kingdom must be determined before His arrival. How else would He know who was a sheep—His, and who was a goat? Even if you don't believe in an actual court room scene (despite its clear description in Daniel and references in Revelation), the kingdom of God must be decided before the second coming of Christ.

His judgment process—visible to the inhabitants of heaven, the twenty-four elders and the other worlds, began in AD1844. The first warning has been given to the earth.

2nd Angel's Message

"And another angel followed, saying, 'Babylon is fallen, is fallen, that great city, because she has made all nations drink of the wine of the wrath of her fornication'" (Revelation 14:8).

"Babylon" This symbol, in its broadest sense, represents Christian churches that have compromised truths for worldly gain, popularity or conformity. There is an ecclesiastical power, which has been labeled as the little horn, the antichrist, the beast— this is Mother Babylon. Further understanding of this symbol Babylon is in the chapter: "Who is Babylon the Great?"

"Fallen" The context of this word carries the meaning of "to light upon" as a pigeon does when it lands on a park bench. Babylon is not destroyed or fallen down, but it is upon us.

This second warning declares that there are Christian Churches who have settled for compromise, allowing error and tradition to supersede the Word of God. Babylon is a symbol for a concept, a false system of religion. Look around at the mainstream Christian churches of today, do they adhere to the plain words of Scripture or do they compromise truth to follow some fable, tradition, or idea of man?

History clearly points out that the Roman Catholic Church changed the day of worship from Saturday to Sunday. It is no secret; and yet thousands of protestant churches— churches who claim to be protesting the changes created by the Catholic Church, are openly deciding to compromise. Any church who holds on to these compromises are part of Babylon and they will partake of God's final wrath if they do not change.

3rd Angel's Message

"Then a third angel followed them, saying with a loud voice, 'If anyone worships the beast and his image, and receives his mark on his forehead or on his hand, 10he himself shall also drink of the wine of the wrath of God, which is poured out full strength into the cup of His indignation. He shall be tormented with fire and brimstone in the presence of the holy angels and in the presence of the Lamb. 11And the smoke of their torment ascends forever

and ever; and they have no rest day or night, who worship the beast and his image, and whoever receives the mark of his name'" (Revelation 14:9-11).

This angel is called the third angel. This gives us the exact number of the previous two messengers. Come out of Babylon. Do not participate with her lies anymore.

If you find yourself worshiping in a Christian church that has a doctrine of belief that contradicts the simple Word of God, come out of her. Separate yourself, or you will find yourself drinking *"the wine of the wrath of God"* for ignoring His commandments.

These three messages were heard beginning in the 1840's. People were stirred to make a decision. They could trust in man and tradition or follow God and His Word. Many chose God's word. Many were then excommunicated from their churches because they were following God's word and not the doctrines of the church. Many of these outcasts began to discover each other. Today there is a community of believers who do not hold to human tradition, but hold on to the pure Word of God. The Seventh-day Adventist Church is a church that has changed over the past hundred years or so because their foundation is based upon their understanding of God's Word and His Word alone. As truths were revealed to the followers, they changed to serve God's Word.

If you are seeking for a community of believers who have a foundation in God's Word over the traditions of men, seek out a Seventh-day Adventist congregation. There are sinners in this church, there are tares that have been sown by the devil, but the doctrines, beliefs, and foundations are grounded in the Word of God and only the Word of God.

The image to the beast is not yet set up. This last message is a warning that soon the earth will be called to make a life altering choice.

End of Time Prophecies

Seven Angels

Reading Revelation 14, three angels have sounded. Four more angels will be discussed, each with a specific task to perform or announce at the End of Time.

Three More Angels

"Then I looked, and behold, a white cloud, and on the cloud sat One like the Son of Man, having on His head a golden crown, and in His hand a sharp sickle. 15And another angel came out of the temple, crying with a loud voice to Him who sat on the cloud, 'Thrust in Your sickle and reap, for the time has come for You to reap, for the harvest of the earth is ripe.' 16So He who sat on the cloud thrust in His sickle on the earth, and the earth was reaped" (Revelation 14:14-16).

This angel signals for Jesus Christ— the Son of Man, to harvest His saints.

"Then another angel came out of the temple which is in heaven, he also having a sharp sickle" (Revelation 14:17).

This angel, different from the last one, is prepared with a sickle to gather together what is left behind after Christ reaps His saints.

"And another angel came out from the altar, who had power over fire, and he cried with a loud cry to him who had the sharp sickle, saying, 'Thrust in your sharp sickle and gather the clusters of the vine of the earth, for her grapes are fully ripe.' 19So the angel thrust his sickle into the earth and gathered the vine of the earth, and threw it into the great winepress of the wrath of God" (Revelation 14:18,19).

This angel, unique from the previous two, has power over fire, signals for the gathering of the vine of the earth. Those gathered at this time will suffer the wrath of God— the fires of hell.

There are two vines. Jesus Christ is the true vine. His precious fruit is harvested with care. The other vine is of this world. *"The field is the world, the good seeds are the sons of the kingdom, but the tares are the sons of the wicked one. 39The enemy who sowed them is the devil, the harvest is the end of the age, and the reapers are the angels. 40Therefore as the tares are gathered and burned in the fire, so it will be at the end of this age"* (Matthew 13:38-40).

We have encountered six unique angels within Revelation 14. There were seven churches, seven seals, and seven trumpets. Seven has been used as a number of completeness. Six is an odd number for Revelation; perhaps there is an angel we missed. Revelation chapter 18 provides the missing angel.

Unified Time-lines

Second Angel's Message

"After these things I saw another angel coming down from heaven, having great authority, and the earth was illuminated with his glory. ₂And he cried mightily with a loud voice, saying, 'Babylon the great is fallen, is fallen, and has become a dwelling place of demons, a prison for every foul spirit, and a cage for every unclean and hated bird!'" (Revelation 18:1,2).

This angel is identical to the second angel of Revelation 14. Both are proclaiming that *"Babylon is fallen."* This redundancy was witnessed in the writings of Daniel. Each vision added more information and detail to the visions before it. Revelation 18 functions just like Daniel did, adding information to Revelation 14.

Third Angel's Message

"And I heard another voice from heaven saying, 'Come out of her, my people, lest you share in her sins, and lest you receive of her plagues'" (Revelation 18:4).

This angel is identical to the third angel of Revelation 14. Both are warning the earth that Babylon is about to be punished— come out from her.

The Great Disappointment

The importance of the first three angels and their messages cannot be ignored. The first message— that God's judgment is upon us, sounded in the early 1840's. The world saw that a great cleansing of the sanctuary was about to occur. Most thought this would be the End of Time and the coming of Christ. Many laid aside their sectarian views and united in proclaiming the coming of Jesus. AD1844 came and went. All felt a great disappointment.

The faithful disappointed ones were not left in darkness. They were led to the Bible to search prophecy. The hand of the Lord opened the door to understanding, and the mistake was explained. The courtroom books described by Daniel were unlocked (Daniel 7:10). The cleansing of the sanctuary was the heavenly Day of Atonement—judgment, not of the cleansing of the earth and Christ's return.

Those who, by faith, accepted the first angel's message also accepted the second angel's message, realizing that Babylon was all around them. Studying the Scriptures, they discovered errors in practice and tradition that contradicted God's Word.

The third angel's message is rooted in worship. With it comes a call to separate yourself from the worship and traditions of Babylon and its daughter churches. The faithful disappointed ones tried to share the truths of Scripture and prophecy with members of their own denominations and churches, but were often met with censor and threats. Many were excommunicated from their congregations for holding on to the light of the three angel's messages.

Revelation 14 spotlights this period of earth's history surrounding AD1844. Revelation 18 reveals that the last two messages will be prominently presented to the world just before the close of probation and the Second Advent of Christ. Babylon is fallen— it is upon us. "*Come out of her my people.*"

The Destruction of Babylon

Chapter 18 of Revelation adds more detail to the third angel's message. Babylon is about to be punished. Her sins have reached to heaven and God's mercy is full. John is given a preview of her destruction.

John uses the Hebrew poetic form of a *chiasm* to present the fall of Babylon.

The *Chiasm* of Revelation 18

(verse 3)	All the nations were deceived.	(verse 23)
(verse 8)	Babylon shall be thrown down.	(verse 21)
(verse 10)	In one hour— judgment.	(verse 19)
(verse 11)	Merchants weep, wail and mourn.	(verse 19)
(verse 15)	Merchants stand at a distance.	(verse 17)

Babylon falls.

(verses 16,17)

The climax of this chapter— the center, is the fall of Babylon.

The Fourth Angel

The third angel's message, beginning in verse 4, cries out that Babylon is about to be destroyed. Another angel is not mentioned until verse 21.

"Then a mighty angel took up a stone like a great millstone and threw it into the sea, saying, 'Thus with violence the great city Babylon shall be thrown down, and shall not be found anymore'" (Revelation 18:21).

This angel is not mentioned in Revelation 14. This angel takes up a millstone and actually destroys Babylon. Nowhere in Revelation 14 is the actual destruction of Babylon mentioned. After the third angel gives his message, in Revelation 14, Christ is seen reaping His fruit. The destruction of Babylon is skipped over. Daniel tells us that before Christ returns to reap His saints, that the little horn— Babylon the great— will be destroyed (Daniel 7:11,26; Daniel 2:35; Daniel 11:45).

The angel with the millstone is the fourth angel of seven. It must be inserted before the last three angels of Revelation 14.

Combining the time-lines of Revelation 14 and 18 gives us a complete view of the final events that will transpire at the End of Time.

End of Time Prophecies

The Last Seven Angels

1st	Rev. 14:6,7	God's judgment has begun.
2nd	Rev. 14:8; Rev. 18:1-3	Babylon is upon us.
3rd	Rev. 14:9-11; Rev. 18:4-8	God's wrath will be poured out.
4th	Rev. 18:21-24	Babylon is destroyed.
5th	Rev. 14:14-16	Christ harvests His saints.
6th	Rev. 14:17	This angel is ready to gather the tares.
7th	Rev 14:18-20; Rev. 19:17,18	The tares suffer the wrath of God.

The Last Plagues
Revelation 15, 16

Once a year, on the Day of Judgment (Atonement), the Israelite high priest would enter into the presence of God. Standing before the mercy seat, the priest would offer a sacrifice that symbolized the atonement for the entire camp. This atonement symbolically covered or paid the penalty required of God's law: *"for the wages of sin is death"* (Romans 6:23). When God accepted the sacrifice, the smoke of His glory would fill the entire tabernacle so that no one, high priest included, could remain in the tabernacle (Exodus 40:34, 35; 1 Kings 8:10, 11).

"And after that I looked, and, behold, the temple of the tabernacle of the testimony in heaven was opened: ₆And the seven angels came out of the temple, having the seven plagues, clothed in pure and white linen, and having their breasts girded with golden girdles. ₇And one of the four beasts gave unto the seven angels seven golden vials full of the wrath of God, who liveth for ever and ever. ₈And the temple was filled with smoke from the glory of God, and from his power; and no man was able to enter into the temple, till the seven plagues of the seven angels were fulfilled" (Revelation 15:5-8 KJV).

The current work of Jesus Christ, our high priest, is the work of atonement. He is now before the Father pleading each case, covering the righteous with His perfect sacrifice. When all has been judged, Jesus Christ— Michael, will stand up (Daniel 12:1), and the tabernacle in heaven will fill with the smoke from the glory of God. It is at this time that God will send out seven angels with the seven last plagues. It is at the conclusion of the judgment in heaven that probation closes. All will have either the seal of God or the mark of the beast— there is no middle ground.

"Then I heard a loud voice from the temple saying to the seven angels, 'Go and pour out the bowls of the wrath of God on the earth'" (Revelation 16:1).

Here begins the time of trouble, also known as Jacob's time of trouble.

"At that time Michael shall stand up, The great prince who stands watch over the sons of your people; And there shall be a time of trouble, Such as never

was since there was a nation, Even to that time. And at that time your people shall be delivered, Every one who is found written in the book" (Daniel 12:1).

"Alas! For that day is great, So that none is like it; And it is the time of Jacob's trouble, But he shall be saved out of it" (Jeremiah 30:7).

The seven last plagues are poured out upon the earth once the trial phase of judgment has finished. Those who chose to accept Jesus Christ, desiring to keep His commandments, have received the seal of God. They are counted as sheep and will receive the reward of eternal righteousness and salvation. Those who slighted Christ's offer of grace and salvation are marked as goats and will have to reap what they have sown. It is this later group that the plagues affect the most.

The Church within the Storm

Ten plagues fell upon Egypt, but it was only the first three plagues (water to blood, abundance of frogs, and lice), that affected both Egyptians and Israelites. The last seven plagues did not fall on those who chose to follow God (Exodus 8:20). God made it clear to the world that His people were unique from the rest of the world.

The Bible never mentions the church being raptured or removed from this period of plagues and tribulations. Christ told His disciples that the church would be in the world during the tribulation period, even warning them that they would have to flee to the mountains.

The disciples asked Christ *"What will be the sign of Your coming, and of the end of the age?"* (Matthew 24:3).

"Therefore when you see the 'abomination of desolation,' spoken of by Daniel the prophet, standing in the holy place (whoever reads, let him understand), 16then let those who are in Judea flee to the mountains. 17Let him who is on the housetop not go down to take anything out of his house. 18And let him who is in the field not go back to get his clothes. 19But woe to those who are pregnant and to those who are nursing babies in those days! 20And pray that your flight may not be in winter or on the Sabbath. 21For then there will be great tribulation, such as has not been since the beginning of the world until this time, no, nor ever shall be. 22And unless those days were shortened, no flesh would be saved; but for the elect's sake those days will be shortened" (Matthew 24:15-22).

Christ revealed events that would transpire both in the lifetime of those hearing His words (the destruction of Jerusalem in AD70), and events that would occur immediately prior to His second coming at the End of Time.

The church endured the destruction of Jerusalem, and the 1260 years of tribulation at the hands of the little horn. The church in the world has witnessed the sun becoming dark (May 19, 1780), the stars falling (November 13, 1833), countless earthquakes, and many false christ's. There is scriptural support that these events will be repeated in rapid succession at the End of Time and on a scale unlike anything witnessed on earth since creation.

"The sun shall be turned into darkness, And the moon into blood, Before the coming of the great and awesome day of the LORD" (Joel 2:31).

"Multitudes, multitudes in the valley of decision! For the day of the LORD is near in the valley of decision. 15The sun and moon will grow dark, And the stars will diminish their brightness. 16The LORD also will roar from Zion, And utter His voice from Jerusalem; The heavens and earth will shake; But the LORD will be a shelter for His people, And the strength of the children of Israel" (Joel 3:14-16).

"For the stars of heaven and their constellations Will not give their light; The sun will be darkened in its going forth, And the moon will not cause its light to shine. 11I will punish the world for its evil, And the wicked for their iniquity; I will halt the arrogance of the proud, And will lay low the haughtiness of the terrible" (Isaiah 13:10,11).

"The city had no need of the sun or of the moon to shine in it, for the glory of God illuminated it. The Lamb is its light" (Revelation 21:23).

"There shall be no night there: They need no lamp nor light of the sun, for the Lord God gives them light. And they shall reign forever and ever" (Revelation 22:5).

God never said He would rapture the church from these events, but He promised to keep His church *"from the hour of trial which shall come upon the whole world, to test those who dwell on earth"* (Revelation 3:10). Noah endured a worldwide flood, safe under the watch care of God in an ark (Genesis 6). Elijah endured a three year drought, being instructed by God to seek solace beside a mountain brook where God commanded ravens to feed him there

End of Time Prophecies

(1 Kings 17:4). When the brook dried up, God sent him to a widows home and provided sustenance for all. Daniel was not spared from the lion's den, but God did spare him from the lions (Daniel 6).

"For in the time of trouble He shall hide me in His pavilion; In the secret place of His tabernacle He shall hide me; He shall set me high upon a rock" (Psalm 27:5).

"No evil shall befall you, Nor shall any plague come near your dwelling; 11For He shall give His angels charge over you, To keep you in all your ways" (Psalm 91:10,11).

"Come, my people, enter your chambers, And shut your doors behind you; Hide yourself, as it were, for a little moment, Until the indignation is past. 21For behold, the LORD comes out of His place To punish the inhabitants of the earth for their iniquity; The earth will also disclose her blood, And will no more cover her slain" (Isaiah 26:20,21).

"He will dwell on high; His place of defense will be the fortress of rocks; Bread will be given him, His water will be sure" (Isaiah 33:16).

A Faith that will Endure

The time of trouble will be severe. It will be unlike anything that has ever been seen. "The season of distress and anguish before us will require a faith that can endure weariness, delay and hunger—a faith that will not faint though severely tried. The period of probation [now going on] is granted to all to prepare for that time."[1]

Now, while our great High Priest is making atonement for us, we should seek to become perfect in Christ; proving His promises and acquainting ourselves with His presence. During the tribulation period and last plagues, there will no longer be a mediator for mankind before the Father. The smoke of the glory of God will have removed everyone from the heavenly tabernacle. Jesus Christ will have completed His work sealing all who are His. While He prepares to receive His kingdom and gather His saints, we must stand, by faith, knowing that our repented sins have been covered. Our faith must endure knowing that though we do not yet see temporal

---

1   White, *The Great Controversy*, 621.

relief from the evils of this world, we can know that His promises are sure.

Martyrdom at this time would serve no purpose, it would not yield a new harvest for God.

"He who is unjust, let him be unjust still; he who is filthy, let him be filthy still; he who is righteous, let him be righteous still; he who is holy, let him be holy still" (Revelation 22:11).

No one can change sides; probation is closed. If God were to allow His saints to die, it would only please Satan to see the loss of human life. Instead Satan and his forces will be infuriated desiring to kill God's people but will be unable to do so.

The Last Plagues
The First Plague

"So the first went and poured out his bowl upon the earth, and a foul and loathsome sore came upon the men who had the mark of the beast and those who worshiped his image" (Revelation 16:2).

This plague separates the sealed of God from those with the mark of the beast. These sores are poured out only on those who have the mark of the beast; those who have chosen not to be sealed by God. It is not clear if everyone marked receives sores or just a portion of them.

The Second Plague

"Then the second angel poured out his bowl on the sea, and it became blood as of a dead man; and every living creature in the sea died" (Revelation 16:3).

This plague affects everything about the sea, including the merchants of the world that use it for transporting their wares.

"For in one hour such great riches came to nothing. Every shipmaster, all who travel by ship, sailors, and as many as trade on the sea, stood at a distance [18]and cried out when they saw the smoke of her burning, saying, 'What is like this great city?'" (Revelation 18:17,18).

The Third Plague

"Then the third angel poured out his bowl on the rivers and springs of water, and they became blood" (Revelation 16:4).

This plague affects the freshwater supply. It cannot be universal or else all life would cease to exist, and there are four more plagues yet to be poured out.

The Fourth Plague

"Then the fourth angel poured out his bowl on the sun, and power was given to him to scorch men with fire. ₉And men were scorched with great heat, and they blasphemed the name of God who has power over these plagues; and they did not repent and give Him glory" (Revelation 16:8,9).

This plague is one of heat, adding to the drought and likely causing famines in certain places. It is during this plague that the world begins to realize that these plagues are supernatural. Instead of repenting (of which it is too late because probation is closed), they blaspheme God, blaming Him for their misery.

The Fifth Plague

"Then the fifth angel poured out his bowl on the throne of the beast, and his kingdom became full of darkness; and they gnawed their tongues because of the pain. ₁₁They blasphemed the God of heaven because of their pains and their sores, and did not repent of their deeds" (Revelation 16:10,11).

Darkness covers the kingdom and throne of the beast. Currently the beast's throne is in Vatican City. While God is not limited as to how He brings darkness to this kingdom, it is interesting to note all the volcanoes surrounding it, and realize that there would be immense darkness if several of these volcanoes began spewing forth ash and dust.

"Their sores" Apparently, the sores of the first plague are not fatal.

Under this plague, mankind still does not acknowledge their guilt and continue to blaspheme God.

The Sixth Plague

"Then the sixth angel poured out his bowl on the great river Euphrates, and its water was dried up, so that the way of the kings from the east might be prepared" (Revelation 16:12).

The reference to the Euphrates drying up is most likely not literal. Revelation 17:15 points to the waters sitting under the scarlet beast as peoples, nations and tongues. This scarlet beast is also called Babylon

(Revelation 17:5). Ancient Babylon sat on the Euphrates River. Cyrus the Persian conquered Babylon by diverting the Euphrates River away from Babylon drying up its waters. His army then entered the city from the lowered river through gates left opened. The language in this plague recalls the fall of Babylon. The scarlet rider called *"Babylon the Great"* will see its support dry up. Where once the world marveled and followed its image, the world now turns, stands afar off, and wails watching Babylon fall (Revelation 18:9-11).

"Kings of the East" The literal translation reads *"Kings from the rising sun."* The rising sun directs our attention to the return of Jesus Christ, appearing from the east (Ezekiel 43:2-5; Matthew 24:30).

Daniel records tidings from the east and north as troubling to Babylon—the king of the north.

"But news from the east and the north shall trouble him; therefore he shall go out with great fury to destroy and annihilate many" (Daniel 11:44).

Both east and north have references to Jesus Christ and His return. The east is the direction that He will appear from (Matthew 24:27). The north is the seat of His throne, Mount Zion (Isaiah 14:13).

Timings of the Plagues

There are three periods of time that keep appearing in the discussion of the time of trouble and the last plagues; *one hour, one day,* and *half an hour*. Symbolically: one day represents a year; one hour is 1/24th of a year or fifteen days (1 yr = 360 days; 1 day = 24 hours; 1/24 of 360 = 15); and half an hour is about seven days.

One Day

"Therefore her plagues will come in one day— death and mourning and famine. And she will be utterly burned with fire, for strong is the Lord God who judges her" (Revelation 18:8).

The plagues come in one day (Isaiah 47:9; Zechariah 14). Reading the seven last plagues it is clear that they are not poured out at once, but one after another. One literal day would not be enough time for the events, especially if famine is to result. One prophetic day, a literal year, better fits the pouring out of the last plagues.

End of Time Prophecies

"And unless those days were shortened, no flesh would be saved; but for the elect's sake those days will be shortened" (Matthew 24:22).

One Hour

"The ten horns which you saw are ten kings who have received no kingdom as yet, but they receive authority for one hour as kings with the beast. ₁₃These are of one mind, and they will give their power and authority to the beast" (Revelation 17:12,13).

The ten horns belong to the scarlet beast. This beast is ridden by Babylon— the mother of harlots. The ten horns represent the nations and merchants of this world who allow Babylon to control them. Babylon the great is the beast from the sea; it is the little horn— the Roman Catholic Church. This power will return to its glory and influence it felt during the dark ages. This power will force the world to comply with its desires.

"And that no one may buy or sell except one who has the mark or the name of the beast, or the number of his name" (Revelation 13:17).

The merchants of the world realize money can be made if they agree to worship the image made to the beast.

"For all the nations have drunk of the wine of the wrath of her fornication, the kings of the earth have committed fornication with her, and the merchants of the earth have become rich through the abundance of her luxury" (Revelation 18:3).

For a prophetic one hour— fifteen days— the world stands unified with the little horn (Catholicism). The first plague is poured out at the end of this hour marking the beginning of judgment. The merchants watch as they see Babylon suffer the wrath of God.

"Standing at a distance for fear of her torment, saying, 'Alas, alas, that great city Babylon, that mighty city! For in one hour your judgment has come.'" "For in one hour such great riches came to nothing. Every shipmaster, all who travel by ship, sailors, and as many as trade on the sea, stood at a distance." "They threw dust on their heads and cried out, weeping and wailing, and saying, 'Alas, alas, that great city, in which all who had ships on the sea became rich by her wealth! For in one hour she is made desolate'" (Revelation 18:10, 17, 19).

Half an Hour

"When He opened the seventh seal, there was silence in heaven for about half an hour" (Revelation 8:1).

One prophetic half hour is the same as seven days. A parallel passage in the scriptures describes another seven days of silence.

"Two by two they went into the ark to Noah, male and female, as God had commanded Noah. 10And it came to pass after seven days that the waters of the flood were on the earth" (Genesis 7:9,10).

Noah, his family, and the animals on the ark sat still for seven days— a prophetic half an hour, before the rains began to fall. Probation had closed for the wicked. The last warnings had been given and now the door to the ark was shut tight and only God could open it. After seven days of "*silence*", the rains began to fall and the wicked were destroyed.

The silence before the flood is a foreshadow of the silence that will be just prior to Christ's return. When the saints of Jesus' kingdom are all confirmed, through the cleansing of the sanctuary, the Father's glory fills the tabernacle pushing everyone out. It is while the heavenly tabernacle is empty that the tribulations and plagues are poured out upon the earth. During the sixth plague, something happens in heaven. Jesus Christ takes off His priestly robes and puts on the robes of a King.

"His eyes were like a flame of fire, and on His head were many crowns. He had a name written that no one knew except Himself. 13He was clothed with a robe dipped in blood, and His name is called The Word of God. 14And the armies in heaven, clothed in fine linen, white and clean, followed Him on white horses. 15Now out of His mouth goes a sharp sword, that with it He should strike the nations. And He Himself will rule them with a rod of iron. He Himself treads the winepress of the fierceness and wrath of Almighty God. 16And He has on His robe and on His thigh a name written: KING OF KINGS AND LORD OF LORDS" (Revelation 19:12-16).

Christ is ready to receive His bride—the New Jerusalem.

"Let us be glad and rejoice and give Him glory, for the marriage of the Lamb has come, and His wife has made herself ready" (Revelation 19:7).

End of Time Prophecies

"I was watching in the night visions, And behold, One like the Son of Man, Coming with the clouds of heaven! He came to the Ancient of Days, And they brought Him near before Him. 14Then to Him was given dominion and glory and a kingdom, That all peoples, nations, and languages should serve Him. His dominion is an everlasting dominion, Which shall not pass away, And His kingdom the one Which shall not be destroyed" (Daniel 7:13,14).

Jesus Christ receives His kingdom.

"Then he said to me, 'Write: Blessed are those who are called to the marriage supper of the Lamb!' And he said to me, 'These are the true sayings of God'" (Revelation 19:9).

"Then I, John, saw the holy city, New Jerusalem, coming down out of heaven from God, prepared as a bride adorned for her husband" (Revelation 21:2).

Jewish weddings lasted days, some as long as a week. Perhaps this seven days of silence on earth is Christ and heaven celebrating Jesus' marriage to His new city—the capital of His kingdom.

The church on earth is represented as chaste virgins who go out to meet the bridegroom (2 Corinthians 11:2).

The seven days of silence may be the wedding party descending from heaven, celebrating the arrival of Jesus' kingdom and the collection of His saints to live with Him for eternity. Ellen White had a vision in which she saw that the saints "were seven days ascending to the sea of glass."[2] This fits the notion that Christ's return is a seven-day jubilee, one that would certainly trouble the king of the north and the devil who gave authority to this king.

The Seventh Plague

"Then the seventh angel poured out his bowl into the air, and a loud voice came out of the temple of heaven, from the throne, saying, 'It is done!' 18And there were noises and thunderings and lightnings; and there was a great earthquake, such a mighty and great earthquake as had not occurred since men were on the earth. 19Now the great city was divided into three parts, and the cities of the nations fell. And great Babylon was remembered before God, to give her the cup of the wine of the fierceness of His wrath. 20Then every island fled away, and the mountains were not found. 21And great hail

---

2   White, *Early Writings*, 16

from heaven fell upon men, each hailstone about the weight of a talent. Men blasphemed God because of the plague of the hail, since that plague was exceedingly great" (Revelation 16:17-21).

This plague matches the last plague that fell on Egypt. The Egyptian plague killed all of the first born who opposed God. The last plague that falls on earth will kill all who oppose God.

During this last plague, all nature is turned upside down. It is during this upheaval of nature, when things look the darkest that Jesus Christ appears in the sky to harvest His flock. *"Joy comes in the morning"* (Psalm 30:5).

The Dead in Christ Arise.

"Behold, I tell you a mystery: We shall not all sleep, but we shall all be changed— 52in a moment, in the twinkling of an eye, at the last trumpet. For the trumpet will sound, and the dead will be raised incorruptible, and we shall be changed" (1 Corinthians 15:51,52).

The saints who were asleep are now raised. This is the resurrection of the living (John 5:29). All of the saints are caught up with Jesus in the clouds.

"But the rest of the dead did not live again until the thousand years were finished. This is the first resurrection" (Revelation 20:5).

The wicked that remain alive are killed; some by the brightness of the Lord's presence, some by hail and other natural disasters.

"Have you entered the treasury of snow, Or have you seen the treasury of hail, 23Which I have reserved for the time of trouble, For the day of battle and war?" (Job 28:22,23).

"And the rest were killed with the sword which proceeded from the mouth of Him who sat on the horse. And all the birds were filled with their flesh" (Revelation 19:21).

In the days of Noah, after the destruction of the world by a flood, God caused a wind to cover up the dead rotting bodies of men and beast (Genesis 8:1). After the destruction of the wicked at Christ's return, the bodies will not be covered. They will lay where they fall. *"And all the birds were filled with their flesh."*

End of Time Prophecies

"Then I saw an angel standing in the sun; and he cried with a loud voice, saying to all the birds that fly in the midst of heaven, 'Come and gather together for the supper of the great God, 18that you may eat the flesh of kings, the flesh of captains, the flesh of mighty men, the flesh of horses and of those who sit on them, and the flesh of all people, free and slave, both small and great'" (Revelation 19:17,18).

"And as for you, son of man, thus says the Lord GOD, 'Speak to every sort of bird and to every beast of the field: Assemble yourselves and come; Gather together from all sides to My sacrificial meal Which I am sacrificing for you, A great sacrificial meal on the mountains of Israel, That you may eat flesh and drink blood. 18You shall eat the flesh of the mighty, Drink the blood of the princes of the earth, Of rams and lambs, Of goats and bulls, All of them fatlings of Bashan. 19You shall eat fat till you are full, And drink blood till you are drunk, At My sacrificial meal Which I am sacrificing for you. 20You shall be filled at My table With horses and riders, With mighty men And with all the men of war,' says the Lord GOD. '21I will set My glory among the nations; all the nations shall see My judgment which I have executed, and My hand which I have laid on them. 22So the house of Israel shall know that I am the LORD their God from that day forward'" (Ezekiel 39:17-22).

"Therefore behold, the days are coming, says the LORD, 'when it will no more be called Tophet, or the Valley of the Son of Hinnom, but the Valley of Slaughter; for they will bury in Tophet until there is no room. 33The corpses of this people will be food for the birds of the heaven and for the beasts of the earth. And no one will frighten them away'" (Jeremiah 7:32,33).

Eternal Life

The people of God have their reward. They travel with Jesus Christ back to heaven to stand on the sea of glass, receive their crowns, participate in the judgment of the wicked, and live eternally. The wicked are all dead. Satan and his angels sit on an empty desolate earth. The millennium follows the seven last plagues.

Armageddon
A Mount Carmel Experience

The word *Armageddon* appears only once in Scripture, and yet it elicits more responses, guesses and fears from people than any other End of Time topic.

"And I saw three unclean spirits like frogs coming out of the mouth of the dragon, out of the mouth of the beast, and out of the mouth of the false prophet. ₁₄For they are spirits of demons, performing signs, which go out to the kings of the earth and of the whole world, to gather them to the battle of that great day of God Almighty. ₁₅'Behold, I am coming as a thief. Blessed is he who watches, and keeps his garments, lest he walk naked and they see his shame.' ₁₆And they gathered them together to the place called in Hebrew, Armageddon" (Revelation 16:13-16).

"**Three unclean spirits**" These gather the whole world to a single place— Armageddon. The purpose of this gathering is to battle God Almighty. This battle may be a physical battle, or a spiritual battle, or a combination of both. The language of these verses gives us powerful clues as to the exact nature of this battle— no guessing is required. The unclean spirits are tasked with the gathering of the world. John saw them coming from the dragon (Satan), the beast (Roman Catholicism), and the false prophet (U.S.A.). John understood what these spirits represented: "*Beloved, do not believe every spirit, but test the spirits, whether they are of God; because many false prophets [spirits] have gone out into the world*" (1 John 4:1).

"For though we walk in the flesh, we do not war according to the flesh. ₄For the weapons of our warfare are not carnal but mighty in God for pulling down strongholds," (2 Corinthians 10:3,4).

The battle of Armageddon is predominately spiritual. It is the struggle for the hearts and minds of real people. Revelation 16:15 lists Biblical themes that correspond to the spiritual battle required for salvation.

"**Blessed is he who watches**" (Matthew 24:42-44; 1 Thess. 5:1-8; Revelation 3:3, 18).

"Keeps his garments" (Matthew 22:11; Zechariah 3:3-5; Isaiah 52:1; Isaiah 61:10; Revelation 3:4).

"Walk naked and see his shame" (Revelation 3:18; Daniel 12:2; Nahum 3:5; 1 Corinthians 15:34; Philippians 3:18,19; Revelation 17:16).

Armageddon: The Mount Carmel Experience

"In Hebrew is called Armageddon" The Greek writing of this Hebrew word includes a breathing mark above the "Ἁ", this is a rough breathing mark which means an "h" sound is added to the word. In Hebrew the words *har* and *megedon* have meanings; *har* means "mountain" and *megedon* has been translated into *megiddo* which means "place of troops", and is a reference to locations in the Bible lands. The problem exists that there is no specific mountain called *Megiddo*. There is a reference to a 20 kilometer ridge running from the Jordan river west towards the Mediterranean sea. The highpoint of this ridge is called Mount Carmel and it is in view of the ancient city of Megiddo.[1]

Mount Carmel is the location where Elijah visibly called out to the nation of Israel to choose between two opinions—God or Baal (1 Kings 18). With the nation gathered on the mountain top, visible to the world, the priests of Baal worshiped Baal asking for a sign of fire to light an altar in his honor. They worshiped all day but to no avail. Finally, Elijah was given a chance to worship the God of Heaven. Before his prayer was complete fire came down from Heaven and devoured the sacrifice, the stones, and the water around it.

It was visible to the entire nation that Elijah's God, the God of Heaven who answered by fire, was the true God.

Perhaps this same event, mimicked by Satan as an angel of light, will transpire at the End of Time ushering in the mark of the beast.

---

1   Paulien, Jon, *The Gospel from Patmos*, (MD: Review and Herald Pub. Assoc., 2007), 287.

The similarities are too great not to think this. Before the close of probation and the great time of trouble, Satan will appear as an angel of light (2 Corinthians 11:14). Through the agency of spiritualism, miracles will be wrought, the sick will be healed, and many undeniable wonders will be performed. Satan will assign his angels roles to play in deceiving the world. He will instruct some to act and speak for men who have died, but now reappear, sounding very religious and giving support to this angel of light—Satan, who is impersonating Christ.[2]

This Mount Carmel experience will not be orchestrated by God. Any simile to the biblical story, including fire from heaven, will be done by Satan and not God. We have been warned, *"Many will come in my name, saying, 'I am the Christ'"* (Matthew 24:5).

The Bible clearly tells us that the next time mankind sees God it will be *"as the lighting comes from the east and flashes to the west"* (Matthew 24:27) and *"Behold, He is coming with clouds, and every eye will see Him, even they who pierced Him. And all the tribes of the earth will mourn because of Him. Even so, Amen"* (Revelation 1:7).

Armageddon is the last battle that matters; it is the one for your eternal life. Your Armageddon may be right at this moment, we are not guaranteed another moment of life. What manner of person will you be?

"But the day of the Lord will come as a thief in the night, in which the heavens will pass away with a great noise, and the elements will melt with fervent heat; both the earth and the works that are in it will be burned up. 11Therefore, since all these things will be dissolved, what manner of persons ought you to be in holy conduct and godliness," (2 Peter 3:10,11).

---

[2] White, *The Great Controversy*, 587.

Who is Babylon the Great?
Revelation 17, 18

The book of Revelation speaks of Babylon. Who or what is this Babylon? Is it the city of Daniel and Nebuchadnezzar? Is it pointing to a modern revival of this city? Is it a symbol of a power, a nation, or some ideology that will exist in the last days?

Where did Babylon come from?

"Cush begot Nimrod; he began to be a mighty one on the earth. 9He was a mighty hunter before the LORD; therefore it is said, 'Like Nimrod the mighty hunter before the LORD.' 10And the beginning of his kingdom was Babel, Erech, Accad, and Calneh, in the land of Shinar" (Genesis 10:8-10).

Cush was the son of Ham, the son of Noah. A city was built in the land of Shinar. Within this city, a tower was built *"whose top is in the heavens"* (Genesis 11:4).

The desired location and purpose of the tower was to be in the heavens, or to be equal with God. The purpose of this tower was to *"make a name for ourselves, lest we be scattered abroad over the face of the whole earth"* (Genesis 11:4).

This desire and purpose suggests that the builders did not trust God; specifically they did not believe His promise to never send another flood to cover the earth (Genesis 9:11). The tower of Babylon (Babel) is a monument to apostasy and unbelief in God. God confused the people's language and scattered them.

"Therefore its name is called Babel, because there the LORD confused the language of all the earth; and from there the LORD scattered them abroad over the face of all the earth" (Genesis 11:9).

Babylon as an empire rose to its greatest power under general Nabopolassar who became its king. When he died in 604BC his son Nebuchadnezzar became king. Nebuchadnezzar and the Chaldean's ruled Babylon until 459BC when Cyrus the Persian conquered the city. The Medes and Persians (Achaemenid rulers) reigned until 331BC when Alexander the Great fully conquered them.

Alexander made great plans for the city of Babylon and wanted to make it the capital of his eastern empire. He rebuilt the temples, dug out a larger harbor in the Euphrates, big enough for 100 war ships, and built dockyards. Unfortunately, Alexander died when he was only 32.

Following Alexander's death his empire broke into four parts. Seleucus I Necator became king over Babylon in 311BC. Soon after his crowning, Seleucus decided to build a new capital city on the Tigris River, forty miles north of Babylon, near Baghdad, naming it Seleucia. He pilfered millions of bricks from Babylon to establish this city. The new metropolitan Seleucia drained Babylon of its people and markets. Sometime after 125BC, Babylon ceased to exist. In the course of time, the Euphrates River, which had flowed through the center of Babylon, changed its course and dried up under Babylon.

The Jewish prophet Jeremiah was a contemporary of Nebuchadnezzar (Jeremiah 39). He prophesied about the end of Babylon centuries before it came about.

"Therefore thus says the LORD: 'Behold, I will plead your case and take vengeance for you. I will dry up her sea and make her springs dry. [37]Babylon shall become a heap, a dwelling place for jackals, An astonishment and a hissing, Without an inhabitant'" (Jeremiah 51:36, 37).

Isaiah also prophesied of Babylon's eternal end.

"And Babylon, the glory of kingdoms, The beauty of the Chaldeans' pride, Will be as when God overthrew Sodom and Gomorrah. [20]It will never be inhabited, Nor will it be settled from generation to generation; Nor will the Arabian pitch tents there, Nor will the shepherds make their sheepfolds there" (Isaiah 13:19, 20).

Today Babylon is still a heap of ruins. No grass grows there and no shepherds pasture their flocks there. In 1982, Saddam Hussein conceived a grand scheme to rebuild the city. He reconstructed the old palace, but there is little evidence that the palace or any other part of the city has been occupied or used.

Who is Babylon the Great?

Who is Babylon the Great, discussed by John in Revelation?

The mention of Babylon, in Revelation, cannot refer to ancient Babylon because God prophesied that it would never be inhabited. The prophecies of Jeremiah and Isaiah tell us that if Babylon, as a city, were to be fully rebuilt and inhabited it would make God a liar.

Apostle Peter in his first epistle writes to the believers of Christ who are scattered throughout a portion of the Roman Empire. The purpose of his letter was to strengthen the believer's faith in the face of suffering and persecution. Peter closes his letter with, "*She [the Church] who is in Babylon, elect[ed to the Gospel] together with you, greets you*" (1 Peter 5:13). Peter was not in Babylon. He was in Rome. It is known that other early Christian writers used the cryptic title "Babylon" when speaking of the Roman Capital— Rome.

The Woman of Scarlet and the Scarlet Beast

"Then one of the seven angels who had the seven bowls came and talked with me, saying to me, 'Come, I will show you the judgment of the great harlot who sits on many waters, ₂with whom the kings of the earth committed fornication, and the inhabitants of the earth were made drunk with the wine of her fornication." ₃So he carried me away in the Spirit into the wilderness. And I saw a woman sitting on a scarlet beast which was full of names of blasphemy, having seven heads and ten horns. ₄The woman was arrayed in purple and scarlet, and adorned with gold and precious stones and pearls, having in her hand a golden cup full of abominations and the filthiness of her fornication. ₅And on her forehead a name was written: MYSTERY, BABYLON THE GREAT, THE MOTHER OF HARLOTS AND OF THE ABOMINATIONS OF THE EARTH'" (Revelation 17:1-5).

The woman, arrayed in scarlet, who rode the beast has the name of Babylon the Great, the Mother of Harlots and the Abominations of the Earth. Before we identify this woman, called Babylon, we will identify the scarlet beast.

The Scarlet Beast

The word beast (*therion*) is a parallel connection to the beasts found in Daniel, specifically chapter 7. In that vision Daniel received various cartoon-like beasts that represented characteristics of succeeding kingdoms. The fourth beast had a set of ten horns. This scarlet beast has ten horns.

The angel appears to John and says "*Come, I will show you.*" John **hears** the angel describe is a woman sitting on water. Moments later John is taken in the Spirit and **sees** "*a woman sitting on a scarlet beast.*"

John *hears* about a woman sitting on water, but *sees* a woman sitting on a beast. The symbols of water and beast are synonymous.

"Then he said to me, 'The waters which you saw, where the harlot sits, are peoples, multitudes, nations, and tongues'" (Revelation 17:15).

The scarlet beast represents the peoples, multitudes, nations, and tongues of the earth— the political nations of the earth. John is given a picture of the future. He *sees* a time when the scarlet woman— called *Babylon the Great*, rides the scarlet beast. The scarlet woman does not always ride the beast; she only rides it for a short time. (Actually, she rides it twice: once as part of the seven kings, and then as the eighth king).

The Timing of the Scarlet Beast

"The beast that you saw was, and is not, and will ascend out of the bottomless pit and go to perdition. And those who dwell on the earth will marvel, whose names are not written in the Book of Life from the foundation of the world, when they see the beast that was, and is not, and yet is" (Revelation 17:8).

Remember this phrase "*was, and is not, and will ascend [go].*" This phrase will identify the exact moment when this beast becomes the scarlet beast ridden by the scarlet arrayed woman.

Whatever this beast is, it will one day go to perdition or destruction.

"Here is the mind which has wisdom: The seven heads are seven mountains on which the woman sits. 10There are also seven kings. Five have fallen, one is, and the other has not yet come. And when he comes, he must continue a short time. 11The beast that was, and is not, is himself also the eighth, and is of the seven, and is going to perdition" (Revelation 17:9-11).

The beast goes through several changes. It has seven heads and ten horns and the seven heads are seven mountains. Heads, horns, and mountains are all symbols used to designate political powers. The seven mountains may also be a direct reference to Rome, which sits on seven mountains. Supporting the concept that we are talking about political powers is the direct phrase "*There are also seven kings*" (Verse 10). Seven heads are seven political powers.

The beast is formed of secular powers, or kings. Five have fallen, the sixth king *is*, and the seventh king has *not yet come*. The beast that "*was and is not and is going to perdition*" is the eighth king. This eighth king is said to be one of the seven.

The scarlet woman rides the last form— king 8. It was also seen riding one of the seven kings.

Can we identify the 8 kings?

The clue rests in verse 9: "*The seven heads are*."

Using Daniel's cartoon beasts, we can count the heads and thus count and label the kings here mentioned.

The lion had one head, the bear one head, the leopard had four heads, and the terrible beast does not have a head. The terrible beast has no animal counterpart. Not even adding wings, or heads or tails to any existing animal could be used to describe the look of this beast. Perhaps, and this is a guess, this beast is an entity similar to our mechanical beasts such as excavators or bulldozers. It would explain the huge iron teeth, and trampling the residue with its '*feet*'. Regardless of our cartoon picture, this beast does not appear to have a full head, not at least until the little horn emerges.

"I was considering the horns, and there was another horn, a little one, coming up among them, before whom three of the first horns were plucked out by the roots. And there, in this horn, were eyes like the eyes of a man, and a mouth speaking pompous words" (Daniel 7:8).

"**Like a man**" Here is the only connection to a head on the fourth beast. The little horn is like a man's head, with eyes and a mouth.

End of Time Prophecies

The counting of heads is important to identifying the eight kings.

King 1	Head 1	Lion = Babylon
King 2	Head 2	Bear = Medes and Persians
King 3,4,5 & 6	Head 3-6	Leopard = Greece

Daniel 11 tells us that Greece was divided into four nations—the kings of the North, South, East and West. In AD31 the last of the three kingdoms were under the control of the king of the North—pagan Rome. John wrote Revelation sometime near AD95. The ruling power or the king at this time, was pagan Rome.

"**Five have fallen**" In AD95, five kings or five heads had fallen.

"**One is**" When John wrote this king number six or the sixth head was the one ruling. At the time of John, Pagan Rome had become the king of the North and was the sixth head or king.

Reviewing Daniel 11 and history we know that Alexander the Great would have his kingdom dived into four parts— four heads. Soon only two heads would remain— the kings of the North and South. 31BC saw the "*robbers of your people*" rise to power, taking on the name, the king of the North. At this time, there was no real ruling king of the South, only one king ruled. When John wrote Revelation 17, the ruling king (king 6) was Rome.

Rome in this capacity was not yet the little horn. Rome, in its pagan or political form had, according to Daniel, no head. King 7 requires a head.

What head remains?

The fourth beast of Daniel 7, Rome, did not have a head—until the little horn power pushed his way up among the ten horns, uprooting three. This little horn appeared to have "*eyes like the eyes of a man, and a mouth speaking pompous words*." Here is the seventh head. Here is the seventh king which in the day of John had not yet come.

"**He must continue a short time.**" The little horn power has been identified as the papacy who sat and controlled political powers and who reigned over the nations of the earth from AD538 to AD1798. This is exactly 1260 years (42 months, 3 ½ prophetic days) or a short time. In AD1798, the popes continued to exist, but their power to control political powers and kingdoms was removed.

Who is King 8?

"The beast that was, and is not, is himself also the eighth, and is of the seven, and is going to perdition" (Revelation 17:11).

"Was, and is not, and will [go]" Did you remember this phrase? The scarlet beast was given this title in verse 8. The scarlet beast is the eighth king. This phrase goes deeper; it is both a title and a description of the scarlet beast with the scarlet rider.

As a title, it is a play on words. *"Holy, holy, holy, Lord God Almighty, Who was and is and is to come!" (Revelation 4:8).*

Jesus Christ— Lord God Almighty— is given the title: "Who was, and is and is to come" (See: Revelation 1:4,5).

The scarlet beast is given the title: *Who was, and is not, and will go.* This is in direct opposition to Christ's title. The scarlet beast is the anti of Christ. Christ is and will come; the beast is not, and will go away, that is, into destruction.

Do not let the verb tenses confuse you. The beast that *was* has the verb form of past tense; this was because these words describe the events that occurred during John's vision of the future. When John was out of the Spirit, that is returned to normal, the angel then used the present tense, that *"One is"* to describe the kings.

"Is of the seven" The scarlet beast was one of the seven heads or seven kings. One of the seven kings will reappear as the scarlet beast.

The scarlet beast exists when the political powers or nations of the world give their power, or control over to the harlot that rides it. From history, we know that the little horn (papacy), once ruled the nations of the earth. This little horn received its deadly wound in AD1798, but was healed. Today we see the little horn, as the papacy, begin to regain its power among the nations of the earth. As of yet no nation has given their power over to the pope, but his influence is being felt in the politics of the world.

The papacy has already joined hands with the United States (false prophet) to remove the Communistic Berlin wall. Recently they have reunited hands in the politics of Cuba. The influence of the pope is beginning to be felt around the world. The scarlet beast is arising and when it, the nations of the world, allow themselves to be controlled or they themselves follow the precepts of the Catholic Church and its leaders, then this prophecy will be complete.

King 7 is the papacy controlling the nations from AD538 – 1798, (prior to it's deadly wound).

King 8 is the papacy controlling the nations after its deadly wound is fully healed.

The beast is the secular powers that rule the earth.

The Mother of Harlots

Who is the great harlot called Babylon?

> Babylon is seen riding or controlling this beast. Babylon is seen controlling the powers that rule the earth.

"And on her forehead a name was written: MYSTERY, BABYLON THE GREAT, THE MOTHER OF HARLOTS AND OF THE ABOMINATIONS OF THE EARTH. 6I saw the woman, drunk with the blood of the saints and with the blood of the martyrs of Jesus. And when I saw her, I marveled with great amazement. 7But the angel said to me, 'Why did you marvel?'" (Revelation 17:5-7).

Why did John marvel with great amazement?

The clue to his amazement sits with the words *"the mother of harlots."* This woman has daughters. It is the daughters that amaze John.

Throughout the Scriptures, a woman is used to symbolize a church. A chaste woman stands for a pure church, while a vile woman, or a harlot, represents an impure or apostate church. (See Isaiah 54:5; Matthew 9:15).

> "Husbands, love your wives, just as Christ also loved the church and gave Himself for her." (Ephesians 5:25).

> "That He might present her to Himself a glorious church, not having spot or wrinkle or any such thing, but that she should be holy and without blemish" (Ephesians 5: 27).

> "For I am jealous for you with godly jealousy. For I have betrothed you to one husband, that I may present you as a chaste virgin to Christ" (2 Corinthians 11:2).

Jesus Christ is the Bridegroom—He is our Maker, our Husband. Those who choose to follow Christ are His bride—His church. Ezekiel 23 describes two women who committed whoredom in the land. One was Samaria, the other Jerusalem. Both harlots represent a body of believers who had departed from God's commands and from His Church. Samaria was once the tribes of Israel, but chose idol worship and the governance of Assyria to God. Jerusalem, the capital for Judah, also turned away from God. She "*doted*" upon the Chaldeans desiring to be like them instead of God's chosen people.

Babylon is the mother of harlots. Babylon and its harlots represent all people who follow false doctrines, errors, and fornications against Jesus Christ. Any church that is joined with the world in compromise is a harlot. It is the will of Christ that His Church be separate from the world in belief and actions, yet remain in the world to be a witness for Him.

John "*marveled with great amazement*" when he saw the woman called Babylon the Great. John was surprised because, like Peter, he had been accustomed to using this term to cryptically represent the city of Rome, but the description just given to him by the angel shocked him. Babylon the Great was not a political entity—it was a religious entity. Not just a religious entity alone, but it was Christian—a Christ-like entity. Babylon is a church that looks, sounds and acts almost like a Christian, but is not. Worse than simply appearing to be Christian, this harlot woman has daughter churches!

The mother of harlots is the Catholic Church. Her daughter churches are any Christian church that follows her traditions, fables, or false beliefs that are contrary to the plain Word of God.

Compare ancient Babylon with the Catholic Church, and realize how accurate the symbol fits.

Babylon defiled Israel with her immorality, teaching Israel to defile the Lord's sanctuary and to profane His Sabbath (Ezekiel 23:17, 39).

Catholicism teaches that the seventh-day Sabbath is no longer the proper day to worship God. They claim that the third commandment teaches us to keep Sunday holy. They have totally removed the second commandment "*You shall not make for yourself a carved image*" and split the tenth commandment in half to make the number remain ten (Exodus 20).

>**The Bible** teaches: Genesis 2:2,3.

Babylon boasted that "*I am, and there is no one else beside me*" (Isaiah 47:8).

Catholicism claims that the pope is infallible— he cannot err when he defines doctrine.

>**The Bible** teaches: Exodus 3:14.

Catholicism claims the church cannot err in what she teaches as faith and morals.

>**The Bible** teaches: Romans 3:23.

Babylon sinned against the Lord (Jeremiah 50:14).

Catholicism teaches that we are to pray to the saints in heaven to honor them.

>**The Bible** teaches: Revelation 22:8,9.

Catholicism teaches that Christ left the power of forgiving sins to the pastors of the Catholic Church.

>**The Bible** teaches: Mark 2:7; Job 14:4; Isaiah 43:25.

Babylon was abundant with treasures (Jeremiah 51:13).

Catholicism loves to adorn itself with gold, scarlet robes, precious gems, and abundant treasures.

The Bible teaches: Revelation 22:8,9.

Catholicism has been a propagator of many false doctrines. She, like Babylon, has corrupted the pure truth's of God's Word and made the nations and many other protestant churches drunk with pleasing fables.

Catholicism:

- Denies that God in Christ dwelt in human flesh— the doctrine of the Immaculate conception.

- Displaces Christ as our Mediator, claiming this is a role of human priests.

- Condemns the way of salvation through faith alone and calls it a *damnable heresy*.

- Re-crucifies Christ daily believing that the sacraments of mass are one and the same as that of the cross— the doctrine of transubstantiation. (This is the sin that kept Moses out of the promised land, after he struck the rock twice (Numbers 20)).

- Believes in the immortality of the soul— a trait only given to God (1 Timothy 6:16). This doctrine opens up errors such as the conscious state of the dead, praying to saints, Mariology (worship of Mary), purgatory, reward at death, prayers to the dead, eternal torment, and universal salvation. None of these are found in the Bible.

- Teaches baptism by sprinkling instead of immersion.

- Teaches the coming of Christ is to be a spiritual event, not of a fleshly or literal nature.

This list is but the tip of the iceberg. The Roman Catholic Christian Church is not a true follower of Christ, but is an apostate or false church.

There are many members within this church body that are unaware of the lies they have been taught. Revelation 14 and 18 speaks of a loud cry that will go out into the entire earth. This cry will bring to light the true character of the Catholic Church. At this time, those who desire to come out of Babylon will be counted as children of God and will receive His seal. Those who stubbornly remain will receive the mark of the beast and all that follows.

"Let no one deceive you by any means; for that Day will not come unless the falling away comes first, and the man of sin is revealed, the son of perdition, 4who opposes and exalts himself above all that is called God or that is worshiped, so that he sits as God in the temple of God, showing himself that he is God" (2 Thessalonians 2:3, 4).

Babylon shocked John. Babylon is a mother. Babylon has daughters that follow after her.

Christians should examine their positions and beliefs to see if in any faith or practice they are guilty of any connection with the great city of confusion—Babylon.

"And I heard another voice from heaven saying, 'Come out of her, my people, lest you share in her sins, and lest you receive of her plagues. 5For her sins have reached to heaven, and God has remembered her iniquities'" (Revelation 18:4, 5).

If you examine your life and discover some practice or pillar of your faith is built upon a lie, or a false doctrine or tradition of man—separate yourself at once.

The signs are rapidly being fulfilled. The mark of the beast has not yet been given. Time permits everyone to make a fearful and trembling searching of his or her own standing. There will only be two classes that will exist at the End of Time: Those totally following the Commandments of God, and those who reject God's laws and decide to follow self, tradition, or the scarlet woman—Babylon.

Do not think that the little horn—the papacy will not return to its strength that it once carried. It is a prophetic Word of God, and it will come true.

Who is Babylon the Great?

Do not think that the mainstream Christian Protestants are free from error. When Rome had the power, she destroyed vast multitudes of those whom she declared heretics. Her protestant daughters have shown this same persecuting spirit. Witness the burning of Michael Servetus by the Protestants of Geneva with John Calvin at their head. Witness the long continued oppression of dissenters by the Church of England. Witness the hangings performed by the Quakers and the whippings at the hands of the Baptists, even the Puritan fathers of New England who themselves were fugitives from the oppression of the Church. Some may try to argue that these things are in the past, but they show evidence that when people who are governed by strong religious prejudice have the power to coerce dissenters, they will do so.

Are you living in Babylon?

The Scarlett woman is Babylon. She is the religious entities of the world united in apostasy against the true God of Heaven.

The scarlet beast is the political nations of the world uniting allowing the religious woman to control them and shape policy.

Are you claiming to be a Christian, but in practice, deed, and worship really worshiping a false set of beliefs? Your only guide of truth is the simple and plain Word of God—the Bible.

The End of Time
Revelation 19, 20

Evil first appeared in the heart of Lucifer, a created angel (Ezekiel 28:15). Why did evil arise? This is a difficult question to answer, but central to any answer is the fact that God created freedom. True freedom requires the option of doing wrong. Satan, Lucifer's fallen name, harbored pride; he felt that he could run the universe better than God—desiring to set up a throne above God's (Isaiah 14:13).

Satan claims that God is unjust, unfair, and is a tyrant who demands love and obedience. This is the heart of the great controversy between Satan and God. Satan has brought charges against God. Satan is condemning God. God, in His infinite wisdom and mercy, is allowing this great controversy to play out in a manner that will resolve all questions about His self-denial, goodness, justice, love and law.

God's method of solving the great controversy and the charges brought against Him are symbolized in the Old Testament sanctuary service and are detailed throughout prophecy. The details on how God will end this drama actually begin back in Daniel.

John Compliments Daniel's Outline

The prophecies, in Daniel, outlined events that would transpire from the life of Daniel (604BC) until the kingdom of Christ (yet future!). Daniel chapter 7 includes a detailed outline that is continued by John in Revelation chapter 19.

Daniel 7 Outline

Daniel 7:1-7	Four beasts represent four kingdoms. *(Babylon, Medes/Persians, Greece, Rome)*
Daniel 7:8	The little horn develops out of Rome.
Daniel 7:9,10	The court room is set in heaven and books are opened.
Daniel 7:11,12	The little horn is slain, *"given to the burning flame."*
Daniel 7:13,14	Christ receives His Kingdom, and then His saints.

End of Time Prophecies

"After these things I heard a loud voice of a great multitude in heaven, saying, 'Alleluia! Salvation and glory and honor and power belong to the Lord our God! ₂For true and righteous are His judgments, because He has judged the great harlot who corrupted the earth with her fornication; and He has avenged on her the blood of His servants shed by her.' ₃Again they said, 'Alleluia! Her smoke rises up forever and ever!' ₄And the twenty-four elders and the four living creatures fell down and worshiped God who sat on the throne, saying, 'Amen! Alleluia!' ₅Then a voice came from the throne, saying, 'Praise our God, all you His servants and those who fear Him, both small and great!'" (Revelation 19:1-5).

Notice the language used regarding the judgment. It is past tense. Revelation 19 picks up after the court room is setup in heaven and after the judgment is complete.

"And I heard, as it were, the voice of a great multitude, as the sound of many waters and as the sound of mighty thunderings, saying, 'Alleluia! For the Lord God Omnipotent reigns! ₇Let us be glad and rejoice and give Him glory, for the marriage of the Lamb has come, and His wife has made herself ready.' ₈And to her it was granted to be arrayed in fine linen, clean and bright, for the fine linen is the righteous acts of the saints. ₉Then he said to me, 'Write: "Blessed are those who are called to the marriage supper of the Lamb!"' And he said to me, 'These are the true sayings of God'" (Revelation 19:6-9).

Who is the Lamb?

The Son of Man— Jesus.

Who is His Bride?

Careful to answer too quickly! His Bride is the New Jerusalem.

The New Jerusalem is *"prepared as a bride adorned for her husband"* (Revelation 21:2). We are the guests called to the marriage feast.

The Marriage of Christ

Christ described the marriage feast with a parable, recorded in Matthew 22:1-14. Many were called to the wedding feast, but only a few were chosen. Only those who heeded the call and wore the freely given wedding garment were allowed to join the wedding feast. Every guest is provided a free wedding garment; it is a gift from the King. By wearing it, the guests show their respect for the King. Refusal to wear the gift insults the King and makes us unfit for the wedding feast. The garment is a symbol of the pure, spotless character that true followers of Christ will possess. Revelation 19:8 describes this as "*the righteous acts of the saints*." Only the covering which Christ provides can make us ready to appear in the presence of God. "*See, I have removed your iniquity from you, and I will clothe you with rich robes*" (Zechariah 3:4). Those found wearing the wedding garments will have their names written in the Lamb's book of life.

"Now I saw heaven opened, and behold, a white horse. And He who sat on him was called Faithful and True, and in righteousness He judges and makes war. 12His eyes were like a flame of fire, and on His head were many crowns. He had a name written that no one knew except Himself. 13He was clothed with a robe dipped in blood, and His name is called The Word of God. 14And the armies in heaven, clothed in fine linen, white and clean, followed Him on white horses. 15Now out of His mouth goes a sharp sword, that with it He should strike the nations. And He Himself will rule them with a rod of iron. He Himself treads the winepress of the fierceness and wrath of Almighty God. 16And He has on His robe and on His thigh a name written: KING OF KINGS AND LORD OF LORDS" (Revelation 19:11-16).

Christ's role as High Priest, as Judge, and Mediator is complete. Daniel 12:1 says, "*At that time Michael shall stand up.*" At that time Christ removes His priestly garments and takes on the role of King of Kings. He has a kingdom. He has guests waiting for the marriage supper. All that remains is to collect His saints and rid the world of sin— forever.

Now, in Revelation 19, is the second coming of Christ.

"For the Lord Himself will descend from heaven with a shout, with the voice of an archangel, and with the trumpet of God. And the dead in Christ will rise first. 17Then we who are alive and remain shall be caught up together with them in the clouds to meet the Lord in the air. And thus we shall always be with the Lord. 18Therefore comfort one another with these words" (1 Thessalonians 4:16-18).

A Lake of Refining Fire

"And I saw the beast, the kings of the earth, and their armies, gathered together to make war against Him who sat on the horse and against His army. 20Then the beast was captured, and with him the false prophet who worked signs in his presence, by which he deceived those who received the mark of the beast and those who worshiped his image. These two were cast

End of Time Prophecies

alive into the lake of fire burning with brimstone. 21And the rest were killed with the sword which proceeded from the mouth of Him who sat on the horse. And all the birds were filled with their flesh" (Revelation 19:19-21).

The little horn (Babylon of Revelation 18) is slain and "*cast alive into the lake of fire.*"

"The lake of fire" This, as mentioned in verse 20, is most likely a foreshadow of the true lake of fire— the fires of hell— that will one day purge the heavens and the earth of sin (1 Peter 3:10; see the chapter: "Hell and Death").

The beast (little horn) and the false prophet are concepts and entities of belief more than they are individuals. How do you burn a concept? Reading Revelation 18:8, that Babylon "*will be utterly burned with fire,*" makes it appear that the fire mentioned at this time is more figurative than literal.

Fire is often used in describing the presence of God. Fire has been used as a symbol of God's judgment. Christ Himself claimed that He "*came to send fire on earth.*" "*Do not think that I came to bring peace on earth. I did not come to bring peace but a sword*" (Luke 12:49; Matthew 10:34). The fire of God is a refiners fire, one that purges the dross or impurities from our lives. Zechariah 13:9 tells us that God "*will refine them [saints] as silver is refined, and test them as gold is tested. They [the saints] will call on My name, and I will answer them. I will say 'This is My people' and each one will say, 'The Lord is my God.'*"

Ezekiel 20:38 and Isaiah 1:25, respectfully, add "*I will purge the rebels from among you.*" "*And thoroughly purge away your dross, and take away all your alloy.*"

Daniel 7:11 and 11:45 show that the little horn will come to his end and will cease to exist as a world controlling power. This is prior to the appearance of Christ in the clouds. Revelation 17:16,17 says that the merchants and the nations of the earth (the ten horns) that once supported her, (Babylon, the harlot, beast, and the little horn are all one and the same) will hate the harlot, make her desolate and naked, eat her flesh, and burn her with fire. *"For God has put it into their hearts to fulfill His purpose."*

This fire tests the character of the false prophet and the beast. This fire proves that they were full of lies and deceit. It is revealed to the whole world that these two entities do not reflect the true character of Christ. They are consumed— that is they cease to exist.

Satan Bound for a Millennium

"Then I saw an angel coming down from heaven, having the key to the bottomless pit and a great chain in his hand. ₂He laid hold of the dragon, that serpent of old, who is the Devil and Satan, and bound him for a thousand years; ₃and he cast him into the bottomless pit, and shut him up, and set a seal on him, so that he should deceive the nations no more till the thousand years were finished. But after these things he must be released for a little while" (Revelation 20:1-3).

The binding of Satan occurs at the end of the atonement process. Christ finished His work, mediating before God. In the Old Testament, when the high priest exited the tabernacle from his work on the Day of Atonement, he would place his hands upon the head of a scapegoat.

"Aaron [the high priest] shall lay both his hands on the head of the live goat, confess over it all the iniquities of the children of Israel, and all their transgressions, concerning all their sins, putting them on the head of the goat, and shall send it away into the wilderness by the hand of a suitable man. ₂₂The goat shall bear on itself all their iniquities to an uninhabited land; and he shall release the goat in the wilderness" (Leviticus 16:21,22).

In a similar manner Christ, our High Priest, will declare to the congregation of the universe that Satan is guilty of all the evil which he caused. Satan will be banished, like the scapegoat, into an empty wilderness.

How is the devil bound?

The word *"bound"* has several connotations within scripture. It can be in a physical sense, like with ropes (Judges 16:6,7), or chains (Mark 5:3). It can be a reference to the curse of sin or of a demonic influence (Luke 13:16). It is even used to connote marriage (1 Corinthians 7:27), or an agreement (Romans 7:2). To understand what sort of binding is placed upon the devil, we must look at the context surrounding its use.

End of Time Prophecies

Where is Satan cast?

Into the bottomless pit.

Abyssos is the Greek word, which the translators write "bottomless pit," or the "deep." The Greek translators of the Septuagint used the word *abyssos* when describing the condition of the earth prior to creation: *"The earth was without form, and void; and darkness was on the face of the deep [abyssos]. And the Spirit of God was hovering over the face of the waters" (Genesis 1:2)*. *Abyssos* appears to describe a place of darkness or secrecy; something that is controlled by mysterious or unknown powers. Psalm 36:3 states that God's judgments are a great deep [*abyssos*].

The bottomless pit appears to be a place of chaos and not of order. It is something that is mysterious and difficult to explain.

Romans 10:7 records: *"who will descend into the abyss?"* The word *abyss*, in this text, might mean the grave (*hades*) or hell (*geenna*), but neither of these Greek words were used! The abyss is truly a mystery. Luke 8:30, 31 records a story where a legion of demons (angels cast out of heaven) beg Christ that He would not command them to go into the abyss. Again, the Greek words *hades* (grave*)*, and *geenna (*hell*)* were not used in this situation.

Revelation and Jude shed light on the abyss. Satan, once a *"covering cherub"* in heaven (Ezekiel 28:16), was cast to the earth, along with a third of the angels who followed him (Revelation 12:4,9). Jude 6 tells us that God has reserved these angels (Lucifer included) under chains of *"darkness for the judgment of the great day."*

The abyss, though mysterious in many ways, appears to be the earth in chaotic form. Christ was buried in a tomb under the earth. The devil and his angels were cast to the earth, reserved for judgment. The earth, prior to becoming organized through creation, was a place of chaos and mystery.

From the context and supporting scriptures, it is plain to see that the binding of the devil describes a time when he is limited or bound to

The End of Time

the wasteland that is then the earth. Satan's binding occurs after the earth has been turned upside down by the last plagues. John echoes the prophets, Jeremiah 46:10 and Ezekiel 39:17-20, when he describes the condition of the earth at the time that Satan is bound. He will have no one to tempt, annoy, or control; for the saints have just been gathered to meet Christ in the air (1 Thessalonians 4:17), and the rest, the wicked, were all slain by the brightness of His coming (Revelation 19:21), and have become a feast for the birds of the air.

The Saints in Heaven for a Millennium

"And I saw thrones, and they sat on them, and judgment was committed to them. Then I saw the souls of those who had been beheaded for their witness to Jesus and for the Word of God, who had not worshiped the beast or his image, and had not received his mark on their foreheads or on their hands. And they lived and reigned with Christ for a thousand years. ₅But the rest of the dead did not live again until the thousand years were finished. This is the first resurrection" (Revelation 20:4,5).

Judgment has several phases: trial, sentencing, appeals and execution of judgment. The trial phase began in heaven in AD1844.

When Christ returns in the air and collects His saints, the sentencing phase will be witnessed. All who are gathered into the clouds are acquitted of their sins— saved by grace through faith in Jesus Christ. Those who remain behind are found guilty of sin and are killed. This is the first death.

The execution of judgment will come at the end of the millennium when the wicked, along with Satan and his angels, will experience the fires of hell— dying the second and final death.

During the millennium, the saints have judgment *"committed to them"* The saints will have the opportunity to judge God's actions. The saints will be able to view every life and see if God's sentencing is fair. The saints will review the lives of the lost, seeing for themselves the love they spurned, and the many pleas of mercy that God presented before them. The saints will be involved in meting out the exact level of punishment due to each of the lost (Jeremiah 32:19; 2 Corinthians 5:10).

End of Time Prophecies

Hell is not an eternal place. It will exist for a moment in time. The end result will be eternal destruction— eternal separation from God— eternal death. The flames of hell will extinguish some in an instant, as if they never even existed (Isaiah 41:11). Others will suffer longer, depending on the works of evil that they have committed. Satan, the father of sin, will suffer the longest, but the Lord's *"anger is but for a moment"* (Psalm 30:5). *"For yet a very little while and the indignation will cease, as will My anger in their destruction"* (Isaiah 10:25).

Hell is discussed further in its own chapter: "Hell and Death."

"Blessed and holy is he who has part in the first resurrection. Over such the second death has no power, but they shall be priests of God and of Christ, and shall reign with Him a thousand years. ₇Now when the thousand years have expired, Satan will be released from his prison ₈and will go out to deceive the nations which are in the four corners of the earth, Gog and Magog, to gather them together to battle, whose number is as the sand of the sea. ₉They went up on the breadth of the earth and surrounded the camp of the saints and the beloved city. And fire came down from God out of heaven and devoured them." (Revelation 20: 6-9)

What happens when the thousand years have expired?

"Satan will be released from his prison" (Verse 7).

Who does Satan then deceive?

The nations of the earth (Verse 8).

What is the camp of the saints?

"The beloved city." The New Jerusalem (Verse 9).

The nations were destroyed, but according to John 5:28,29 there will be another resurrection, this one, a resurrection of condemnation. At the end of the Millennium Jesus Christ will return to the bottomless pit, the earth that was in turmoil due to the plagues, and will execute judgment— punishment and eternal death for the wicked.

Jesus Returns to the Earth

"And in that day His feet will stand on the Mount of Olives, Which faces Jerusalem on the east. And the Mount of Olives shall be split in two, From east to west, Making a very large valley; Half of the mountain shall move toward the

north And half of it toward the south. ₅Then you shall flee through My mountain valley, For the mountain valley shall reach to Azal. Yes, you shall flee As you fled from the earthquake In the days of Uzziah king of Judah. Thus the LORD my God will come, And all the saints with You" (Zechariah 14:4,5).*

Jesus Christ returns to earth with His saints and their mansions in the New Jerusalem. At this time the wicked dead are raised to life. The wicked exist as they did prior to the millennium. Satan is now loosed, he has people to deceive and nations to control.

Execution of the Judgment

"They went up on the breadth of the earth and surrounded the camp of the saints and the beloved city" (Revelation 20:9).

The saints have descended with God inside of the New Jerusalem city. At this moment, every human who ever lived are brought together, some are inside the city, and others are outside. Now is the statement of Revelation 1:7: *"Behold, He is coming with clouds, and every eye will see Him, even they who pierced Him. And all the tribes of the earth will mourn because of Him. Even so, Amen."*

Satan seeing another opportunity to win the war marshals the vast host who are outside the city. He is determined not to yield. Together the wicked throng and Satan's angels descend upon the camp of the saints. This is the last battle.

"Then I saw a great white throne and Him who sat on it, from whose face the earth and the heaven fled away. And there was found no place for them. ₁₂And I saw the dead, small and great, standing before God, and books were opened. And another book was opened, which is the Book of Life. And the dead were judged according to their works, by the things which were written in the books. ₁₃The sea gave up the dead who were in it, and Death and Hades delivered up the dead who were in them. And they were judged, each one according to his works" (Revelation 20:11-13).

Christ now appears on a great white throne. Every eye, both redeemed and lost, becomes fixed upon the Savior. The wicked are painfully conscious of every sin which they have committed. They see just where their feet diverged from the path of purity and holiness. All behold the enormity of their guilt. *"For it is written: 'As I live, says the LORD, Every knee shall bow to Me, And every tongue shall confess to God.' ₁₂So then each of us shall give account of himself to God"* (Romans 14:11,12).

Satan's character remains unchanged. The spirit of rebellion again boils up within and he attempts to arouse his subjects back to battle. The wicked are filled with anger but seeing their case is hopeless they turn their rage against Satan.

"Because you have set your heart as the heart of a god, ₇Behold, therefore, I will bring strangers against you, The most terrible of the nations; And they shall draw their swords against the beauty of your wisdom, And defile your splendor. ₈They shall throw you down into the Pit, And you shall die the death of the slain In the midst of the seas" (Ezekiel 28:6-8).

Satan and the wicked will receive their final punishment. Every knee will acknowledge that Jesus is God. If their punishment were to be stayed they would be like Judas, repenting because of the punishment and not because they desire to follow, obey, and honor God.

"Then Death and Hades were cast into the lake of fire. This is the second death. ₁₅And anyone not found written in the Book of Life was cast into the lake of fire" (Revelation 20:14,15).

"Then the beast was captured, and with him the false prophet who worked signs in his presence, by which he deceived those who received the mark of the beast and those who worshiped his image. These two were cast alive into the lake of fire burning with brimstone" (Revelation 19:20).

Here is the second death. The judgment sentence is served.

"Upon the wicked He will rain coals; Fire and brimstone and a burning wind Shall be the portion of their cup" (Psalm 11:6).

"But the day of the Lord will come as a thief in the night, in which the heavens will pass away with a great noise, and the elements will melt with fervent heat; both the earth and the works that are in it will be burned up" (2 Peter 3:10).

Fire comes down from God out of the heavens and proceeds to burn up the wicked, their leader Satan and the entire cursed heavens and earth. The wicked receive their recompense in the earth. In the cleansing flames, the wicked are at last destroyed—forever. The earth is purified and every trace of the curse is swept away.

The End of Time Outline

The Little Horn Appears.
(Revelation 13:1-10; Matthew 24:9-12)

The False Prophet Appears.
(Revelation 13:11-18)

The Little Horn's Wound is Healed.
(Revelation 13:3; Daniel 8:25)

The King of the South Attacks the King of the North.
(Daniel 11:40)

The King of the North Attacks the King of the South with Chariots, Horsemen and Many Ships.
(Daniel 11:40-44)

Satan Impersonates Christ.
(Matthew 24:11,12,23-27; Revelation 16:13-16; 2 Thessalonians 2:3-9)

The Last Angel Sounds Its Message of Warning to the World.
(Revelation 18:1-4; Revelation 14:9,10; Matthew 24:14; Joel 2:23,24)

**The Mark of the Beast is Created.
A Mount Carmel Experience Forces all to Choose God or the Mark.**
(Revelation 13:3,4,15-17; Isaiah 56:1-5; Matthew 24:15-27; Daniel 11:45)

The Scarlet Beast is Formed and Rules with Babylon 15 days.
(Revelation 17:11-13; Revelation 13:4,7,8)

The World Makes War with the Lamb and His Children.
(Revelation 17:14; Matthew 24:9,10)

Probation Closes; He Who is Unjust, Let Him Be Unjust Still; He Who is Righteous, Let Him Be Righteous Still.
(Revelation 22:11)

The Little Horn Falls as a Result of its Plagues.
(Revelation 18:7,8; Daniel 11:45; Revelation 16:2-20; Revelation 14:9,10; Psalm 91:3-10; Isaiah 33:16; Isaiah 41:17; Psalm 121:5-7)

The Time of Trouble.
(Matthew 24:16-22; Acts 14:22; Daniel 12:1; Revelation 3:10; 2 Timothy 3:12; John 16:33; Romans 5:3-5; 2 Thessalonians 1:4,5; Psalm 91)

It Is Done! Is Announced from Heaven.
(Revelation 16:17)

A Great Earthquake. Islands and mountains move out of place.
(Revelation 16:17-20; Isaiah 13; Zephaniah 1:14-18; Revelation 6:14-16)

Jesus Christ Returns in the Clouds Above.
(1 Thessalonians 4:16,17; Matthew 24:30; Acts 1:11;
2 Thessalonians 2:9; Titus 2:12,13; Revelation chapter19)

The Saints Are Gathered to be with Christ. The First Resurrection.
(Daniel 12:2; John 5:28,29; Matthew 26:64; Revelation 1:7;
1 Thessalonians 4:16,17; Jeremiah 25:33; Matthew 13:39-42)

Hail and the Brightness of Christ Destroys the Wicked.
(Revelation 19:21; Revelation 16:21; Jeremiah 25:33; Ezekiel 39:17-22;
Zechariah 14:12,13; 2 Thessalonians 2:8; Isaiah 28:17;
Isaiah 30:30; 1 Corinthians 15:52)

Satan Bound to a Desolate and Empty Earth– The Bottomless Pit.
(Revelation 20:2; Genesis 1:1)

Saints Spend the Millennium in Heaven Reviewing God's Judgment.
(Revelation 20:4; 1 Corinthians 4:5; Daniel 7:22; Revelation 15:2,3)

The New Jerusalem with the Saints Return to the Earth.
(Revelation 21:2; Revelation 20:7-9)

The Resurrection of Condemnation. The Wicked are Raised.
(John 5:28,29; Revelation 21:2; Revelation 20:7-9; Isaiah 24:22;
Revelation 14:20; Zechariah 14:4,5,9)

Every Knee Bows Before Jesus Christ Claiming That He is Lord God.
(Isaiah 45:20-25)

Judgment via the Lake Of Fire (Hell) is Meted Out to the Wicked, and to Satan. All Burn until they Exist No More.
(2 Peter 3:10-13; Revelation 20:14,15; Revelation 14:18-20;
1 Corinthians 15:26; Revelation 22:5; Malachi 4:1; Isaiah 34:8)

The Saints Live in a Universe Free from Sin— Forever.
(Revelation ch.21, 22; Isaiah 65:17-25; Isaiah 14:7; Psalm 37:29)

A Time-line for the End of Time
The Prophecy of the Future

Prophecy is designed to be trusted only when one of two events occur: 1) God explicitly reveals the exact answer, or 2) History has passed and the prophecy was true.

Creating an outline of future prophetic events must be met with skepticism and caution. Having said this, the Bible does reveal a lot of clues that can assist in the creation of a proper outline.

The book of Daniel is a prophetic book, one that gives us foreknowledge of events that will take place during the End of Time. In some instances, God revealed the exact answers to the symbols, in other instances we had to wait for history to transpire before we could unlock the mysteries within Daniel.

The book of Revelation is just that, it is a book that reveals or uncovers. It reveals who Jesus Christ is and what His work encompasses, but it reveals more of Daniel's closed book. Revelation 5 reveals that Jesus Christ is able to unlock the closed book. John was privileged to hear this revelation and he shared most of it with us.

The time-lines of Daniel have all concluded; that is, there are no more periods of time like the 2300 days, 1260 years, or 3 ½ years mentioned in the Bible, all have been fulfilled. However, the prophecies are not yet complete. We still live in a world of sin and Michael— Jesus Christ our Prince, has not yet stood up and delivered *"everyone who is found written in the book [of life]"* (Daniel 12:1).

Revelation confirms that all of the set time-lines are to be *"no more."* The seven thunders (Revelation 10:1-6), told us that there would be no more time-lines with set dates. Daniel's 2300 days (Daniel 8), which includes the 1335, 1290 and 1260 time-lines, concluded in AD1844. After this point in history, there would be no more time-lines given for man to follow; this marked the beginning of the End of Time.

End of Time Prophecies

Though the time-lines have concluded, and though we are not yet free from sin, Jesus did not leave us without clues regarding the events that would transpire at the End of Time. His disciples, desiring to know what the End of Time would look like asked:

"Tell us, when will these things be? And what will be the sign of Your coming, and of the end of the age?" (Matthew 24:3).

Christ left clues to the Christians in Jerusalem so they could escape to the mountains in AD70 when they saw the proper signs. God has left us clues about these last day events.

"Many shall be purified, made white, and refined, but the wicked shall do wickedly; and none of the wicked shall understand, but the wise shall understand" (Daniel 12:10).

The *"wise shall understand."* There are several passages throughout the scriptures that provide a consecutive list of events that will transpire at the End of Time: Daniel 11:40-45; Revelation 13; Matthew 24; Revelation 16; Revelation 6:12-16; Revelation 17:11-16; Revelation 18. The first three passages are the primary ones used to create the following outline of the End of Time.

Revelation, by its very name, reveals. The book of Daniel, a prophetic book, foretells the future. Because prophecy is an outline of events that will transpire it will be the framework by which the outline of the End of Time events will be done. Daniel 11:40-45 lists events that have not yet transpired. Using these prophetic events and looking for parallel concepts, terms and references, it is possible to get an outline of the events that will transpire as we near the End of Time.

What follows is an outline of these final events. Many of these events are not simple pinpoints in time, some happen simultaneously and others develop over time.

Bold headings are solid foundations, meaning they will occur before Christ returns in the clouds for His saints. There are no times given between headings (except the possibility of the 1 hour rule of the kings). Each heading may occur rapidly within hours, days or months. What is guaranteed is that every event, every text listed must occur before the Son of God appears in the clouds above.

The Little Horn Appears

"Then I stood on the sand of the sea. And I saw a beast rising up out of the sea, having seven heads and ten horns, and on his horns ten crowns, and on his heads a blasphemous name" (Revelation 13:1).

This began in AD538.

"Now the beast which I saw was like a leopard, his feet were like the feet of a bear, and his mouth like the mouth of a lion" (Revelation 13:2).

"The dragon gave him his power, his throne, and great authority" (Revelation 13:2).

The dragon is Satan from Revelation 12:9.

The beast is papal Rome; it ruled from AD538 – 1798.

Matthew 24 is a multipurpose outline of prophetic events. Christ used the same words to describe three periods that His followers would experience. First Christ's words accurately described the events of the early Christians leading up to the destruction of Jerusalem in AD70. His words then gave warning and strength to the Christian church as they endured the atrocities performed at the hands of a church who had rule over the civil authorities called the little horn, from AD538 – 1798. These same words of Christ will be a comfort and a guide to Christians living in the last days.

"Then they will deliver you up to tribulation and kill you, and you will be hated by all nations for My name's sake. 10And then many will be offended, will betray one another, and will hate one another. 11Then many false prophets will rise up and deceive many. 12And because lawlessness will abound, the love of many will grow cold" (Matthew 24:9-12).

Revelation 13, like Matthew 24, describes the history of the beast (the little horn) both in its 1260 year rule (AD538-AD1798) and once its wound is fully healed at the End of Time.

"And I saw one of his heads as if it had been mortally wounded, and his deadly wound was healed. And all the world marveled and followed the beast. 4So they worshiped the dragon who gave authority to the beast; and they worshiped the beast, saying, "Who is like the beast? Who is able to

End of Time Prophecies

make war with him?" ₅*And he was given a mouth speaking great things and blasphemies, and he was given authority to continue for fortytwo months.* ₆*Then he opened his mouth in blasphemy against God, to blaspheme His name, His tabernacle, and those who dwell in heaven" (Revelation 13:3-6).*

"**Mortally wounded**" The deadly wound was issued in AD1798 when the pope was taken prisoner and lost power and authority over the civil powers of the world.

"**Fortytwo months**" This is the period of "authority" that the little horn was given to rule. 42 months = 1260 days = 3 ½ years. Prophetically this time is 1260 years.

The False Prophet Appears

"Then I saw another beast coming up out of the earth" (Revelation 13:11).

Here is a description of the United States of America who gained independence in AD1776, near the time that the sea beast (the little horn) lost its power. The U.S. developed in a part of the world that did not have the developed nations, and peoples of the world—designated as waters, but it developed in the wilds of America—the earth.

"And he had two horns like a lamb" (Revelation 13:11). The **Nation of America** began as a lamb, but will begin to speak and act like a dragon. *"And spoke like a dragon" (Revelation 13:11).*

"He performs great signs, so that he even makes fire come down from heaven on the earth in the sight of men" (Revelation 13:13).

If this fire is a reference to literal fire it may be a description of the atomic bombs used by the United States in sight of the world. The first successful explosion of an atomic bomb was in 1942. Three years later, two were dropped on Japan ending World War II.

The Little Horn's Wound is Healed

"And I saw one of his heads as if it had been mortally wounded, and his deadly wound was healed" (Revelation 13:3).

The wound of the little horn, inflicted in AD1798, began to be healed in AD1929. In 1929 the Roman Catholic Church and the Italian government, under Benito Mussolini, signed the Lateran Treaty, which regularized relations between them and recognized an independent Vatican City under papal authority. The little horn's wound was healed; he had control over a civil authority, and soon would begin to reach out to the nations of the earth to regain the control it once enjoyed.

"And all the world marveled and followed the beast" (Revelation 13:3).

The papacy is gaining status among world leaders who have forgotten history during the dark ages. The world now marvels at the pope and soon will follow him wherever he leads.

King of the South Attacks the King of the North

"At the time of the end the king of the South shall attack him" (Daniel 11:40).

The king of the South is Islam. Daniel 11:25 foretold the rise of Islam, which began in AD629.

The king of the North is still papal Rome.

This attack will stir up the world having them ask: *"Who is like the beast? Who is able to make war with him?"* (Revelation 13:4).

"The beast that was, and is not, is himself also the eighth, and is of the seven, and is going to perdition" (Revelation 17:11).

This beast, composed of earthly nations, is not yet fully the scarlet beast (Revelation 17), because Babylon—the joint union of papal Rome and mainstream Christianity, does not yet control the nations of the earth. But the movement in this direction is clearly evident.

The King of the North Attacks the King of the South

"The king of the North shall come against him like a whirlwind, with chariots, horsemen, and with many ships" (Daniel 11:40).

The king of the North retaliates against the king of the South. The question stands: How can the papal king of the North come against Islam with chariots, horsemen and many ships of war? Vatican City is too small to attack Islam or any radical branch of it such as Isis or al-Qaeda all by itself.

End of Time Prophecies

"And I saw three unclean spirits like frogs coming out of the mouth of the dragon, out of the mouth of the beast, and out of the mouth of the false prophet. 14For they are spirits of demons, performing signs, which go out to the kings of the earth and of the whole world, to gather them to the battle of that great day of God Almighty" (Revelation 16:13,14).

The three unclean spirits are parallel to Revelation 18:2 coming from the dragon (devil), beast (papal Rome), and false prophet (U.S.A.). These spirits begin to work in uniting the nations of the earth together under a common cause. These spirits work throughout the End of Time and are not to be pinpointed to a specific time only.

Under this event, the nations of the world unite under a single cause, but their minds are still controlled by themselves. Soon, after this event, the nations of the earth will give their control, their mind, power, and authority totally over to the control and influence of the little horn (Revelation 17:13).

The false prophet (U.S.A.) will be seen as an integral part in uniting the nations of the world to the cause of defending the little horn, the king of the North. This is not a strange concept as the false prophet and the sea beast (papal Rome) have already united in history. Under President Reagan, they joined hands working together to remove the Communist wall. Recently President Obama joined hands with the pope as the U.S. reestablished ties with Cuba.

"And he [the false prophet] deceives those who dwell on the earth by those signs which he was granted to do in the sight of the beast, telling those who dwell on the earth to make an image to the beast who was wounded by the sword and lived" (Revelation 13:14).

Fighting to avenge the attack on the papacy, the nations of the earth will be asked to set up an image to the papacy. This image will be a unifying of Christian beliefs that mirror, or reflect the image of the papal church. Already there is a growing sentiment among the mainstream protestant churches that there should be a union based upon common points of doctrines. To secure such a union, any doctrine or subject in which not all are able to agree upon, must be ignored—even if it is contrary to Biblical truths.

A Time-line for the End of Time

This image is not yet a mandatory requirement of all the earth, but this will change thereby creating the mark of the beast.

"And he shall enter the countries, overwhelm them, and pass through" (Daniel 11:40).

The king of the South (Islam) is overwhelmed, and loses.

"He shall also enter the Glorious Land," (Daniel 11:41).

The little horn shall enter the glorious land. The glorious land is the land of Canaan, the Promised Land, the land of Jerusalem and surrounding lands.

"And many countries shall be overthrown; but these shall escape from his hand: Edom, Moab, and the prominent people of Ammon" (Daniel 11:41).

Islam loses. Those supporting Islam are destroyed. Those who once believed in Islam either follow the little horn and its ideologies or follow the God of the Bible.

"He shall stretch out his hand against the countries, and the land of Egypt shall not escape" (Daniel 11:42).

"He shall have power over the treasures of gold and silver, and over all the precious things of Egypt; also the Libyans and Ethiopians shall follow at his heels" (Daniel 11:43).

Satan Impersonates Christ

This occurs sometime before the mark of the beast is fully setup. This occurs before Michael stands up and the time of trouble.

"Then many false prophets will rise up and deceive many. $_{12}$And because lawlessness will abound, the love of many will grow cold" (Matthew 24:11,12).

"Then if anyone says to you, 'Look, here is the Christ!' or 'There!' do not believe it. $_{24}$For false christs and false prophets will rise and show great signs and wonders to deceive, if possible, even the elect. $_{25}$See, I have told you beforehand. $_{26}$Therefore if they say to you, 'Look, He is in the desert!' do not go out; or 'Look, He is in the inner rooms!' do not believe it" (Matthew 24:23-26).

End of Time Prophecies

At this time there will be two Gospels being proclaimed into the world.
1) The Gospel of Jesus Christ is supported by God the Father, Jesus the Messiah, and the Holy Spirit— the Holy Trinity.
2) The Gospel of deception looks a lot like the Biblical Gospel but this one includes errors and traditions of man, the most notable tradition being the worship of Sunday in place of the fourth commandments' seventh-day Sabbath— Saturday. This deceptive gospel is supported by the false trinity: the dragon (who will be impersonating as an angel of light), the beast (papal Rome) and the false prophet (U.S.A. and its allies).

The Last Message of Warning to the World

"And I heard another voice from heaven saying, 'Come out of her, my people, lest you share in her sins, and lest you receive of her plagues'" (Revelation 18:4).

This is the last warning, the third angel's message, given to the inhabitants of earth. Now is the last chance to choose God and His truth or be deceived following your own ideas or the ideas of men.

"For all the nations have drunk of the wine of the wrath of her fornication, the kings of the earth have committed fornication with her, and the merchants of the earth have become rich through the abundance of her luxury" (Revelation 18:3).

The Mark of the Beast is Created

"And he shall plant the tents of his palace between the seas and the glorious holy mountain;" (Daniel 11:45).

"Therefore when you see the 'abomination of desolation,' spoken of by Daniel the prophet, standing in the holy place (whoever reads, let him understand), 16then let those who are in Judea flee to the mountains. 17Let him who is on the housetop not go down to take anything out of his house. 18And let him who is in the field not go back to get his clothes. 19But woe to those who are pregnant and to those who are nursing babies in those days! 20And pray that your flight may not be in winter or on the Sabbath. 21For then there will be great tribulation, such as has not been since the beginning of the world until this time, no, nor ever shall be. 22And unless those days were shortened, no flesh would be saved; but for the elect's sake those days will be shortened" (Matthew 24:15-22).

Here is the Mount Carmel experience predicted in Revelation 16:16 as Armageddon. Mt. Carmel was chosen as the most conspicuous place to test God's people. Satan will repeat this event, possibly even calling down fire from the heavens to persuade the people of the earth to follow him.

"He was granted power to give breath to the image of the beast, that the image of the beast should both speak and cause as many as would not worship the image of the beast to be killed. 16He causes all, both small and great, rich and poor, free and slave, to receive a mark on their right hand or on their foreheads, 17and that no one may buy or sell except one who has the mark or the name of the beast, or the number of his name" (Revelation 13:15-17).

The mark is fully put into place. Anyone who honors the image to the beast— worshiping on the day selected by Babylon (the union of Christian churches with Catholicism), will receive the mark of the beast. It is interesting to note that the Christian churches were called Protestants because they once protested against the Catholic Church, but now they join hands compromising beliefs to create harmony and union.

"And I saw one of his heads as if it had been mortally wounded, and his deadly wound was healed. And all the world marveled and followed the beast. 4So they worshiped the dragon who gave authority to the beast; and they worshiped the beast, saying, 'Who is like the beast? Who is able to make war with him?'" (Revelation 13:3,4).

The Scarlet Beast is Formed

"The beast that was, and is not, is himself also the eighth, and is of the seven, and is going to perdition" (Revelation 17:11).

This beast is the Roman Catholic Church (the woman dressed in scarlet) united with mainstream Christianity riding the civil ten horned scarlet beast composed of the world's civil powers. The scarlet woman controls the beast.

"The ten horns which you saw are ten kings who have received no kingdom as yet, but they receive authority for one hour as kings with the beast. 13These are of one mind, and they will give their power and authority to the beast" (Revelation 17:12,13).

The ten horns represent the nations of the earth that give their power over to the papal beast.

End of Time Prophecies

"It was granted to him to make war with the saints and to overcome them. And authority was given him over every tribe, tongue, and nation. ₈All who dwell on the earth will worship him, whose names have not been written in the Book of Life of the Lamb slain from the foundation of the world" (Revelation 13:7,8).

"One hour with the beast" In prophetic timing this is 15 days. When the Mt. Carmel experience is over, the scarlet beast (the kings of the earth) will be under the control of Babylon (the combination of protestant Christianity with Roman Catholicism). I believe this begins an actual period of 15 days that the kings will rule with the little horn beast.

The World Makes War with the Lamb and His Children

"These will make war with the Lamb" (Revelation 17:14).

During this time, the remnant of God will be under duress.

"Then they will deliver you up to tribulation and kill you, and you will be hated by all nations for My name's sake. ₁₀And then many will be offended, will betray one another, and will hate one another" (Matthew 24:9,10).

The Little Horn Falls

"In the measure that she glorified herself and lived luxuriously, in the same measure give her torment and sorrow; for she says in her heart, 'I sit as queen, and am no widow, and will not see sorrow'" (Revelation 18:7).

I believe, like Nebuchadnezzar in Daniel 4 who boasted that he, on his own, made the nation of Babylon great, that when the little horn stands up to boast about her greatness, she will fall. This, I believe, occurs 15 days (one prophetic hour) after the mark of the beast is put into place and the kings of the earth, with one mind, have given their power over to the little horn— the sea beast. The fall of the little horn begins at the time of trouble and occurs over time.

"Yet he shall come to his end, and no one will help him" (Daniel 11:45).

The Time of Trouble

"Therefore her plagues will come in one day— death and mourning and famine" (Revelation 18:8).

A Time-line for the End of Time

"For then there will be great tribulation, such as has not been since the beginning of the world until this time, no, nor ever shall be. ₂₂And unless those days were shortened, no flesh would be saved; but for the elect's sake those days will be shortened" (Matthew 24:21, 22).

"At that time Michael shall stand up, The great prince who stands watch over the sons of your people; And there shall be a time of trouble, Such as never was since there was a nation, Even to that time. And at that time your people shall be delivered, Every one who is found written in the book" (Daniel 12:1).

The plagues, symbols of God's wrath, are not poured out while Jesus Christ, as High Priest, is still ministering in the Most Holy Place of the Heavenly Sanctuary.

Carrying over the idea that 1 hour is 15 literal days, I believe the plagues begin to fall exactly 15 days after the mark of the beast is fully enforced.

"One Day" Prophetically one literal year. *"And unless those days were shortened, no flesh would be saved; but for the elect's sake those days will be shortened"* (Matthew 24:22). The plagues are scheduled, in my opinion, to last one year, but God is a God of mercy and shortens the length of His wrath.

The plagues are poured out only on those who have the mark of the beast. These plagues are similar to the last seven of Egypt's ten plagues. The first three were poured out on the entire nation of Egypt, Israelites included, but the last seven were only poured out on all who did not honor and worship the God of Heaven.

Merchants Lose Money and Hate the Beast

"Then the fifth angel poured out his bowl on the throne of the beast, and his kingdom became full of darkness; and they gnawed their tongues because of the pain. ₁₁They blasphemed the God of heaven because of their pains and their sores, and did not repent of their deeds. ₁₂Then the sixth angel poured out his bowl on the great river Euphrates, and its water was dried up, so that the way of the kings from the east might be prepared" (Revelation 16:10-12).

"And the merchants of the earth will weep and mourn over her, for no one buys their merchandise anymore:" (Revelation 18:11).

End of Time Prophecies

"The fruit that your soul longed for has gone from you, and all the things which are rich and splendid have gone from you, and you shall find them no more at all" (Revelation 18:14).

Here is the central reason for Babylon's fall. They honored the riches of creation instead of the Creator. Their heart was on self, on pride, and not on the God of the universe.

"It is Done!" is Announced from Heaven

"Then the seventh angel poured out his bowl into the air, and a loud voice came out of the temple of heaven, from the throne, saying, 'It is done!'" (Revelation 16:17).

"When He opened the seventh seal, there was silence in heaven for about half an hour" (Revelation 8:1).

"**Half an hour**" This, in literal terms, is seven days. A possible explanation for this silence in heaven centers around the marriage festival and the seven days of travel that Jesus Christ, with his retinue of angels, will enjoy as they empty out heaven celebrating the Kingdom of Christ and His return to earth to gather His saints.

A Great Earthquake rocks the earth.

"I looked when He opened the sixth seal, and behold, there was a great earthquake; and the sun became black as sackcloth of hair, and the moon became like blood. 13And the stars of heaven fell to the earth, as a fig tree drops its late figs when it is shaken by a mighty wind. 14Then the sky receded as a scroll when it is rolled up, and every mountain and island was moved out of its place. 15And the kings of the earth, the great men, the rich men, the commanders, the mighty men, every slave and every free man, hid themselves in the caves and in the rocks of the mountains, 16and said to the mountains and rocks, 'Fall on us and hide us from the face of Him who sits on the throne and from the wrath of the Lamb! 17For the great day of His wrath has come, and who is able to stand?'" (Revelation 6:12-16).

Islands and Mountains move out of place.

"And there were noises and thunderings and lightnings; and there was a great earthquake, such a mighty and great earthquake as had not occurred since men were on the earth. 19Now the great city was divided into three parts, and the cities of the nations fell. And great Babylon was remembered before God, to give her the cup of the wine of the fierceness of His wrath. 20Then every island fled away, and the mountains were not found" (Revelation 16:18-20).

A Time-line for the End of Time

Jesus Christ Returns in the Clouds Above

"Then the sign of the Son of Man will appear in heaven, and then all the tribes of the earth will mourn, and they will see the Son of Man coming on the clouds of heaven with power and great glory" (Matthew 24:30).

Christ, at this time, does not touch the surface of the earth! It is only after the millennium that Christ and the New Jerusalem will touch the earth, landing on the Mount of Olives (Zechariah 14:4).

Hail and the Brightness of Christ Destroys the Wicked

"And great hail from heaven fell upon men, each hailstone about the weight of a talent. Men blasphemed God because of the plague of the hail, since that plague was exceedingly great" (Revelation 16:21).

Saints are gathered to be with Christ

"And He will send His angels with a great sound of a trumpet, and they will gather together His elect from the four winds, from one end of heaven to the other" (Matthew 24: 31).

"And at that time your people shall be delivered, Every one who is found written in the book. ₂And many of those who sleep in the dust of the earth shall awake, Some to everlasting life, Some to shame and everlasting contempt. ₃Those who are wise shall shine Like the brightness of the firmament, And those who turn many to righteousness Like the stars forever and ever" (Daniel 12:1-3).

The Millennium

"Then I saw an angel coming down from heaven, having the key to the bottomless pit and a great chain in his hand. ₂He laid hold of the dragon, that serpent of old, who is the Devil and Satan, and bound him for a thousand years; ₃and he cast him into the bottomless pit, and shut him up, and set a seal on him, so that he should deceive the nations no more till the thousand years were finished. But after these things he must be released for a little while" (Revelation 20:1-3).

Christ Returns with His Saints
The Great White Throne and the Judgment of the Wicked

"Then I saw a great white throne and Him who sat on it, from whose face the earth and the heaven fled away. And there was found no place for them" (Revelation 20:11).

End of Time Prophecies

"And in that day His feet will stand on the Mount of Olives, Which faces Jerusalem on the east. And the Mount of Olives shall be split in two, From east to west, Making a very large valley; Half of the mountain shall move toward the north And half of it toward the south. ₅Then you shall flee through My mountain valley, For the mountain valley shall reach to Azal. Yes, you shall flee As you fled from the earthquake In the days of Uzziah king of Judah. Thus the LORD my God will come, And all the saints with You" (Zechariah 14:4,5).

Hell and the Lake of Fire

"Now when the thousand years have expired, Satan will be released from his prison ₈and will go out to deceive the nations which are in the four corners of the earth, Gog and Magog, to gather them together to battle, whose number is as the sand of the sea. ₉They went up on the breadth of the earth and surrounded the camp of the saints and the beloved city. And fire came down from God out of heaven and devoured them. ₁₀The devil, who deceived them, was cast into the lake of fire and brimstone where the beast and the false prophet are. And they will be tormented day and night forever and ever" (Revelation 20:7-10).

"Then Death and Hades were cast into the lake of fire. This is the second death. ₁₅And anyone not found written in the Book of Life was cast into the lake of fire" (Revelation 20:14,15).

"But the day of the Lord will come as a thief in the night, in which the heavens will pass away with a great noise, and the elements will melt with fervent heat; both the earth and the works that are in it will be burned up" (2 Peter 3:10).

The New Jerusalem on Earth— Forever!

"Now I saw a new heaven and a new earth, for the first heaven and the first earth had passed away. Also there was no more sea. ₂Then I, John, saw the holy city, New Jerusalem, coming down out of heaven from God, prepared as a bride adorned for her husband" (Revelation 21:1,2).

"The wolf also shall dwell with the lamb, The leopard shall lie down with the young goat, The calf and the young lion and the fatling together; And a little child shall lead them. ₇The cow and the bear shall graze; Their young ones shall lie down together; And the lion shall eat straw like the ox. ₈The nursing child shall play by the cobra's hole, And the weaned child shall put his hand in the viper's den. ₉They shall not hurt nor destroy in all My holy mountain, For the earth shall be full of the knowledge of the LORD As the waters cover the sea" (Isaiah 11:6-9).

The Second Coming of Christ
The Gathering of His Saints

The gospel of Jesus Christ is the heart of Christianity. It is the hope that encouraged Adam and Eve after sin. It is the hope that propelled Moses through the wilderness, Daniel in the lion's den, and the disciples to believe in Jesus Christ. The gospel of Jesus Christ is the good news that Jesus Christ—God in human flesh, died for your sins, was buried paying the price for our sins, and rose again the third day (1 Corinthians 15:1-11). However, the gospel of Christ cannot end there, for if it does we are still doomed. Our hope is in the promise that Jesus gave to His listeners.

"Let not your heart be troubled; you believe in God, believe also in Me. 2In My Father's house are many mansions; if it were not so, I would have told you. I go to prepare a place for you. 3And if I go and prepare a place for you, I will come again and receive you to Myself; that where I am, there you may be also" (John 14:1-3).

Jesus spoke openly of his return, His second coming. The Bible is clear about the nature, timing, and events that will occur at His second coming. It is important that you study the method of His return so that you will not be deceived by Lucifer—the angel of light who will appear with signs and miracles that will be very real and very convincing.

Jesus Christ will return during the last plague. Do not be deceived by those who claim that some secret rapture of the saints will occur prior to this last plague. Christ's coming is not in secret.

"Now when He had spoken these things, while they watched, He was taken up, and a cloud received Him out of their sight. 10And while they looked steadfastly toward heaven as He went up, behold, two men stood by them in white apparel, 11who also said, 'Men of Galilee, why do you stand gazing up into heaven? This same Jesus, who was taken up from you into heaven, will so come in like manner as you saw Him go into heaven'" (Acts 1:9-11).

"Behold, He is coming with clouds, and every eye will see Him, even they who pierced Him. And all the tribes of the earth will mourn because of Him. Even so, Amen" (Revelation 1:7).

End of Time Prophecies

The Bible never states that the saints will enter heaven at death, or that there will be some secret rapture. The Bible is clear that those who have died, like Noah, Abraham, David, Sarah and others did not yet receive the promises of eternal life and a mansion in heaven. Jesus Christ promised that He would return personally, and gather His saints home (Hebrews 11: 13-16).

"But now Christ is risen from the dead, and has become the firstfruits of those who have fallen asleep. 21For since by man came death, by Man also came the resurrection of the dead. 22For as in Adam all die, even so in Christ all shall be made alive. 23But each one in his own order: Christ the firstfruits, afterward those who are Christ's at His coming" (1 Corinthians 15:20-23).

The Trumpet of God

"Behold, I tell you a mystery: We shall not all sleep, but we shall all be changed— 52in a moment, in the twinkling of an eye, at the last trumpet. For the trumpet will sound, and the dead will be raised incorruptible, and we shall be changed. 53For this corruptible must put on incorruption, and this mortal must put on immortality" (1 Corinthians 15:51-53).

"For this we say to you by the word of the Lord, that we who are alive and remain until the coming of the Lord will by no means precede those who are asleep. 16For the Lord Himself will descend from heaven with a shout, with the voice of an archangel, and with the trumpet of God. And the dead in Christ will rise first. 17Then we who are alive and remain shall be caught up together with them in the clouds to meet the Lord in the air. And thus we shall always be with the Lord" (1 Thessalonians 4:15-17).

The second coming is not a silent event. There is a trumpet, there is shouting and there is the voice of the Archangel who will call the sleeping saints—those who have died, to awake to everlasting life.

"Then the seventh angel poured out his bowl into the air, and a loud voice came out of the temple of heaven, from the throne, saying, 'It is done!'" (Revelation 16:17).

It is during this last plague upon the earth that Jesus will rescue His people. Prior to this rescue, Satan, using the nations of the earth under his control, will issue a decree that all who worship the true law of God will be destroyed. He will declare that all of these plagues are because of a select few who remain stubborn to his rule. The nations of the earth will conspire to root out this hated sect.

The Second Coming of Christ

It will be determined to strike in one night a decisive blow in an attempt to silence them. It is now, in the hour most dark that Jesus Christ will interpose for the deliverance of His chosen.[1]

"Weeping may endure for a night, But joy comes in the morning" (Psalm 30:5).

"For to everyone who has, more will be given, and he will have abundance; but from him who does not have, even what he has will be taken away. 30And cast the unprofitable servant into the outer darkness. There will be weeping and gnashing of teeth. 31When the Son of Man comes in His glory, and all the holy angels with Him, then He will sit on the throne of His glory" (Matthew 24:29-31).

"Since it is a righteous thing with God to repay with tribulation those who trouble you, 7and to give you who are troubled rest with us when the Lord Jesus is revealed from heaven with His mighty angels, 8in flaming fire taking vengeance on those who do not know God, and on those who do not obey the gospel of our Lord Jesus Christ" (2 Thessalonians 1:6-8).

"Now, brethren, concerning the coming of our Lord Jesus Christ and our gathering together to Him, we ask you, 2not to be soon shaken in mind or troubled, either by spirit or by word or by letter, as if from us, as though the day of Christ had come. 3Let no one deceive you by any means; for that Day will not come unless the falling away comes first, and the man of sin is revealed, the son of perdition." "And then the lawless one will be revealed, whom the Lord will consume with the breath of His mouth and destroy with the brightness of His coming" (2 Thessalonians 2:1-3, 8).

Jesus Christ appears in a cloud surrounded by thousands upon thousands of His angels. He calls to the saints, dead and alive, and they float up to meet Him in the air. Once all of the saints have been rescued, the wicked are destroyed by the brightness of His coming (2 Thessalonians 2:8) and by hail (Job 38:22,23; Isaiah 28:17; 30:30). The wicked are dead. They are left for the fowls of the air to feast upon.

"Then I saw an angel standing in the sun; and he cried with a loud voice, saying to all the birds that fly in the midst of heaven, 'Come and gather together for the supper of the great God, 18that you may eat the flesh of kings, the flesh of captains, the flesh of mighty men, the flesh of horses and of those who sit on them, and the flesh of all people, free and slave, both small and great'" (Revelation 19:17, 18).

---

1   White, *The Great Controversy*, 635.

End of Time Prophecies

"And the rest were killed with the sword which proceeded from the mouth of Him who sat on the horse. And all the birds were filled with their flesh" (Revelation 19:21).

"My heritage is to Me like a speckled vulture; The vultures all around are against her. Come, assemble all the beasts of the field, Bring them to devour!" (Jeremiah 12:9).

"And as for you, son of man, thus says the Lord GOD, 'Speak to every sort of bird and to every beast of the field: 'Assemble yourselves and come; Gather together from all sides to My sacrificial meal Which I am sacrificing for you, A great sacrificial meal on the mountains of Israel, That you may eat flesh and drink blood. 18You shall eat the flesh of the mighty, Drink the blood of the princes of the earth, Of rams and lambs, Of goats and bulls, All of them fatlings of Bashan. 19You shall eat fat till you are full, And drink blood till you are drunk, At My sacrificial meal Which I am sacrificing for you. 20You shall be filled at My table With horses and riders, With mighty men And with all the men of war," says the Lord GOD" (Ezekiel 39:17-20).

The first resurrection has been completed (John 5:28,29). The saints have all been harvested personally by Jesus Christ and are en route to God's home in heaven. Satan will be bound and cast into the bottomless pit for a thousand years— the millennium. The hope of the gospel message has come true. We are Saved! The blight of sin still remains, this will be cleansed during the fires of hell.

Evidence of Christ's Return
Visible
Every eye will see Christ return.
Matthew 24:27; Acts 1:11

Noise
Christ will appear with a shout and with the trump of God.
1 Thessalonians 4:16; Revelation 16:18

Air
Christ will meet His saints in the air;
He will not touch the ground at this time.
1 Thessalonians. 4:17

Clouds
Christ will be in the clouds with an army of angels.
Revelation 19:11-16; Luke 21:27

Hell and Death
The Biblical Truth

Hell and its related concept of death should be understood from a Biblical perspective and without any taint of human ideas, traditions or fantasies.

Death is the result of sin. Sin is disobeying God's Word. The first ever mention of death came from God's own words.

"And the LORD God commanded the man, saying, 'Of every tree of the garden you may freely eat; 17but of the tree of the knowledge of good and evil you shall not eat, for in the day that you eat of it you shall surely die'" (Genesis 2:16, 17).

God was speaking to His newly formed creatures. Adam was formed from the dust of the ground and God's breath of life (Genesis 2:7). Eve was formed of Adam's flesh and bones, specifically a rib bone that God used to form into a woman, an equal partner for Adam (Genesis 2:21).

God said *"If you sin, you will die."*

What does it mean to die?

The Bible requires no guessing, the answer is found from God's own words.

"So the LORD God said to the serpent: 'Because you have done this, You are cursed more than all cattle, And more than every beast of the field; On your belly you shall go, And you shall eat dust All the days of your life. 15And I will put enmity Between you and the woman, And between your seed and her Seed; He shall bruise your head, And you shall bruise His heel.' 16To the woman He said: 'I will greatly multiply your sorrow and your conception; In pain you shall bring forth children; Your desire shall be for your husband, And he shall rule over you.' 17Then to Adam He said, 'Because you have heeded the voice of your wife, and have eaten from the tree of which I commanded you, saying, You shall not eat of it: Cursed is the ground for your sake; In toil you shall eat of it All the days of your life. 18Both thorns and thistles it shall bring forth for you, And you shall eat the herb of the field. 19In the sweat of your face you shall eat bread Till you return to the ground, For out of it you were taken; For dust you are, And to dust you shall return'" (Genesis 3:14-19).

Death was a curse; it would change the face of creation forever, bringing about sorrow and pain. Death would ultimately be the end of life. Death is separation from God. Death occurs when you return to the dust of the ground from where you were created. To understand death we must understand life.

Life

What is life?

"And the LORD God formed man [of] the dust of the ground, and breathed into his nostrils the breath of life; and man became a living soul" (Genesis 2:7 KJV).

The formula for creating life.

Dust + God's Breath = A soul

God formed man from two items: Dust and His breath of life. Putting these two things together *then* man *became* a living soul. God did not put a living soul into man!

Many try to argue that God inserted a soul into man, but this is error. God did not use the formula: Dirt + Soul = Soul.

It is like making pancakes. The formula is: Flour + Water = Pancakes.

You don't take a pancake and add water or add flour to create a pancake. Dirt + God's Breath = Soul, a living being.

Understanding the two components needed to make a living soul helps us to understand death. If you remove the dirt, or the spark of life then the soul (the living being), does not exist.

The concept of a soul, according to the Bible, is simply the concept of a living being. Psalm 74:19 uses the word soul (*nepes*) when speaking about the life of a turtle dove. Humans and animals *are* souls. A soul is simply a living person, proved by the following texts.

A soul: can sin (Leviticus 4:2), touch (Leviticus 5:2), swear (Leviticus 5:4), eat (Leviticus 7:18), grow weary (Job 10:1), crave, be hungry, be empty (Isaiah 29:8), long, cling, melt from heaviness, and faint (Psalm 119), be cast down and dejected (Psalm 42:5, 11), be hungry and be satisfied (Psalm 107:9), can desire fruit (Micah 7:1).

Hell and Death

Common Biblical Words Describing Life

English	Hebrew	Definition
Dust	apar	refers to fine, dry dust.
Breathed	napah	to breath upon, to blow upon.
Nostril	ap	nose.
Breath	nesama	breath, blast of breath, life force.
Life	hay	state of living, life, lifetime.
Became	haya	to be, happen, change of state.
Soul	nepes	life, entire being.

Death

The doctrine of death is a simple one; it is the absence of life. In death there is no praising God (Psalm 115:17); there is no remembrance or thoughts (Psalm 6:5; 146:3, 4; Ecclesiastes 9:5); it is as though we are asleep (John 11:11-14; Daniel 12:2; Acts 7:60; 1 Thessalonians. 4:13, 14). There is no immortal soul that continues to live, thrive, or exist during death (1 Timothy 6:16; Romans 2:7; 1 Corinthians 15:51-54). Using the pancake example if you remove the flour you have boiling water; remove the water and you have burnt flour. Removing one item does not leave you with a pancake.

The concept that a soul exists outside of a body at death is Satan's greatest deception.

"Then the serpent said to the woman, 'You will not surely die. ₅For God knows that in the day you eat of it your eyes will be opened, and you will be like God, knowing good and evil'" (Genesis 3:4, 5).

Satan clearly is calling God a liar. Satan says you will not die, some part of you will continue to exist, furthermore you will be like God, for God is a spirit (John 4:24).

Those who teach that a soul returns to heaven or enters hell at death are following the greatest lie ever told. It would not be a stretch to

End of Time Prophecies

say that believing in an immortal soul is akin to believing, paying homage or even worshiping Satan instead of the Creator.

The concept that death is simply the absence of life is confirmed in the concepts of the two resurrections (John 5:29), and in the description of Christ's return with the last trumpet to raise the dead to life (1 Corinthians 15:52-55).

If we are souls living in heaven at death, what need would there be for a second coming of Christ? What purpose would the atonement process be; that of judging who are to be saved and who are not? Wouldn't the saved already be spirits or souls floating in heaven? Clearly, there is no part of us that remains at death. The Bible is clear.

The Biblical concept of death is simple and beautiful. In death there is no sorrow or pain. There is no torture, either physical or mental, where the deceased have to watch loved ones suffer through the trials of life.

"For what happens to the sons of men also happens to animals; one thing befalls them: as one dies, so dies the other. Surely, they all have one breath; man has no advantage over animals, for all is vanity. $_{20}$All go to one place: all are from the dust, and all return to dust" (Ecclesiastes 3:19,20).

This is the simple truth that God revealed to Adam and Eve prior to sin. This is called mortality. If our soul or spirit or any part of us were to continue to exist, it would be immortal— we would be like God. No one is immortal— this belongs only to God (1 Timothy 6:16).

The Jews and the authors of the New Testament were fully aware that at death nothing continued to exist. Peter preached, and Luke confirmed (Acts 2) that the patriarch David is both dead and buried and even after the resurrection and ascension of Jesus Christ, David had still not ascended into heaven.

Matthew (9:24) and John (11:11) both record death as a sleep and not a transformation into a spirit or a soul.

The author of Hebrews (I like to think it's Paul) summed it up best:

"These [the people of faith] all died in faith, not having received the promises, but having seen them afar off were assured of them, embraced them and confessed that they were strangers and pilgrims on the earth. 14For those who say such things declare plainly that they seek a homeland. 15And truly if they had called to mind that country from which they had come out, they would have had opportunity to return. 16But now they desire a better, that is, a heavenly country. Therefore God is not ashamed to be called their God, for He has prepared a city for them" (Hebrews 11:13-16).

The Reward of Christ

The list of God's faithful saints include such greats as Abel, Noah, Abraham, Sarah, Samson, Samuel, and many others. Every one mentioned has "obtained a good testimony through faith [But they] did not [yet] receive the promise [of eternal life.]" (Hebrews 11:39). The scriptures go on to say that God would not give them the reward of eternal life without us.

"For this we say to you by the word of the Lord, that we who are alive and remain until the coming of the Lord will by no means precede those who are asleep. 16For the Lord Himself will descend from heaven with a shout, with the voice of an archangel, and with the trumpet of God. And the dead in Christ will rise first. 17Then we who are alive and remain shall be caught up together with them in the clouds to meet the Lord in the air. And thus we shall always be with the Lord. 18Therefore comfort one another with these words" (1 Thessalonians 4:15-17).

"And behold, I am coming quickly, and My reward is with Me, to give to every one according to his work" (Revelation 22:12).

"For the Son of Man will come in the glory of His Father with His angels, and then He will reward each according to his works" (Matthew 16:27).

Nowhere in scripture is eternal life promised to be given prior to His second coming. Eternal life has been given to a select few: Enoch (Genesis 5:24) and Elijah (2 Kings 2:1-15), both saw eternal life without seeing death. Moses (Jude 9) and a select few (Matthew 27:52,53) were raised to life after their death. We know Moses is experiencing eternal life as he was seen with Elijah on the mountain top (Matthew 17:1-4). Elijah and Moses represent the promises of Christ. Some will die, like Moses, but if their hope rests in Jesus, they will be resurrected at His coming. Others— perhaps some reading this sentence, will experience the End of Time and will remain alive like Elijah and see their reward.

Jesus' reward of eternal life is with Him. He brings it with Him at His second coming. The devil has warped God's concept of death. Many today live a deceived life, believing that they will live forever— either in heaven or hell. This is a lie.

Hell

The concept of hell has been warped by traditions and fables of men who believe in a life spirit existing after death. The idea of a red devil carrying a pitchfork and living in a place of eternal flames, who is in control of torturing sinners, is a deception created by Satan. This view of hell supports the devil's first lie; "*You shall not die.*" Furthermore, it gives Satan a realm to rule allowing him to rule like God. This concept of hell, especially the eternal torment of sinners, leads men to believe that the Creator is a heartless and cruel God.

Where is hell? Does it exist today?

"Therefore as the tares are gathered and burned in the fire, so it will be at the end of this age. 41The Son of Man will send out His angels, and they will gather out of His kingdom all things that offend, and those who practice lawlessness, 42and will cast them into the furnace of fire. There will be wailing and gnashing of teeth" (Matthew 13:40-42).

The fires of hell will be at the End of Time. Hell does not exist today. The angels (2 Peter 2:4), the unjust (2 Peter 2:9), and the wicked dead (Revelation 20:5) are reserved for the day of judgment and destruction (Job 21:30,32; Jude 6).

"But the day of the Lord['s judgment] will come as a thief in the night, in which the heavens will pass away with a great noise, and the elements will melt with fervent heat; both the earth and the works that are in it will be burned up" (2 Peter 3:10).

The lake of fire takes place on planet earth. Hell will be on earth. Hell will be the consumption of the heavens and the earth by fire.

Hell and Death

"Now I saw a new heaven and a new earth, for the first heaven and the first earth had passed away. Also there was no more sea" (Revelation 21:1).

The Second Death

"But the cowardly, unbelieving, abominable, murderers, sexually immoral, sorcerers, idolaters, and all liars shall have their part in the lake which burns with fire and brimstone, which is the second death" (Revelation 21:8).

"Then Death and Hades were cast into the lake of fire. This is the second death. 15And anyone not found written in the Book of Life was cast into the lake of fire" (Revelation 20:14,15).

Hell will be a place of torment and burning, but it will also be the place of the second death.

"Do not marvel at this; for the hour is coming in which all who are in the graves will hear His voice 29and come forth— those who have done good, to the resurrection of life, and those who have done evil, to the resurrection of condemnation" (John 5:28,29).

Death, as proven, is the absence of life. Those who enter the first death, death as we know it today, will be raised again either to the resurrection of life or to the resurrection of condemnation.

Those who find themselves separated from God and not counted as saints will find themselves resurrected at the second one, the resurrection of condemnation. This will occur after the millennium and after the saints have been in heaven proving, testing, or confirming that the judgments of God are pure and just.

Those who are raised in the second resurrection will be punished for their unforgiven sins. The method of this punishment is ultimately death—eternal death. The method of this death will be fire and brimstone. There will be some level of pain and torture, based on the life of the unrepentant sinner, but it is a temporary pain that will eventually end. God is a merciful God.

The Fires of Hell

Hell is the cleansing process that God has reserved for sin. The fires of hell will burn up— purify— the heavens and the earth. All traces of sin will be removed forever. Sin cannot remain in the universe of God. The concept that hell now exists or will exist as some otherworldly realm is a lie.

"Where can I go from Your Spirit? Or where can I flee from Your presence? 8If I ascend into heaven, You are there; If I make my bed in hell, behold, You are there" (Psalm 139: 7,8).

God is in hell. He is everywhere. If sin is to be eradicated, then hell must have some conclusion. We are told that there will be a new heaven and a new earth, therefore the fires that melted the old heavens and earth must one day be extinguished.

Do not get hung up on the word everlasting. Jude 7 says that Sodom and Gomorrah suffered eternal fire. These cities are not burning today despite the plain Word of God that says eternal fire. These fires wiped out the cities— forever. They have never been rebuilt. They were removed for all eternity, never given a second chance to be rebuilt.

Jeremiah 17:27, speaking of the destruction that would come on Jerusalem many centuries later, said that it would burn with an unquenchable fire. Jerusalem is not still burning today. A fire that is unquenchable will consume everything it comes in contact with. Nothing will be untouched by its flames. Only when all has been consumed and there is no more fuel for the flames, will the fire be complete and find its end. The Bible is clear: anything— person, place, or thing— that enters into the fires of hell will be destroyed. No trace of them will exist (Psalm 37:36; Obadiah 1:16).

The word everlasting, in most scriptural texts, does not reference the fires of Hell. *"And these will go away into everlasting punishment, but the righteous into eternal life"* (Matthew 25:46). The punishment— eternal destruction (death), is everlasting, not the punishing or the continual process of being tortured. After the second death there will never be another resurrection or chance at life.

Daniel 12:2 says the contempt is everlasting, not the torture. 2 Thessalonians 1:9 says that the destruction is complete and everlasting, not the torture or fires of hell.

Hell is a future event, one promised to those who are not found in the first resurrection. Hell will be a moment in time; it could be days, weeks or shorter, but it will have a beginning and an end.

Hell will result in the second death of which there is no return. Those who experience hell will cease to exist; they will die and never exist again. Hell eradicates sin from God's universe. No trace of sin will exist after the lake of fire. There will not be some hold, prison, or realm where sinners will exist for God's perfect universe to see, run into or even remember.

"For behold, I create new heavens and a new earth; And the former shall not be remembered or come to mind" (Isaiah 65:17).

The New Jerusalem
Revelation 21

Central to the new earth is God's residence on earth. Like His presence in the tabernacle for ancient Israel, God's presence will once more inhabit the home of His people.

John is able to see this new city. He is even given some descriptions about it size, composition, and layout.

"Then one of the seven angels who had the seven bowls filled with the seven last plagues came to me and talked with me, saying, 'Come, I will show you the bride, the Lamb's wife.' 10And he carried me away in the Spirit to a great and high mountain, and showed me the great city, the holy Jerusalem, descending out of heaven from God, 11having the glory of God. Her light was like a most precious stone, like a jasper stone, clear as crystal. 12Also she had a great and high wall with twelve gates, and twelve angels at the gates, and names written on them, which are the names of the twelve tribes of the children of Israel: 13three gates on the east, three gates on the north, three gates on the south, and three gates on the west" (Revelation 21:9-13).

There are three parts to the New Jerusalem city: The city, its wall, and an outer wall.

The City

"The city is laid out as a square; its length is as great as its breadth. And he measured the city with the reed: twelve thousand furlongs. Its length, breadth, and height are equal" (Revelation 21:16).

The city and streets are made from pure gold like transparent glass. The city is designed like a cube, with its length equal to its width equal to its height. I do not believe every structure within the city is of equal height, but the tallest ones do not exceed the length or width of the city.

The base of the city is laid out in a square with its length equal to its breadth and has a perimeter of 12,000 furlongs. One side of the city is 3000 furlongs or 375 miles in length. The tallest building within this city also reaches to a height of 375 miles.

End of Time Prophecies

The Wall of the City

A wall sits on the perimeter of the city. This wall has twelve foundations; each one named for one of the twelve apostles.

"Now the wall of the city had twelve foundations, and on them were the names of the twelve apostles of the Lamb. 15And he who talked with me had a gold reed to measure the city, its gates, and its wall" (Revelation 21:14).

Each of the twelve foundations are formed from a unique precious stone.

"The foundations of the wall of the city were adorned with all kinds of precious stones: the first foundation was jasper, the second sapphire, the third chalcedony, the fourth emerald, 20the fifth sardonyx, the sixth sardius, the seventh chrysolite, the eighth beryl, the ninth topaz, the tenth chrysoprase, the eleventh jacinth, and the twelfth amethyst" (Revelation 21:19-20).

"And when they had entered, they went up into the upper room where they were staying: Peter, James, John, and Andrew; Philip and Thomas; Bartholomew and Matthew; James the son of Alphaeus and Simon the Zealot; and Judas the son of James." "And they cast their lots, and the lot fell on Matthias. And he was numbered with the eleven apostles" (Acts 1:13 & 26).

Gems in the New Jerusalem

The gems used in the city present a few problems to modern interpretations of the Bible. The inspired writers of the Bible were limited in their descriptions of events and items by the words familiar to their knowledge. This is evident when describing some of the rocks and gems mentioned in the scriptures. Ancient writers named gems by their color. Modern science uses chemical compositions to accurately identify a specific gemstone regardless of its color. Diamonds can be clear, blue, or black, and yet all are composed of the same molecular carbon foundation.

For example the gem Topaz is commonly used in the scriptures (Revelation 21:20; Exodus 28:17). Topaz comes in many colors from yellows to greens. Its chemical compound ($Al_2F_2SiO_2$) is specific. Studying gems and their history, it is seen that greenish yellow gems were mined from an island called Topazias, thus these gems were at one time called Topaz gems. The problem is no Topaz is found on this island. There is a yellow green gem found on this island, but its scientific name is Peridot (Mg_2SiO_4). If the scriptures were written today I believe the word Topaz would be called Peridot.

It is difficult to have pinpoint accuracy with the exact stones that will be used. Regardless of their proper scientific name we do understand that it will be beautiful beyond imagination.

The Outer Wall

The outer wall is separate from the wall of the city. (Ezekiel 40:5; Revelation 21:14). This outer wall is composed of jasper, clear as crystal. This is in contrast to the pure gold of the city. Red is a common jasper color and some have speculated that this is a symbol of Christ's blood, showing us that only those who have been cleansed by the blood of Christ will have access to the New Jerusalem city.

"Then he measured its wall: one hundred and forty-four cubits, according to the measure of a man, that is, of an angel. 18The construction of its wall was of jasper; and the city was pure gold, like clear glass" (Revelation 21:17,18).

John records one part of this wall, but does not record the perimeter of this outer wall. I believe the perimeter of the outer wall is given to us by Ezekiel.

"These are the exits of the city. On the north side, measuring four thousand five hundred cubits 31{the gates of the city shall be named after the tribes of Israel}, the three gates northward: one gate for Reuben, one gate for Judah, and one gate for Levi; 32on the east side, four thousand five hundred cubits, three gates: one gate for Joseph, one gate for Benjamin, and one gate for Dan; 33on the south side, measuring four thousand five hundred cubits, three gates: one gate for Simeon, one gate for Issachar, and one gate for Zebulun; 34on the west side, four thousand five hundred cubits with their three gates: one gate for Gad, one gate for Asher, and one gate for Naphtali. 35All the way around shall be eighteen thousand cubits [measures]; and the name of the city from that day shall be: THE LORD IS THERE" (Ezekiel 48:30-35).

This perimeter is said to be four sides of 4500 **units** for a total perimeter of 18,000 **units**. I use the word **units** here instead of cubits for a reason. The actual word used in the Hebrew is *midda* which means "measurement." The translators of the New King James Bible *assumed* that the units were cubits. When John writes his description of the city he describes the size of the city in furlongs. Cubits and Furlongs are hugely different. A cubit is 18 inches; a furlong is 1/8 of a mile. If Ezekiel's units were cubits, then the outer wall would not be large enough to surround the city. Using the length of furlongs, matching the Greek words in Revelation's description, gives us a workable number.

Eight furlongs is equivalent to one mile. 4,500 furlongs would be 562.5 miles long for each side of the outer wall.

The Twelve Gates

"The twelve gates were twelve pearls: each individual gate was of one pearl. And the street of the city was pure gold, like transparent glass" (Revelation 21:21).

These gates are made from a single pearl! How big was the clam? These, I believe are in the outer wall, outside of the city proper. The twelve gates were named for the twelve tribes of Israel (Revelation 21:12). There are several lists of the tribes of Israel in the Scriptures. It may be the list from Ezekiel or John's list in Revelation 7. We will find out when we get to heaven.

The New Jerusalem

Is There Room Enough?

God's city is designed with you in mind.

"In My Father's house are many mansions; if it were not so, I would have told you. I go to prepare a place for you. ₃And if I go and prepare a place for you, I will come again and receive you to Myself; that where I am, there you may be also" (John 14:2,3).

How many mansions does God have prepared for us?

On the surface this may sound like a stupid question. God is able to create as much space as needed to for these mansions... right? Since God revealed to John the dimensions of His city, there must be a purpose for these numbers. I like to think that it is so that we can look at the dimensions and find an answer to the question: **Is there room for me?**

Is there enough space to hold every human who ever lived?

Can every human truly have his or her own mansion?

Let's do the math

Living space

The total area of the city is 375 miles × 375 miles or

1,980,000 feet × 1,980,000 feet = 3,929,400,000,000 square feet of total area (3.9 trillion).

This area is not all living space. There must be room for gold streets, a river, a tree of life, a banquet table and a throne with its own room.

Let's assume that the living space will occupy only one quarter (¼) of the city.

¼ of the total area = 980,100,000,000 square feet (980 billion).

Mansion Size

Let's dream big and assume our individual mansion will be 50,000 Sq.Ft. (An average 2-4 bedroom home is 2,000 - 3,000 square feet.)

On the first floor there is room for 19,602,000 mansions. (Living area ÷ Mansion size)

The city's tallest building extends to a height of 375 miles, or 1,980,000 feet. Some Biblical scholars tell us that Adam was nearly 15 feet tall. He is going to need a mansion with lots of head room. Let's make the ceilings to be nearly 30 feet tall. This will provide 66,000 floors on which to build mansions.

The Answer

The total number of mansions that could cover a quarter of the city.

1.254 Trillion Mansions; (19 million per floor × 66,000 floors)

Is there room enough?

Statistics estimate between 200 and 500 billion humans have ever lived on planet earth. (Assuming a young earth of six or seven thousand years old).

Even using the high number of 500 billion there would be plenty of mansions to house every human who ever lived.

God has a mansion prepared just for you.

Will you be there?

A New Heaven and a New Earth
After the End of Time

The End of Time marks a new beginning. Sin and all it cursed is fully eradicated. The only evidence that a curse ever existed are the scars left on the person of Jesus Christ. His nail scarred hands and feet, along with the scar from the sword thrust into His side, forever remind the living of the price of love.

"Now I saw a new heaven and a new earth, for the first heaven and the first earth had passed away. Also there was no more sea" (Revelation 21:1).

John is given a glimpse of this new life.

What will life be like after sin?

The Bible reveals many clues as to what life will be like in heaven and on the earth made new.

The Lamb is the Light

"The city had no need of the sun or of the moon to shine in it, for the glory of God illuminated it. The Lamb is its light. 24And the nations of those who are saved shall walk in its light, and the kings of the earth bring their glory and honor into it. 25Its gates shall not be shut at all by day (there shall be no night there)" (Revelation 21:23-25).

"Your sun shall no longer go down, Nor shall your moon withdraw itself; For the LORD will be your everlasting light, And the days of your mourning shall be ended" (Isaiah 60:20).

All Sickness is Removed

"Then the eyes of the blind shall be opened, And the ears of the deaf shall be unstopped. 6Then the lame shall leap like a deer, And the tongue of the dumb sing. For waters shall burst forth in the wilderness, And streams in the desert" (Isaiah 35:5,6).

Dominion is Restored

"Then God said, 'Let Us make man in Our image, according to Our likeness; let them have dominion over the fish of the sea, over the birds of the air, and over the cattle, over all the earth and over every creeping thing that creeps on the earth'" (Genesis 1:26).

End of Time Prophecies

"They will see the Son of Man coming on the clouds of heaven with power and great glory" (Matthew 24:30).

Man lost their dominion when they submitted to Satan and sinned against God. Jesus Christ—the Son of Man, was born as a human and conquered sin. Through His power dominion has been restored to mankind.

Our Created Purpose

"Then the LORD God took the man and put him in the garden of Eden to tend and keep it. ₁₆And the LORD God commanded the man, saying, "Of every tree of the garden you may freely eat" (Genesis 2:15,16).

"Then God blessed them, and God said to them, 'Be fruitful and multiply; fill the earth and subdue it; have dominion over the fish of the sea, over the birds of the air, and over every living thing that moves on the earth'" (Genesis 1:28).

"And they shall rebuild the old ruins, They shall raise up the former desolations, And they shall repair the ruined cities, The desolations of many generations" (Isaiah 61:4).

"The LORD will open to you His good treasure, the heavens, to give the rain to your land in its season, and to bless all the work of your hand. You shall lend to many nations, but you shall not borrow" (Deuteronomy 28:12).

"They shall build houses and inhabit them; They shall plant vineyards and eat their fruit. ₂₂They shall not build and another inhabit; They shall not plant and another eat; For as the days of a tree, so shall be the days of My people, And My elect shall long enjoy the work of their hands. ₂₃They shall not labor in vain, Nor bring forth children for trouble; For they shall be the descendants of the blessed of the LORD, And their offspring with them" (Isaiah 65:21-23).

We were created to work. We were to be stewards of the earth. We were to tend it, grow food with it to eat, live in it, and multiply upon it. Isaiah speaks of a rebuilding. We will return to tending the garden, and will rebuild homes. We will live life as we were first created to do. We were not created to sit idle. We will continue to grow and learn. 1 Peter 1:12 gives evidence that even the angels continue to learn. If we knew it all—we would be God. God cannot learn! He knows it all.

No More Thorns

"Instead of the thorn shall come up the cypress tree, And instead of the brier shall come up the myrtle tree; And it shall be to the LORD for a name, For an everlasting sign that shall not be cut off" (Isaiah 55:13).

"'The wolf and the lamb shall feed together, The lion shall eat straw like the ox, And dust shall be the serpent's food. They shall not hurt nor destroy in all My holy mountain,' Says the LORD" (Isaiah 65:25).

We Will Worship God

"'And it shall come to pass That from one New Moon to another, And from one Sabbath to another, All flesh shall come to worship before Me,' says the LORD" (Isaiah 66:23).

"Therefore they are before the throne of God, and serve Him day and night in His temple. And He who sits on the throne will dwell among them. 16They shall neither hunger anymore nor thirst anymore; the sun shall not strike them, nor any heat; 17for the Lamb who is in the midst of the throne will shepherd them and lead them to living fountains of waters. And God will wipe away every tear from their eyes" (Revelation 7:15-17).

"He who testifies to these things says, 'Surely I am coming quickly.' Amen. Even so, come, Lord Jesus! The grace of our Lord Jesus Christ be with you all. Amen."

(Revelation 22:20,21)

Index

42 months
  1260 days, 91, 96
  but for a time, 118
  Little Horn Power, 65, 279, 302

70 AD, 220, 259, 300

144,000, 197
  redeemed in heaven, 239

408 BC
  Jerusalem rebuilt, 75
  temple dedicated, 93

457 BC
  Artaxerxes' decree, 92
  start of 2300 days, 83

458 BC, 78

508 AD
  1335 year Time-line, 94
  Clovis supports Papacy, 66, 217
  turning point for Papacy, 117

538 AD
  42 months, 279
  1260 year Time-line begins, 66, 96, 225
  black horse, Seal 3, 187
  little Horn appears, 301
  Ostrogoths removed, 116
  Pergamos, 171
  pope is head of all churches, 217

1260 year Time-line, 96, 172, 301
  42 months, 91, 224
  1798 AD, 174
  little Horn Power, 65, 69, 279
  Ostrogoths out of Rome, 117
  papacy in power, 235
  tribulation of the Church, 259
  United States, 234

1290 Years, 91, 117
  1335 year Time-line, 94

1335 Years, 91, 93, 117
  508 AD, 217
  1844 AD, 218

1798 AD, 217, 280
  42 months, 301
  508 AD, 95
  538 AD, 96
  1260 year Time-line, 96
  1290 year Time-line, 95
  Berthier, General, 69
  deadly wound, 67, 117
  little Horn Power, 279
  Philadelphia, 175
  Sardis, 174
  United States, 234

1844 AD, 81, 93, 129, 177, 178, 218
  457 AD, 83
  2300 year Time-line, 83
  cleansing of the sanctuary, 83, 157
  God's judgment, 117, 293
  Philadelphia, 175
  three angel's messages, 249
  time of the end, 124
  woe 3, 213

2300 days, 83, 91, 299
  70 week Prophecy, 71
  457 BC, 92
  1844 AD, 81, 94
  cleansing of the sanctuary, 83

Abomination of Desolation, 79, 93, 122, 217, 258, 306

Abyssos, 209, 292

Alaric the Visigoth, 95, 116, 205, 216

End of Time Prophecies

Alexander the Great, 50, 215
  Babylon plans, 274
  goat with notable horn, 60, 104

Anti-Christ, 193

Arianism, 115

Armageddon, 269

Atonement.
      See Cleansing of the Sanctuary

Attila the Hun, 216

Babylon, 250, 273
  fallen, 250
  fall of, 37
  great, The, 273

Beast from the Earth, 234

Beasts, 46
  bear raised up, 48
  dreadful and terrible, 51
  four living creatures, 179, 201
  leopard with four wings, 50
  lion with wings, 47

Byzantine Empire, 207, 209, 210, 217

Canonization of the Bible, 55

Chaldeans, 48

Chiasm, 107

Cleansing of the Sanctuary, 83

Clovis, 217
  508 AD, 95
  converts to Catholicism, 66, 116

Counterfeit Prophecy
  deceits and errors created by the Papacy, 68
  Israel, 139
  little Horn Power, 65
  Nebuchadnezzar's tree, 32
  wheat vs tares, 135

Crusades, 120

Daniel
  lion's den, 41

Day for a Year, 35

Dead in Christ Arise, 267

Death, 317

Devil, 195, 230

Dragon's War, 229

East, 127

E.G. White
  144,000, 199, 201
  messenger, 177
  seven days of silence, 266

Eight Kings, 277

End of Time Outline, 297

False Prophet, 195

Fiery furnace, 23

Foolish Virgins, 81

Four Horses, 183

Gaiseric the Vandal, 206, 216

God's Judgment, 218, 249, 298
  1844, 293

Greece, 105, 216
  beast three, 50
  goat, 60
  kings 3,4,5 & 6, 278
  power moves to Greece, 104

Half an Hour, 265

Hebrew Captives, 9

Hell, 317

Horns of Prophecy, 49
  little Horn, 61

Isaac versus Ishmael, 141

Index

Islam, 303
  King of the South, 118

Israel, 139
  church today, 151
  counterfeit, 139
  walks away from God, 147

Jerusalem
  destruction of, 79
  mountain, 21
  New Jerusalem, 327

Jesus Christ
  Archangel, 133
  baptism, 75
  crucifixion, 76
  current work, 155, 257
  evidence of His Return, 316
  Michael, 129, 131
  Prince of the Covenant, 113
  return To Earth, 294
  Satan impersonates, 196
  second coming, 313
  stone, 20

Last Plagues, 257

Litch, Josiah, 122, 211

Little Book, 182, 219

Little Horn
  characteristics of, 65
  historical evidence, 67
  Roman Catholicism, 66

Mark of the Beast, 137, 236
  cast alive in lake of fire, 296
  how received, 236
  image to the beast, 305
  Mount Carmel experience, 270
  Nebuchadnezzar's Image, 26
  not yet in place, 201, 284
  plagues poured out upon, 261, 309
  sunday worship, 237
  worship, 125, 307

Medes, 215
  459 BC, 274
  beast Two, 48
  captures Babylon, 39
  king 2, 278
  Persians, 49
  ram with two horns, 59
  two horned ram, 59

Metal Statue, 13

Michael. *See* Jesus Christ

Mount Carmel, 270

Muhammad, 119

Nebuchadnezzar
  humbled, 27
  metal statue dream, 13

New Jerusalem. *See* Jerusalem

Nicolaitans, 169

Odoacer the Heruli, 62, 115, 216

One Day, 263

One Hour, 264

Ottoman Empire, 122, 211, 217, 218

Papacy
  538 AD, 117
  apostate christian religion, 188
  beast of the sea, 235
  crusades, 120
  deceits, 68
  infallible, 68
  king 7, 217, 280
  King of the North, 114
  Sabbath, changes it to sunday, 238
  The Beast, 194
  wound is healed, 303

Persians. *See* Medes

End of Time Prophecies

Prayer
  Daniel mourns three full weeks, 99
  Daniel's choice, 42
  Daniel's prayer of thanks, 16
  seventy weeks, 72

Prophecy
  tools for interpreting, 5

Prophetic Timings, 33
  cows, 33
  day for a year, 35
  prophetic calendars, 34

Revelation, 153
  apocalypse of Christ, 153

Rise of the Empires, 215

Roman Catholicism. *See* Little Horn

Rome
  dreadful and terrible beast, 61
  King of the North, 110
  ten kingdoms, 115

Sabbath, 241

Satan
  angel of light, 195
  conflict with Michael, 133
  sin began with, 135

Satan's deceptions, 136

Sea Beast, 232

Seal of God, 198, 239
  Sabbath, 241

Second Coming, 313

Seven Churches, 165
  Ephesus, 168
  Laodicean, 176
  Pergamos, 171
  Philadelphia, 175
  Sardis, 174
  Smyrna, 170
  Thyatira, 172

Seven Seals, 179

Seven Thunders, 219

Seven Trumpets, 203

Seventy Weeks, 71
  Jesus' Baptism, 75
  start date, 74

Soul
  immortality, 283
  life and death, 318

Symbols of Prophecy
  beast, 46
  compass direction, 104
  horn, 49, 62
  lamps of fire, 180
  metals, 19
  mountain, 21
  olive trees, 225
  seven Spirits of God, 166
  seven stars, 165
  smoke of the incense, 203
  stone, 20
  times, 31

Ten Kingdoms, 115

Tests of Inspiration, 56

The Beast, 194

Three Angels Messages, 247

Throne Room, 179

Time-line for the End of Time, 299

Time Lines of Prophecy, 91
  1260 years, 96
  1290 years, 95
  1335 year, 93
  2300 years, 92

Index

Times
  3 ½ years, 224
  42 months, 224
  1260 days, 224
  2300 years, 83
  half an hour, 191

Translations of the Bible, 55

Two Witnesses, 223

United States
  lamb-like beast, 235

Visions
  cartoon beasts, 45
  Daniel's last vision, 103
  metal statue, 13
  Nebuchadnezzar's tree, 28
  rams and goats, 59
  seventy weeks, 71

Wheat and tares, 136

Woes, 208
  first woe, 208
  second woe, 210
  third woe, 212

Worship The Image, 23

We invite you to view the complete
selection of titles we publish at:

www.AspectBooks.com

Scan with your mobile
device to go directly
to our website.

Please write or email us your praises, reactions, or
thoughts about this or any other book we publish at:

info@AspectBooks.com

Aspect Books titles may be purchased in bulk for
educational, business, fund-raising, or promotional use.
For more information, please e-mail:

BulkSales@AspectBooks.com

Finally, if you are interested in seeing
your own book in print, please contact us at

publishing@AspectBooks.com

We would be happy to review your manuscript for free.

www.ingramcontent.com/pod-product-compliance
Lightning Source LLC
Chambersburg PA
CBHW060551230426
43670CB00011B/1780